I0127915

Violent Extremists

Violent Extremists

Understanding the Domestic and International Terrorist Threat

THOMAS R. MOCKAITIS

Praeger Security International

BLOOMSBURY ACADEMIC

NEW YORK · LONDON · OXFORD · NEW DELHI · SYDNEY

BLOOMSBURY ACADEMIC
Bloomsbury Publishing Inc
1385 Broadway, New York, NY 10018, USA
50 Bedford Square, London, WC1B 3DP, UK
29 Earlsfort Terrace, Dublin 2, Ireland

BLOOMSBURY, BLOOMSBURY ACADEMIC and the Diana logo
are trademarks of Bloomsbury Publishing Plc

First published in the United States of America by ABC-CLIO 2019
Paperback edition published by Bloomsbury Academic 2024

Copyright © Bloomsbury Publishing Inc, 2024

Cover photos: (Ekaterina Pokrovsky/Dreamstime.com); (Gunnar Curry/Dreamstime.com);
(Emily Molli/NurPhoto/Sipa USA via AP Images); (Alessandro Di Marco/ANSA via AP)

All rights reserved. No part of this publication may be reproduced or
transmitted in any form or by any means, electronic or mechanical,
including photocopying, recording, or any information storage or retrieval
system, without prior permission in writing from the publishers.

Bloomsbury Publishing Inc does not have any control over, or responsibility for,
any third-party websites referred to or in this book. All internet addresses given
in this book were correct at the time of going to press. The author and publisher
regret any inconvenience caused if addresses have changed or sites have
ceased to exist, but can accept no responsibility for any such changes.

Library of Congress Cataloging-in-Publication Data
Names: Mockaitis, Thomas R., 1955-author.
Title: Violent extremists : understanding the domestic and international
terrorist threat / Thomas R. Mockaitis.
Description: Santa Barbara : Praeger/ABC-CLIO, [2019] |
Series: Praeger security international |
Includes bibliographical references and index.
Identifiers: LCCN 2019007383 (print) | LCCN 2019011751 (ebook) |
ISBN 9781440859496 (eBook) | ISBN 9781440859489 (print)
Subjects: LCSH: Radicalism–United States. | Radicalism–Religious aspects–Islam.
White supremacy movements–United States. Terrorism–Prevention–United States.
Classification: LCC HN49.R33 (ebook) | LCC HN49.R33 M63 2019 (print) |
DDC 303.48/4–dc23
LC record available at https://lccn.loc.gov/2019007383

ISBN: HB: 978-1-4408-5948-9
PB: 979-8-7651-2633-2
ePDF: 978-1-4408-5949-6
eBook: 979-8-2161-6217-9

Series: Praeger Security International

To find out more about our authors and books visit www.bloomsbury.com
and sign up for our newsletters.

In Memoriam:
Gene Robkin—mentor, colleague, and friend

Contents

Preface

Almost 30 years have gone by since I wrote my first book. Published at the end of the Cold War, *British Counterinsurgency, 1919–1960* (London: Macmillan, 1990) was well received as an historical work. However, many experts questioned its relevance to the contemporary world. Insurgency and terrorism, they insisted, belonged to a dead colonial past. Unfortunately, the collapse of the Soviet Union did not herald an era of peace, as many had hoped and some expected, but rather a new period of uncertainty. The power vacuum caused by the withdrawal of the United States and Soviet Union from many areas led to a series of brutal civil conflicts. The failure of the Somali state, the breakup of Yugoslavia, and the Rwandan genocide occurred in rapid succession. Then came the shock of the Oklahoma City bombing, attacks on the U.S. embassies in Kenya and Tanzania, and, of course, 9/11. The United States has been at war since the end of 2001. We live in an era of continuous, low-level conflict with no end in sight.

The world has given me plenty to write about over the past three decades. This book, like several of its predecessors, has a simple purpose: to situate a pervasive threat in a healthy context, replacing ignorance and fear with understanding. Although it avoids political opining, it does challenge the fearmongering done by some politicians. I argue that terrorism is a persistent problem but not an existential threat and that domestic extremism is more worrisome than international terrorism. Many politicians and commentators tend to exaggerate the former and downplay or even ignore the latter. The book concludes with suggestions on how to counter the threat of extremism, particularly the ideology that fuels it.

The decades have seen as much change in my own life as in the world. When I published my first book, I was the proud father of three young sons. I am now the doting grandfather of two grandsons and two grand-daughters. Along with my students, these family members keep me optimistic about the future. They also motivate me to work hard so that the future remains bright for them long after I am gone.

As with any such undertaking, I have amassed a considerable debt of gratitude to the people who have supported me in writing this book. My colleagues at the Center for Civil-Military relations have been a source of encouragement and a sounding board for ideas. My department has always supported and recognized my scholarly work. My graduate student assistant, Prashant Jivanlal Varia, from the DePaul College of Computers and Digital Media did excellent research for the section on cyberterrorism. DePaul University funded his position. Last but certainly not least, my wonderful wife of 38 years, Martha Ross-Mockaitis, has been a constant source of love and support through the long and at times frustrating task of research and writing.

As I was completing the manuscript, my dear friend Gene Robkin died. Many times, as I was working through ideas for this manuscript, I wanted to discuss them with him, as I had with so many other projects in the past. In appreciation of his guidance and friendship, I am dedicating this book to him. The last thing he said to me before he died was, "Speak truth to power." I always will, but it won't be as easy without his wisdom and encouragement.

Introduction

In 2007, I published *The "New" Terrorism: Myths and Reality* with a very specific purpose in mind. The book aimed to debunk a popular myth. In the aftermath of 9/11, a bevy of newly minted experts loudly proclaimed the uniqueness of the al-Qaeda phenomenon and, along with the media, exaggerated the threat it posed to the United States and its people. I sought to demonstrate how, contrary to popular belief, terrorism had been evolving over the preceding decades and to place it in a healthy perspective relative to other threats. I aimed to separate the new from the old characteristics of the phenomenon and to situate terrorism within the broad spectrum of security risks facing the United States. Above all, I wanted to dampen down the pervasive fear that had so many people convinced that they could become victims at any moment.

Like its predecessor, this book also aims to debunk myths and to situate contemporary terrorism in the context of threats facing the United States. Over the past decade, the myths have changed, but the fear remains, intensified by a new populist political rhetoric that seeks scapegoats to blame for the country's problems. This rhetoric exaggerates the threat posed by the Islamic State in Iraq and Syria (ISIS), encourages fear of immigrants, and creates an atmosphere of Islamophobia, which makes it easier for ISIS to recruit followers. Ironically, many of the same people who hype the Islamist threat tend to ignore or dismiss the more serious danger posed by domestic hate groups. Rather than see homegrown, racially motivated violence as terrorism, they discount it as the work of "lone wolves"—unstable individuals acting alone—rather than as part of a larger pattern of violence encouraged by the inflammatory rhetoric of a broad ideological movement whose ideas some groups have explicitly embraced and many individuals tacitly accept.

Public opinion polls corroborate this distorted view of terrorism. A spring 2017 survey conducted by the Pew Charitable Trust found that 42 percent of Americans were "very concerned" about Islamist extremism, and another 30 percent were "somewhat concerned."[1] Responses varied by political ideology, with 86 percent of those on the right indicating that they were very or somewhat concerned as opposed to only 57 percent of those on the left.[2] In another survey conducted in August 2017, only 32 percent of respondents considered white nationalism as a "very serious threat," and only 25 percent perceived it as a "somewhat serious threat."[3] Data on actual attacks demonstrate the inaccuracy of these perceptions. According to an April 2017 Congressional Budget Office Report, 85 terrorist attacks causing 225 fatalities have taken place on American soil between September 11, 2001, and December 31, 2016. Radical Islamists killed 106 of these victims, and right-wing extremists 119.[4] These figures reveal two important truths: the chances of any American being killed in a terrorist attack of any kind are extremely remote, and right-wing terrorism has proven to be as lethal as Islamist extremism. Domestic terrorism may in fact be more dangerous. Almost half the fatalities caused by ISIS-inspired terrorists occurred in a single incident, the June 2016 Orlando nightclub shooting, in which 49 people died. Right-wing extremists have perpetrated attacks far more frequently, accounting for 62 of the 85 incidents.[5] To the death toll must be added 13 more victims killed in 2018: 11 members of the Tree of Life Synagogue in Pittsburgh and 2 African Americans murdered by a white supremacist in Louisville.

In addition to exaggerating the Islamist threat while underestimating the right-wing domestic one, the public in general and some policy makers in particular misunderstand the nature of terrorism today. This misunderstanding has led to a bad counterterrorism strategy that concentrates disproportionately on destroying terrorist organizations without adequately addressing the underlying causes of terrorism or countering the ideology that motivates those who perpetrate it. This mistaken approach has resulted in billions of dollars wasted on placebo security, a military focused on destroying the Islamic State in Syria and Iraq (ISIS), and a public gripped by xenophobia.

This book aims to replace myth, misunderstanding, and inflammatory rhetoric with a careful examination of terrorism in the contemporary world focusing on threats facing the United States. While I hope it will be of use to others, the book specifically speaks to Americans for whom terrorism has become the new bogeyman, a replacement for the communist threat of the Cold War. Some politicians and commentators have deliberately exaggerated the threat of foreign extremistism for political gain. Terrorism does pose a real danger to the country, but that danger has to be kept in a realistic perspective. It pales in comparison with gun violence, climate change, and rogue regimes such as North Korea. The book focuses on the terrorist threats posed by two broad ideological movements: Islamist jihadism and right-wing extremism. My analysis rests on two premises. First, terrorism is a persistent problem but not an existential threat. Like corruption and organized crime, it has the capacity to do damage but cannot destroy or even substantially alter our way of life unless we allow it to do so. Barring their acquisition of a weapon of mass destruction (WMD), terrorists have limited ability to cause casualties. Gang violence has killed far more Americans than ISIS operatives, and the murder rate in most U.S. cities far exceeds that of U.S. citizens killed by extremists. Second, terrorist threats today are multidimensional. They exist as ideological movements, hierarchical groups, and complex networks. A radical ideology motivates people to form or join a terrorist group, usually located in a particular place and often concerned with local grievances. As it expands, the group may create a network of cells and operatives regionally and/or internationally. The three dimensions represent not only a linear progression but also a synergistic whole, interconnected parts of the same phenomenon. Sometimes a leader (or leaders) will coordinate activity in all three dimensions. At other times, actors within each dimension operate independently. Extremist groups also encourage walk-on terrorists—people who adopt the ideology without belonging to the group. Commonly known as "lone wolves" or "homegrown extremists," these perpetrators are carrying out an increasing number of attacks.

These lone wolves have added a new, troubling dimension to terrorism. Classic lone wolves operated independently of any group or movement, often motivated by their own bizarre worldview. Most suffered from mental illness or some recognizable social pathology. Today, lone wolves seldom suffer from any diagnosable condition. Rather than concoct their own ideology, they usually adopt the ideology of an existing group or movement with which they may have a loose association but no formal affiliation. They carry out attacks in accordance with a general mandate to strike at the enemy but without any specific direction or even guidance. The organization or movement on whose behalf they claim to act may disavow or embrace them after the fact, as convenience dictates. ISIS has gone so far as to invite like-minded individuals to strike a blow for the cause whenever and wherever possible, promising to own and even praise any act carried out in the name of its ideology. Far-right extremist groups, on the other hand, prefer to disavow the violent people they inspire. As they seldom communicate their intentions before striking, lone wolves do not create the communications "chatter" characteristic of cells and networks. The Internet and social media have made it possible for sympathizers to absorb extremist ideology from afar and even to learn terrorist methods online. The ready availability of firearms with high-capacity magazines, bomb-making materials, and vehicles that can be used to run down pedestrians makes it possible for an individual acting on his/her own to do considerable damage.

This book's form follows its function. Chapter 1 examines the nature of violent extremism, the structure of groups and networks, and the nature of ideology. It considers the profile of terrorist recruits and discusses the radicalization process. Chapter 2 traces the origin and development of Islamist jihadism, the ideology motivating al-Qaeda and its affiliates, especially al-Qaeda in the Land of the Two Rivers (a.k.a., al-Qaeda in Iraq, the group from which ISIS evolved). Chapter 3 covers ISIS from its inception to the present, examining it as the latest manifestation of Islamist extremism. Chapter 4 looks at the complex threat posed to the United States by domestic extremist groups espousing racist, antigovernment, and neo-Nazi ideology. Chapter 5 takes up the issue of lone-wolf terrorism, considering how the threat posed by these individuals has changed over the past decades. Chapter 6 explores nightmare scenarios, the worst possible attacks extremists might carry out using WMD and cybertools. The book concludes with lessons to be drawn from contemporary extremism and recommendations for combating it.

CHAPTER 1

Understanding Extremism

TERRORISM AND EXTREMISM

For such a pervasive phenomenon, terrorism has proven difficult to define. The federal government, individual states, and various organizations have crafted different definitions. Academics disagree, and the international community has yet to achieve consensus on what the term means. To ordinary people watching the carnage in Paris, Barcelona, or Charleston, however, debates over definition must seem arcane and pointless. "Surely," the average man or woman on the street will insist, "we know a terrorist attack when we see one." This commonsense realization points the way to a functional definition based on agreed-upon characteristics: if it walks like a duck and quacks like a duck, it's a duck.

Understanding terrorism begins with understanding terror. "Terror" names an emotion, but it also designates acts that produce that emotion. Whether he or she uses an airplane, a suicide vest, a car bomb, or a firearm, the perpetrator of a terrorist attack seeks to spread fear. Terror targets not only those it kills and maims but also those who witness the attack, either firsthand or through various media. It frightens people into believing that they may become a victim at any moment and tries to convince them that only by giving in to the demands of the perpetrators will they be safe. Terror instills fear disproportionate to the damage it causes and the casualties it inflicts. If an attack gets people to change their behavior, it has succeeded.

Like any weapon or tactic, terror can be employed by different actors. States, insurgent groups, criminal enterprises, and extremist organizations have all used terror, but they have employed it in different ways. States are the oldest practitioners of terror. The Romans executed Jesus Christ by nailing him on a cross to suffer an agonizing public death. They wished to send an unmistakable message: those who defy Rome will suffer the same fate. Insurgents seeking to gain control of a state from within will also use terror to prevent people supporting the government. Criminal enterprises sometimes murder members of rival groups and informants within their own ranks in a gruesome fashion as a warning to others who would cross them.

The use of terror by states, insurgents, and criminals has some characteristics in common. Because these actors have specific objectives they pursue with a rational strategy, they generally make limited use of terror and keep it highly focused. They want people to clearly understand what will make them a target of violence in order to induce them to behave in a certain way. To be effective, state terror must be predictable. The indiscriminate violence of the French Revolutionary "reign of terror" (1793–94) and the Red Terror perpetrated by Joseph Stalin in the Soviet Union (1936–38) proved unsustainable. Governments can, however, get away with short, intense campaigns of terror, especially when directed against minorities. In 2017, the Burmese military launched a campaign of terror against the Rohingya, forcing them to flee the country. Because they seek to win the "hearts and minds" of people in the state they want to control, insurgents also keep their use of terror focused and limited. If they do not, they alienate the people whose support they are trying to gain. For their part, criminals usually understand that violence is bad for business. They use terror sparingly and usually only against people in their underworld. Too much violence may provoke a backlash from civil society and the authorities who protect it. The Saint Valentine's Day Massacre of 1929 produced such public outrage that the federal government brought more resources to bear on Al Capone and his criminal organization in Chicago. The Mafia learned from that mistake; going forward, it kept its use of violence below a threshold of public tolerance.

Conversely, violent extremist organizations (VEOs), more popularly known as terrorist groups, use terror more extensively and with far less discrimination than states, insurgents, or criminals. They often embrace an ideology that divides the world into "them" and "us" and use it to designate entire populations as evil and deserving of destruction. In 1998, Osama bin Laden issued a *fatwa* (religious proclamation) to kill Americans whenever and wherever they could be targeted. "The ruling to kill the Americans and their allies—civilians and military—is an individual duty for every Muslim who can do it in any country in which it is possible to do it," bin Laden told his followers.[1] VEO terror is a macabre form of theater with two audiences: the enemy society it seeks to frighten and the supporters it wishes to empower. To maximize its effect, VEO terror seeks to produce mass casualties—the more dramatic the attack, the greater its emotional impact.

In recent years, the term "terrorist group" has been replaced in official U.S. literature by the designation "violent extremist organization." The change is not merely a matter of semantics. Academics and law enforcement officials have come to recognize that these organizations are not defined solely or even primarily by their use of terror, as the term "terrorist group" would suggest, but rather by the ideology that drives their behavior. The Federal Bureau of Investigation (FBI) defines violent extremism as "encouraging, condoning, justifying, or supporting the commission of a violent act to achieve political, ideological, religious, social, or economic goals."[2] A group or organization need not engage in violence directly to be designated extremist. It need only inspire others to do so. Determining what constitutes "encouraging, condoning, justifying, or supporting" can be very difficult, especially from a legal standpoint. "Inciting" violence may be a crime; condoning or even encouraging it is not.

The line separating insurgent groups from VEOs has become so fine that some analysts have all but erased it. They describe organizations such as the Provisional Irish Republican Army (PIRA) and the Basque separatist group Euskadi Ta Askatasuna (Bosque for "Basque Homeland and Liberty") as "ethnonationalist" terrorist groups.[3] This approach causes no end of confusion and has fueled the exaggerated fear of terrorism. Over the past half century, the vast majority of terror attacks have been perpetrated by groups involved in local conflicts. The *Global Terrorism Index 2017* concluded that over the past 17 years, 99 percent of incidents "occurred in countries that are either in conflict or have high levels of political terror."[4] This data clearly indicates that despite popular preoccupation with its international dimensions, most terrorism is deeply rooted in local affairs.

WEAPONS AND TACTICS

VEOs employ a variety of tactics in carrying out attacks. They engage in "asymmetric warfare," which the U.S. Department of Defense defines as the use of methods designed to "circumvent or negate an opponent's strengths while exploiting his weaknesses."[5] VEOs cannot challenge powerful countries like the United States by direct, conventional means, so they attack them indirectly with a variety of unconventional weapons and improvised tactics. Most of these weapons have limited capacity to cause harm, but they are readily available and hard to defend against.

Bombs have long been a preferred weapon of extremists. In 1881, Russian revolutionaries used a homemade, hand-thrown bomb to assassinate Tsar Alexander II. Vehicle bombs have proven even more effective because they can be driven to the target and carry a large quantity of explosives. On September 16, 1920, an Italian American anarchist detonated a horse-drawn cart filled with explosives and shrapnel on Wall Street in the financial district of Manhattan, killing 38 and wounding 143. Car bombs have been used so frequently that they have been dubbed the "poor man's cruise missile." Zionist insurgents used car bombs to drive the British from Palestine in the late 1940s, and Palestinians used them in their struggle with

Israel. Both the Catholic PIRA and the Protestant Ulster Volunteer Force used car bombs during the Northern Ireland Conflict (1969–98). On October 23, 1983, a suicide bomber from the Islamic Jihad Organization drove a truck filled with explosives into the U.S. Marine compound in Beirut, Lebanon, killing 307 people. The deadliest vehicle bomb attack on U.S. soil occurred on April 19, 1995, when Timothy McVeigh detonated a truck bomb next to the Murrah Federal Building in Oklahoma City, killing 168 people. Vehicle bombs continue to be used in Iraq and Syria to this day.

Suicide vests have also proven to be highly effective terrorist weapons. The bomber straps on a vest containing explosives and shrapnel, covers it with clothing, walks up to the target, and detonates the bomb, killing or wounding all those around him or her. The vest may also be detonated remotely. Men, women, and even children have been used as suicide bombers. Women and children have the advantage of being designated as noncombatants under the Geneva Conventions and so may be able to approach their target more easily.[6] Children have a limited understanding of death and can be more easily indoctrinated by terrorist groups.[7] Women have the added advantage of being able to feign pregnancy, enabling them to carry more explosives on their bodies. On May 21, 1991, a female suicide bomber working for the Sri Lankan Tamil separatist group Liberation Tigers of Tamil Elam (LTTE) assassinated Indian Prime Minister Rajiv Gandhi and killed 14 others.

Suicide attacks have distinct advantages that make them attractive to terrorists. Killing people is much easier to do if the murderer is willing to die. A suicide bomber can strike with precision. The suicide bomber who assassinated Indian Prime Minister Rajiv Gandhi walked right up to him before detonating her suicide vest, thus assuring the death of the intended target. A terrorist suicide operation does not require an extraction plan for the attacker, and the authorities have no one to interrogate after the attack.[8] LTTE made extensive use of suicide terrorism in its struggle with the government of Sri Lanka, developing a dedicated unit known as the "Black Tigers" to carry out such operations. In recent years, however, most suicide attacks have been carried out by Islamist extremists. Because the ideology of al-Qaeda and ISIS promises eternal life to anyone who dies a martyr to the cause, they have an easier time attracting suicide terrorists than do secular groups. Even so, most extremists would rather live to fight another day. They prefer to place their bombs and, if possible, walk away.

Mass transit has long been an attractive target for terrorist bombers. In March 2004, an al-Qaeda terrorist cell bombed commuter trains in Madrid, Spain, killing 193 people and wounding more than 2,000 others. The following year, another al-Qaeda terrorist cell placed bombs on three London underground trains and a double-decker bus, killing 52 people along with the 4 suicide bombers. Two weeks later, a follow-up attack did not succeed because all four bombs placed on trains failed to detonate. In both the Madrid and London attacks, the terrorists detonated their devices as close to the same time as possible to maximize the fear and disruption they caused. For almost a decade after these two incidents, no major attack on trains occurred, although there were some failed attempts. Then on March 22, 2016, Islamic State terrorists bombed an underground train in the heart of Brussels an hour after the same cell bombed a check-in area at Brussels International Airport. The two attacks claimed 35 lives, including that of the three suicide bombers.

Bombs have also been used to destroy airliners. In 1985, a bomb concealed in the luggage compartment brought down an Air India Boeing 747 off the coast of Ireland. Three years later, Libyan terrorists blew up Pan Am Flight 103 over Lockerbie, Scotland. In addition to these successful attacks, a number of terrorist attempts to blow up aircraft have failed. On December 22, 2001, Richard Reid tried to bring down American Airlines Flight 63 en route from Paris to Miami using explosives hidden in his shoes. He hoped to blow a hole in the fuselage and destroy the plane through the resulting explosive decompression of the cabin. Fortunately, his shoes got wet before he boarded the plane, and the fuse failed to light. On Christmas Day, 2009, Umar Farouk Abdulmutallab tried to destroy Northwest Flight 253 as it approached Detroit from Amsterdam. The bomb contained in his underwear failed to detonate, and passengers detained him until the aircraft landed.

Until September 11, 2001, few people imagined that an aircraft could be hijacked and turned into a flying bomb. Previously, hijackers had taken captured planes to a secure location and released passengers in return for concession or in exchange for prisoners. On 9/11, 19 al-Qaeda terrorists seized four airplanes, crashing two into the twin towers of the World Trade Center in New York City and one into the Pentagon in Washington, DC. A fourth plane crashed in a field near Pittsburgh, Pennsylvania, when passengers sought to regain control of the aircraft. Nearly 3,000 people died in the attacks. After 9/11, airlines secured cockpit doors, retrained flight crews, and restricted access to gate areas. As a result of these precautions, terrorist have not been able to repeat their dramatic success.

As threatened states got better at securing airports, government buildings, and other high-value targets, VEOs adapted. In November 2008, 10 members of Lashkar-e-Taiba introduced the world to a bold new terrorist tactic. They landed in small boats at the port of Mumbai, India, and, using small arms and bombs, held the city hostage for two days, killing more than 160 people. The attack proved to be a harbinger of things to come. In December 2015, Islamic State in Iraq and Syria (ISIS) terrorists conducted a series of well-coordinated attacks in Paris, France, using firearms and explosives. They struck cafés, a concert hall, and a sports stadium, killing 130 people. Attacks of this type reveal that crowds and venues have become preferred targets. Cities abound in such venues, which are very difficult to protect. Because terrorists seek mass casualties, one site may be as good as another. If one restaurant proves hard to hit, they can strike the one next door.

Although some attacks have been carried out by teams of terrorists, others have been perpetrated by lone individuals. Modern firearms are so lethal that one person can perpetrate a mass casualty attack. On June 17, 2015, white supremacist Dylan Roof entered a Charleston, South Carolina, church and murdered nine African American church members attending a Bible study. He hoped to start a race war. On June 12, 2016, Omar Mateen entered a nightclub in Orlando, Florida, with a semiautomatic rifle and pistol and opened fire. Before the carnage ended, he had killed 49 people and wounded 58 others. He had previously called 911 to tell police he had pledged allegiance to ISIS. Both Roof and Mateen fit the pattern of the lone-wolf terrorist, but they also espoused ideologies of known VEOs.

Guns and bombs are not the only weapon available to terrorists. In October 2010, al-Qaeda in the Arabian Peninsula (AQAP) published in its *Inspire Magazine* an article titled "The Ultimate Mowing Machine," which provided instructions on how to use a pickup truck to mow down pedestrians.[9] Few supporters of AQAP answered the call to create an improvised tank, but the followers of ISIS have made continuous use of the tactic. On July 14, 2016, an ISIS sympathizer drove a truck through Bastille Day revelers in Nice, France, killing 86 people. On November 28 of the same year, another terrorist drove through a crowd of students at Ohio State University in Columbus, injuring 11 people. Three weeks later, a Tunisian terrorist hijacked a truck and used it to kill 12 people at a Berlin Christmas market. Vehicle attacks occurred throughout the following year. On March 22, 2017, a British man ran down pedestrians on Westminster Bridge in London. A few weeks later an Uzbek man killed four people when he deliberately rammed pedestrians in Stockholm, Sweden. Terrorists conducted another vehicle attack on London Bridge in June, and an ISIS cell used a truck to kill 13 people in Barcelona in August. Then on Halloween, an Uzbek-American who had sworn allegiance to the Islamic State used a rental truck to kill eight people on a bike path in Manhattan. Islamist extremists have not, however, been the only terrorists to use vehicles to kill people. On June 19, 2017, a white British man, plowed into a crowd of Muslims leaving evening prayers at the Finsbury Park Mosque in London, killing one and injuring 11 others. A white supremacist attending a Unite the Right rally drove his car into a group of counterdemonstrators in Charlottesville, Virginia, on August 17, 2017, killing one woman and injuring 19 others.

The nightmare terrorist scenario involves extremists getting hold of a weapon of mass destruction (WMD). WMDs are chemical, biological, radiological, and nuclear materials used to produce mass casualties. There have been only a few WMD terrorist attacks, and those have had limited success. On March 20, 1995, the Aum Shinrikyo cult released Sarin nerve gas on a Tokyo subway, killing 12 people and injuring more than 5,000. In 1984, members of the Rajneesh Commune in Wasco County, Oregon, conducted a bioterror attack using salmonella. They wanted to infect enough people to prevent them voting in the elections for county commissioners so that Rajneesh candidates would win. After poisoning two commissioners by giving them tainted glasses of water, they sent out two-person teams to lace 10 salad bars with the bacteria. No one died, but 751 people became ill.[10]

No group has yet been able to perpetrate a terror attack using nuclear or radiological material. A nuclear attack would require building or securing a nuclear device and detonating it in a target-rich environment, such as a city. Fortunately, making a bomb requires facilities and expertise currently beyond the capability of terrorist groups. Even states sympathetic to a VEO would be extremely reluctant to give it a bomb for fear of retaliation from the country against which the extremists used it. In 1997, the television documentary show *60 Minutes* ran a feature story in which former Russian General Aleksander Lebed claimed that the Soviet military had suitcase nuclear bombs and that 100 of them had gone missing at the end of the Cold War. Critics have, however, cast doubt on the story and even on the feasibility of building such a device.[11]

Radiological dispersal devices (RDDs), commonly called "dirty bombs," pose a more realistic potential threat. These weapons use a conventional explosive device to spread radioactive material over an area, rendering it uninhabitable for a protracted period of time. Frightening though this prospect sounds, building such a device would not be easy. It would require a significant amount of radioactive material to contaminate even a small area and a sophisticated bomb to disperse it properly. The radioactive material could be cleaned up, and the deaths it caused (primarily from cancer and other health-related issues) would be few and take years to occur. The fear such a device would inspire is thus out of proportion to the threat it poses. For that reason, the Nuclear Regulatory Commission has described the dirty bomb as a "weapon of mass disruption" rather than a "weapon of mass destruction."[12]

Terrorists have proven to be creative and adaptive. They constantly seek new weapons and tactics to ply their trade. Governments must strive to stay one step ahead of them. That involves considering not only what they have done in the past but also what they might do in the future. Remotely piloted aircraft, commonly known as "drones," pose a considerable potential threat. Drones come in a variety of sizes, from large military vehicles capable of traveling great distances and delivering lethal payloads to toys no bigger than a human hand. Companies like Amazon are already planning to use drones to deliver orders directly to buyers' doorsteps. Unfortunately, if such aircraft can deliver packages, they can also carry bombs.

A drone might also cause an airliner to crash if it were drawn into the plane's engine. A few near misses by recreational drones and commercial aircraft have already occurred. Other than restricting the use of drones around airports, the government has done little to regulate the use of this new technology.

Cyberterrorism has been the subject of considerable speculation and much hype. Films like *Live Free or Die Hard* have presented nightmare scenarios in which cyberterrorists hack into traffic systems to change signals and cause numerous auto accidents. So far, however, cyberattacks have been perpetrated by states against other states to disrupt government and commercial systems, as Russian hackers did against Estonia in 2007, or to steal proprietary information from manufacturers, as China has frequently been accused of doing, or by criminals stealing data for economic gain.

TERRORIST IDEOLOGY

There is more to terrorism, however, than attacks carried out against innocent civilians using a variety of weapons to produce mass casualties and spread fear. Ideology distinguishes VEOs from other groups and individuals who use terror. Everyone has an ideology, a complex worldview comprising conscious beliefs and unconscious assumptions. Ideologies can be religious, secular, or a blend of both. Socialism, capitalism, fascism, nationalism, and a host of other "isms" have motivated human behavior for good and ill over the centuries. In the context of these intellectual movements, the term "terrorism" is highly problematic because it implies that the use of terror is an end in itself, rather than a means to an end. This tendency to define organizations solely in terms of their tactics provides another reason for replacing "terrorism" with "violent extremism."

Ideologies vary with the extremist groups that espouse them. At one time or another, every major world religion has been perverted to create an ideology that justifies violence. Secular ideologies like Marxism and environmentalism have also been used to justify extremism. Whatever their differences, however, all ideologies espoused by extremist groups have one characteristic in common: at their core lies a grievance narrative and an empowerment narrative. A grievance narrative articulates what the group perceives as wrong with the world.[13] An extremist organization usually has little difficulty identifying legitimate grievances among the people it claims to represent. The PIRA rightly decried a century of oppression suffered by Catholics at the hands of Protestants in Northern Ireland. In the United States during the 1990s the Earth Liberation Front conducted arson attacks against targets deemed a threat to the environment, including a ski resort in Vail, Colorado. During the 1970s and 1980s Red Army Faction blamed capitalism and the class system for the ills of Germany and the world.

A laundry list of grievances, no matter how egregious, will not by itself inspire violent extremism. Terrorists also need to be convinced that they can eliminate or ameliorate the grievance of their group, even if they themselves die in the process. An empowerment narrative tells the aggrieved that they are not powerless, that they can effect meaningful change through violence. VEOs build their empowerment narrative on success. The more attacks they carry out, the stronger the case they can make that violence works. For this reason, the anarchists of the nineteenth century (arguably the first modern terrorists) described terrorist attacks as "propaganda of the deed."[14] The 9/11 attacks had two audiences. To the American people, al-Qaeda proclaimed: "We can hit and hurt you at any time." To its supporters, the group declared: "We are not powerless." A campaign of violence enhances the empowerment narrative and attracts followers who share the grievance narrative. Success thus breeds success.

VEO ideology based upon religion provides a particularly strong empowerment narrative. All of the world's great religions have been a force for good, and none is inherently violent. Each has, however, been perverted by some of its followers at one time or another to justify violence. Employed in this manner, religion empowers extremists by providing a divine mandate for their cause. People who believe that they are doing God's will can justify any action, no matter how horrific. They are often willing to die, especially if they believe that they will be rewarded with eternal life in paradise for their faithfulness.

RADICALIZATION

Radicalization is the process by which individuals come to accept the grievance and empowerment narratives. Academics, analysts, and policy makers are struggling to understand the process by which people become radicalized. Whatever differences exist among those who study the phenomenon, experts all agree on a few key points. First, radicalization is a far more complex process than previously imagined. Second, there are different paths to radicalization. Third, the factors that impel some people to join an extremist group vary with time and place. As one expert astutely concluded, "Radicalization tends to combine social, political and cultural circumstances with individual processes and interpersonal relations. This is a complex web, and it shows that there is no single route to radicalization, at least on the individual level."[15]

This complexity notwithstanding, some experts have tried to develop behavioral models to explain the radicalization process. One, developed by Mitchell Silber and Arvin Bhatt for the New York Police Department, claims to explain how Americans become jihadis. They define four distinct phases of radicalization: preradicalization, identification, indoctrination, and jihadization. They insist that observable behaviors or "signatures" characterize each phase.[16] Human rights groups and academics have criticized this and other law enforcement models for treating radicalization as a "conveyor belt" in which each stage leads inexorably to the next.[17] They point out that little empirical research supports these models and note the highly problematic nature of the few studies that have been conducted. The studies are based on the dubious assumption that overt observable changes in behavior accompany radicalization and that changes in behavior drawn from a list of characteristics automatically signal that the individual is headed down the path toward violent extremism.[18]

Recognizing the complexity of radicalization and the difficulty of modeling the process does not, however, mean that vulnerable populations cannot be identified. Marginalized people need little persuasion to accept the validity of the grievance narrative presented by extremist groups that claim to act on their behalf. Communities whose residents lack opportunity or face overt discrimination based on their race, ethnicity, religion, or social status may become fertile recruiting grounds for VEOs. However, the vast majority of people in these communities never accept the empowerment narrative offered by extremist organizations. Of those who do, only a tiny percentage engage in violence. Furthermore, recruits come from the mainstream as well as from the margins of societies.

Identifying at-risk individuals is even more difficult than recognizing the vulnerable populations to which they belong. A variety of factors impel people to join extremist groups. In desperately poor areas, offers of even modest sums of money motivate some individuals to join. Others have suffered a personal loss and seek revenge. Traumatized people living in refugee camps may be especially prone to recruitment for this reason. Young people in minority communities, especially children of immigrants, also seem particularly at risk. First-generation youth often feel alienated both from their parents' world and the society in which they live. This double alienation can make them particularly vulnerable to radicalization.[19] Others seek adventure, an escape from the boredom of ordinary life. However, the vast majority of people in any of these categories never engage in violent or even illegal nonviolent behavior. Potential recruits do not fit a simple profile, and variations by country and VEO further complicate matters. Simplistic profiling often leads to stereotyping and the stigmatizing of entire communities, which further alienates marginalized people, making them even more vulnerable to radicalization.

The difficulty of developing a reliable terrorist recruit profile and the dangers of stereotyping do not preclude identifying warning signs of radicalization. Behavioral changes may be indicators, but only when they are part of a larger pattern. The case of Rizwan Farook, who, along with his wife Tashfeen Malik, killed 14 people in San Bernardino, California, in December 2105, illustrates this point. After the attack, Farook's father described how, in the months before the attack, his son had grown a beard and become more religious. These behaviors in and of themselves were no cause for concern, but Farook also expressed anger toward coworkers who allegedly made fun of his appearance, and he showed his father a gun he had purchased. Unfortunately, the father did not report the incident to police or anyone else. The San Bernardino shooting illustrates another important point about profiling: family and close associates, not law enforcement, are most likely to spot the warning signs of radicalization.

To a significant degree, radicalization and recruitment are specific to each extremist group and the social and cultural contexts in which it operates. As will be seen, other than the desire to act on strong feelings of alienation and anger, those who join ISIS have little in common with those who become members of U.S. hate groups. Ideology and the process by which people adopt it vary considerably between VEO groups. Recruits to a particular group may join for different reasons, depending on their location and circumstances. A Syrian in a Turkish refugee camp may undergo a different process in becoming an ISIS recruit than would a young man in Paris, Brussels, or London.

Understanding how people become radicalized also requires figuring out who radicalizes them. Before the advent of the Internet and the development of social media, that question could be easily answered. Conversion to the cause required one-to-one human contact. Personal interaction still plays a crucial role in radicalization, but the interaction does not always occur face-to-face in the physical world. As will be seen in discussions of specific groups, chat rooms and other forms of virtual communication can play an important role in the radicalization process. Whether terrorist recruits can "self-radicalize" solely through the Internet and social media remains a subject of intensive study and considerable debate. A limited number of case studies suggest that radicalization usually requires human interaction at some point, with social media accelerating the process. "Lone-wolf" terrorists, however, may be the exception to this pattern. They often embrace an extremist ideology without formally joining any group, so they require no recruiter to enlist them.

In cases of direct interaction, the recruiter must know the individual well enough to build trust. Often a relationship between them already exists: siblings, close friends, or spouses may be agents of radicalization. Trust also attaches to a person in a position of authority. Intelligence services in the United States, Canada, and Western Europe have long been concerned about radical imams preaching to youth in mosques. Even when the imams do not espouse radical views, youth leaders at the mosque may be agents of radicalization. Charismatic leaders whom potential recruits do not know personally but respect may also persuade them to join a VEO. White supremacist gatherings like the "Unite the Right" rally in Charlottesville, Virginia, in August 2017 provide attendees an opportunity for radicalization. As with other aspects of violent extremism, however, the agents of radicalization will vary by group, location, and circumstances.

ORGANIZATIONS, NETWORKS, AND MOVEMENTS

As nonstate actors engaged in illegal activity, VEOs must operate clandestinely. They require an organizational structure that maximizes their ability to function while minimizing their likelihood of being detected. Some VEOs organize themselves as hierarchies. Their structure resembles that of a corporate personnel diagram, with designated leaders and subordinates organized by task or function characterized by clear lines of authority. This organization allows for centralization of command and control and efficient operation, but it has definite weaknesses. Hierarchical structures are particularly vulnerable to decapitation strikes, the removal of those in leadership roles. Target its leaders, and the group no longer functions. Clearly defined lines of communication also make it easier for law enforcement to identify and apprehend group members. Each individual arrested will know the names of his or her superiors and subordinates. Hierarchical organizations work best when the VEO has a safe haven in which its leaders can operate. PIRA, which waged a 30-year campaign of terror in Northern Ireland, located its general staff in the Irish Republic, out of reach of the British security forces.

The vulnerability of hierarchical organizations has led VEOs to adopt network structures. The simplest and oldest form of network organization is the hub-and-spoke model. This model retains the centralized authority of the traditional hierarchical organization, but it loosens the connection to subordinate bodies. The leadership hub connects to semiautonomous cells via a single point of contact, usually the cell leader (the "spoke"). This model provides greater security and flexibility than a strict hierarchy, but it still leaves the organization vulnerable to decapitation. Take out the hub, and the spokes lose direction. If the hub can be located in a safe haven, however, this structure can be effective.

The vulnerability of the hierarchical and even of the hub-and-spoke models has led violent extremists to adopt decentralized network structures. Networks consist of nodes and the connections among them. A node may be a single individual or a group. Analysts classify networks based upon the nature of the connections between nodes. "Chain" networks link a series of nodes in succession, like the string of lights on a Christmas tree. "Core" or "star" networks link nodes to a central leader or body but also allow nodes to communicate with one another. They are essentially variations of the hub-and-spoke model. "Mesh" or "all-channel" networks allow nodes to connect with one another without linking to a central hub. Extremist networks may employ any one or a combination of these network models. Their networks can be local, regional, or international.

Complex international terrorist networks may contain "clusters" or sub-networks located regionally. The Internet, cell phones, and social media have increased the range and effectiveness of networks by facilitating communication between nodes over great distances. Networks offer advantages over other forms of organization. They are hard to detect, highly adaptive, and difficult to disrupt, and they easily regenerate. Mapping them requires considerable data, and targeting individual nodes has limited effect.[20]

Violent extremism manifests itself not only as discrete groups and complex networks but also as broad ideological movements. White supremacy (often designated as "white nationalism") in the United States illustrates this point. At its core lies a constellation of beliefs, attitudes, and assumptions about the superiority of Caucasian people. Most of the adherents to this belief system never join a group, and most of those who do never become violent. Many extremist groups do not openly advocate violence. On the other hand, some individuals who never join a white supremacist group engage in violence on behalf of the ideology. An extremist movement thus creates a milieu of ideas that produce a variety of violent and nonviolent manifestations.

HISTORIC TRENDS AND PATTERNS

Terror has been used by states since the beginning of civilization, but, according to David Rapoport, modern terrorism dates to the last quarter of the nineteenth century when a wave of anarchist terror struck Europe and the United States. Revolutionary groups in Tsarist Russia perpetrated much of the violence, but several prominent incidents occurred in the United States, including the Haymarket Square bombing in Chicago in 1886 and the assassination of President William McKinley in Buffalo, New York, in 1901. A second wave of terrorism accompanied the anticolonial insurgencies of the mid-twentieth century. A third wave of leftist terrorism occurred in the 1960s and 1970s, and a fourth wave of religious terrorism began with the 1979 Islamic revolution in Iran and continues to the present.[21] Not all VEOs and terrorist campaigns fit neatly into Rapoport's waves, but his model does reveal that terrorism waxes and wanes over time and is associated with larger historical movements.

Geography provides another useful lens through which to view patterns of violent extremism. The University of Maryland Global Terrorism Database project has mapped attacks from 1970 to 2015 and developed an intensity scale based upon the number of incidents in a given area. The map reveals that the incidence of terrorist violence correlates with local conflicts, organized criminal activity, and other forms of social unrest. As would be expected, the Middle East has been an area of intense terrorist activity for decades owing to the struggle between Israel and various

Palestinian groups and a long series of local wars. The protracted struggle between the Revolutionary Armed Forces of Colombia (FARC) and the Colombian government and widespread narcotic production and trafficking has made that country a hotbed of terrorism. Central America saw a high incidence of terrorism by governments and insurgents in the 1980s due to conflicts in Nicaragua and El Salvador. A 30-year insurgency by Tamil separatists produced numerous terrorist attacks in the small island nation and its neighbor India. Nigeria and Somalia have also been wracked by civil conflict characterized by terrorism as has Northern Ireland.[22]

The close relationship between civil wars and terrorism continues today. The *Global Terrorism Index 2017* reported that from 1985 to 2016, 95 percent of terrorist attacks were linked to local conflicts.[23] Countries with the highest number of combat deaths also have the highest number of terrorist fatalities. From 2012 to 2016, Syria, Iraq, Yemen, and Afghanistan had both high combat and high terrorism death rates.[24] A combination of weak governance and the propensity of belligerents in civil wars to employ a combination of conventional and unconventional tactics explains this correlation.[25] Terrorist attacks in war zones also target military and government personnel more frequently than terrorist attacks in more stable areas.[26] Areas with unusually high incidents of organized crime also experience high levels of terrorism, perhaps because such criminal activity often results from weak governance. This pattern is clearly visible in the terrorism statistics for Mexico and the Central American drug corridor. The correlation between terrorism and other forms of conflict suggests that in most cases, nonstate actors use terror as one tactic among many in a locally focused campaign rather than as a strategy in a global ideological struggle.

This terrorist data suggests the need to disaggregate genuinely ideologically driven, extremism from terror employed as a tactic in other types of conflict. Even ideologically motivated international VEOs, however, usually originate in a specific country or region. Attacks farther afield often result from a spillover effect. Al-Qaeda attacked the United States because the U.S. government supported what it considered apostate regimes in the Muslim world, particularly Egypt and Saudi Arabia. It targeted the far enemy to facilitate its struggle with the near one. Broad ideological justifications for violence frequently mask or at least complement profoundly local grievances. PIRA carried out terrorist attacks in England but only as a means to the end of forcing the British out of Northern Ireland. Boko Haram is a vicious Islamist VEO, but its origins lie in a north-south, Christian-Muslim split within Nigeria reflected in economic disparity between the two regions. The local origins of so much terrorism has profound implications for counterterrorism. A strategy for countering an international terrorist network without understanding its local origins has little chance of success.

The Global Terrorism Data Base also indicates that, contrary to popular belief, the United States is not a hotbed of terrorist activity, although it may suffer more frequent lone-wolf attacks. Three incidents account for the vast majority of terrorist deaths on American soil over the past 25 years: the bombing of the Alfred P Murrah Federal Building in 1995 (168 dead), the 9/11 attacks (2,977 dead), and the 2016 Orlando nightclub shooting (49 dead). From September 12, 2001, to December 31, 2016, VEO attacks in the United States killed 225 people, with 119 of them murdered by Islamist jihadis and 106 by right-wing extremists.[27] Forty-one percent of the deaths caused by Islamist radicals occurred in a single incident, the 2016 Orland nightclub shooting, and an ISIS sympathizer, not the organization itself, perpetrated the massacre. Most terrorist attacks fail, and the majority of the rest kill or injure far fewer people than generally believed. From 2012 to 2016, 27,000 terrorist attacks worldwide resulted in no casualties; during the same period, only 8.5 percent of attacks killed more than five people.[28]

Terrorism is thus a persistent problem but not an existential threat to the United States. That it has loomed so large in American political discourse attests to the enormous emotive power of terrorist attacks. Many people exaggerate the danger terrorism poses to them personally. Actuarial data collected by insurance companies puts the chance of dying in a terrorist attack at 1 in 20 million, 100,000 times less likely than being hit by an asteroid (1 in 200,000). The average American is more likely to be killed by a bear while visiting Yellowstone National Park (1 in 2.1 million) and far more likely to be murdered in an ordinary crime by another American (1 in 18,690) than to be killed by a violent extremist.[29] Politicians willing to encourage fear for partisan gain exacerbate the distorted popular perception of the terrorist threat.

Death and injury are not, however, the only consequences of terrorism. VEO campaigns have significant economic consequences. The direct short-term costs of the 9/11 attacks amounted to $27.2 billion, but indirect and long-term expenditures drove that figure to $3.3 trillion.[30] Since then the estimated annual global economic cost of terrorism peaked in 2014 at $1.6 billion and then declined significantly to approximately $90 billion in 2015.[31] The increase in terrorism during 2016 may, however, have caused the figure to rise again. At least some of the cost of terrorism stems from overreaction and fear. Putting extra security guards in train stations after the March 2016 Brussels attacks, even when there was no evidence that ISIS planned similar attacks in the United States, cost money but did nothing to make Americans safer. What we do to ourselves out of fear can be as damaging as what the terrorists do to us out of malice.

Recognizing that terrorism does not pose an existential threat to the United States or its allies does not mean pretending that it poses no threat at all. However, it does mean keeping the threat in a healthy perspective, both in absolute terms and relative to other threats facing the country. Violent extremism in all its forms must be addressed, but it should be countered with a strategy and tactics that do not compromise the core values of the nation. Curtailing freedoms and civil liberties in the interests of a vaguely defined concept of security amounts to taking ourselves hostage to our own fears. Spending millions of dollars on placebo security that makes us feel safe without enhancing real security wastes money. If we allow fear to guide us, the terrorists have won.

THREATS FROM THE LEFT

Readers may question the omission of left-wing extremism from this study. At this point in history, however, those espousing far-left ideologies do not pose a serious threat to the United States. From 1992 through August 2017, left-wing extremists killed 23 people in the United States.[32] Many of these deaths have been attributed to black nationalism, including the murder of five Dallas police officers by Michael Xavier Johnson following a Black Lives Matter rally in July 2016. Johnson had no connection to the movement, but his online activity did reveal an interest in Black Power groups.[33] One such group, the New Black Panther Party, espouses a racist and anti-Semitic ideology, so it can hardly be considered "left wing."

Although leftist terrorist groups like the anarchists of the early 20th century and the Red Army faction that plagued Germany in the 1970s have posed a significant threat in the past, no contemporary leftist organization has risen to their level of violence. The "Antifa" (short for antifascist) movement has gained strength since the election of Donald Trump. Antifa activists may belong to a specific group or simply act on the movement's beliefs. Like black-bloc protesters in Germany during the 1970s, antifa members dress in black, confront far-right groups at rallies, and conduct demonstrations of their own. They have been willing to fight their counterparts on the street and have vandalized property, but they do not use bombs or firearms and have killed no one. They do need to be monitored by law enforcement, but at present, they pose no serious threat. Their activities do not come close to matching violence perpetrated by far-right extremists.

TODAY'S HYBRID THREATS

Despite certain similarities, violent extremism today differs from violent extremism in the past. Extremist movements, groups, and networks have existed throughout the modern era, but never before have they been so complex and so multidimensional. Today, VEOs exist in hybrid form, operating simultaneously as groups, networks, and ideological movements. The United States faces two such hybrid threats—one international, the other domestic. The international threat is widely recognized but poorly understood. Most people know something about al-Qaeda and ISIS, but they do not see them as manifestations of the same ideological movement.

They understand far less about the global network of groups, cells, and individuals linked to one or both organizations. Failure to understand the multidimensional, hybrid nature of the threat has led to an emphasis on defeating the core organizations in the mistaken belief that doing so will end the threat. Most people probably believe that al-Qaeda has been defeated because the United States killed Osama bin Laden and degraded his organization to the point where it has virtually disappeared from the news. They may misinterpret its inaction over the past few years as a sign of defeat when the organization might be rebuilding. The public may also expect that with the loss of ISIS territory in the Middle East, terrorist attacks in the United States and Europe will decline when they might, in fact, increase. As one part of the hybrid entity (the core organization) weakens, another part (the network) picks up some of the slack.

A growing domestic extremist threat has been developing alongside the international one, but it has received far less attention. "White nationalism" is a broad ideological movement based on the belief in the racial superiority of Caucasians and their fear of being displaced by "inferior" peoples. The movement embraces a constellation of beliefs and encompasses a variety of groups and organizations. The difference between groups, however, is often little more than a matter of emphasis. Domestic extremists are equal-opportunity haters. Neo-Nazis, for example, blame liberal Jews for affirmative action, thus linking anti-Semitism with racism and misogyny. Islamophobic groups attract people who oppose immigration, especially from Latin America. Antigovernment organizations claim to fight for local autonomy and states' rights, but they often interpret these rights as the freedom to discriminate against people of color and religious minorities. Groups that target LGBTQ (lesbian, gay, bisexual, transgender, and questioning) people usually harbor prejudice against other minorities. The United States needs to devote more resources to countering the threat from within while it continues to combat the threat from without.

CHAPTER 2

Radical Islamism and the Rise of Al-Qaeda

On February 23, 1998, the little-known son of a Saudi billionaire issued a fatwa (religious proclamation) against the United States. The proclamation accused the country of crimes against Islam, most notably support for Israel and "occupation" of Saudi Arabia during the 1990–91 Gulf War. America's sins, the writer proclaimed, were "a clear declaration of war on God, his messenger and Muslims." He then issued a chilling call to arms:

The ruling to kill the Americans and their allies—civilians and military—is an individual duty for every Muslim who can do it in any country in which it is possible to do it, in order to liberate the al-Aqsa Mosque [Jerusalem] and the holy mosque [Mecca] from their grip, and in order for their armies to move out of all the lands of Islam, defeated and unable to threaten any Muslim.[1]

Few Americans had heard of Osama bin Laden, and even fewer took his threat seriously. That would soon change. Less than six months later, his terrorist group detonated truck bombs outside the U.S. embassies in Nairobi, Kenya, and Dar es Salaam, Tanzania, killing 224 people. Al-Qaeda (Arabic for "the base") had put itself on the radar as a significant security threat, but it would take a devastating attack on the U.S. homeland on September 11, 2001, to make its name a household term and bin Laden a symbol of infamy.

Many people assume that the ideology that has inspired so much violence over the past two decades began with bin Laden's declaration of war on the United States. However, this belief system has its roots much further in the past, and it will continue to manifest itself in various forms for the foreseeable future. What has been popularly dubbed "radical Islam" motivated al-Qaeda, motivates ISIS, and will motivate similar groups in the future. This ideology matters more than those who espouse it, for as long as it exists, it will inspire new groups, networks, and individuals willing to engage in terrorism. Understanding radical Islamism as an ideological movement is, therefore, crucial to understanding international terrorism today. Ideology is the foundation of this multidimensional threat.

ISLAM, ISLAMISM, AND THE IDEOLOGY OF AL-QAEDA

The extent of terrorism conducted in the name of Islam has led many to wonder whether the religion has a propensity to inspire extremism not found in other faiths. A closer look at history and the contemporary word reveals the absurdity of this claim. Every religion has been perverted in the interests of violent extremism. From the Crusades to the colonization of Africa, Asia, and the Americas, Christians have been quite willing to murder in the name of God. Today Buddhists persecute Muslim Rohingya in Thailand. Hindus have murdered Sikhs and Muslims. And even the Anti-Defamation League, an organization devoted to combating anti-Semitism, has condemned the Jewish Defense League. Clearly, no faith community has a monopoly on either love or hate. Furthermore, much seemingly religious violence has other causes. Catholics and Protestants in Northern Ireland did not fight over theology but for political and economic power in the province. The Bosnian conflict pitted Muslims, Roman Catholics, and Orthodox Christians against one another, but religious differences did not cause the conflict. The Syrian civil war has a sectarian dimension, but at its core, it is a struggle for political control. Ethnic nationalism has been the cause of far more bloodshed than religion.

Nonetheless, the teachings of Islam have been used to justify terrorism. The belief system that animated bin Laden and his followers is an extreme version of Islamism (sometimes called the "new Islamic discourse"), a broad intellectual movement within Sunni Islam concerned with how Muslims should practice their faith in the context of the modern world. In particular, Islamists have struggled with reconciling their faith with Western secular ideologies like nationalism, capitalism, and socialism.[2] Islamism has its roots in a much older revival movement known as "*Salafism*." Derived from the Arab word "*salaf*," meaning "devout ancestor," the movement began in the ninth century as an effort to make the *Uma* (community of the faithful) live as they had in the days of the Prophet Mohammed. Another Salafist movement occurred in the fourteenth century, led by the scholar Taqi ibn Taymiyyah. The Salafist movement that had the greatest influence on bin Laden and his followers took place in eighteenth-century Arabia. In 1745, the cleric Muhammad Ibn al-Wahhab (1703–92) formed an alliance with the Saud family, rulers of Najd (a kingdom in the Arabian Peninsula). In 1932, Abdul Aziz Ibn Saud became the first ruler of modern Saudi Arabia, and Wahhabism became the form of Islam practiced in the country.

Wahhabism represents an ultraconservative form of Islam. It insists society be governed by strict shariah law, both family and criminal, and demands adherence to clearly defined gender roles that subordinate women. The attitude of Wahhabism toward other Muslims has had a profound impact on al-Qaeda's ideology. Mainstream Islam teaches that only Allah may judge the faith of a Muslim. Wahhabis, however, insist that they can declare those who do not adhere to their beliefs *takfirs* (apostates), making them de facto non-Muslims who can be killed with impunity.[3] Wahhabis also embrace a more militant notion of *jihad*, the Islamic duty to struggle to live a good life (greater jihad) and to wage defensive war when necessary (lesser jihad). While traditional Islam allows for defensive war against non-Muslims threatening the Uma, Wahhabism allows jihad to be waged against takfirs as well and has encouraged offensive war to spread the faith. Although many Americans conflate Wahhabism and Islam, Wahhabis make up less than 5 million of the world's 1.6 billion Muslims.[4] Found primarily in Saudi Arabia and the Persian Gulf states, Wahhabi Islam today is ultraconservative but not inherently violent. Only a tiny percentage of its adherents support terrorism. Its theology has nonetheless been co-opted by extremists.

Osama bin Laden grew up in Saudi Arabia under the influence of Wahhabism, but that experience alone does not explain his embrace of violent extremism. Raised in the same conservative environment, his half-brother Salim turned out to be an international playboy. Two other forces shaped what would become al-Qaeda's defining ideology. The first was a radical Islamist movement that began in Egypt during the 1920s and developed throughout the twentieth century. The second was a series of historical events that rocked the Arab world from 1967 through 1991 and convinced bin Laden that God was punishing Muslims for deviating from the true path of Islam defined in the *Holy Quran* and the *Hadiths* (sayings of the Prophet Mohammed).

In 1928, an Egyptian Salafist cleric named Hassan al-Banna formed the Muslim Brotherhood. Like Taymiyyah, he advocated a return to the Islam of the eighth century, and like Wahhab, he advocated jihad against apostates as well as infidels. The brotherhood espoused two broad goals that would be adopted by bin Laden:

1. Freeing the Islamic homeland from all foreign authority, for this is a natural right belonging to every human being which only the unjust oppressor will deny.
2. The establishment of an Islamic state within this homeland, which acts according to the precepts of Islam, applies its social regulations, advocates its sound principles, and broadcasts its mission to all of mankind.[5]

Al-Banna rejected the idea that war on behalf of the faith was the "lesser jihad" and argued that Muslims must be prepared to fight "in order to rescue the territories of the Muslims and repel the attacks of the disbelievers."[6]

After al-Banna was assassinated in 1949, a new spokesman emerged. Sayyid Qutb shared his predecessor's contempt for the Western ideologies at work in postcolonial Egypt. He espoused even more militant views than al-Banna, rejecting what he considered the apologist view of jihad as purely defensive war. Jihad must be waged

to establish God's authority in the earth; to arrange human affairs according to the true guidance provided by God; to abolish all the Satanic forces and Satanic systems of life; to end the lordship of one man over others since all men are creatures of God and no one has the authority to make them his servants or to make arbitrary laws for them.[7]

Opposition to monarchy led Qutb and the Brotherhood to support the 1952 coup to overthrow the corrupt King Farouk. However, Qutb soon fell afoul of the coup leader and Egypt's new ruler, Colonel Gamal Abdul Nasser, who wished to govern the country as a secular republic and promoted Arab nationalism, both of which Salafists opposed. Nasser had Qutb executed in 1966, but the Brotherhood survived and has been involved in Egyptian politics ever since.

Qutb's writings had a profound influence on young bin Laden, according to one of the al-Qaeda leader's college friends, Jamal Khalifa.[8] Sayyid Qutb's brother Mohammed taught at King Abdulaziz University in Saudi Arabia when bin Laden attended the school. Mohammed shared Sayyed's opposition to secularism, nationalism, and communism. Like his brother, he embraced violent jihad and believed it could be waged against takfirs as well as infidels. Unlike his brother, however, Mohammed emphasized an inevitable struggle between Islam and the United States. Sayyid had lived in the United States and condemned its decadence and materialism, but he did not see it as a direct threat to his goal of restoring the governance of the Muslim world to its historic roots. At the time of his death, the Soviet Union and its atheistic communist ideology seemed to pose a greater threat, especially so because of its close ties with Nasser.[9]

During his time at university, bin Laden also fell under the influence of the radical cleric Abdullah Azzam. Azzam taught that Muslims had a sacred duty to defend Islam wherever it was threatened. He is thus credited with articulating the idea of global jihad, which became a central tenet of al-Qaeda's ideology.[10] "Jihad is the most excellent form of worship, and by means of it the Muslim can reach the highest of ranks," Azzam declared.[11]

By the end of the 1970s, bin Laden had absorbed all the elements of the ideology that would inspire al-Qaeda and ISIS. Salafist jihadism (also known as Islamist extremism or radical Islamism) rejects secularism and western political ideologies such as nationalism, communism, and liberal democracy. It views the governments of most Muslim states as apostate regimes and calls for their overthrow. Only Islamic republics governed by strict sharia law conform to the teachings of the *Quran*. Muslims who do not adhere to this strict version of Islam could be declared takfirs and killed as if they were infidels. Violent jihad is not a lesser act but a sacred duty of all Muslims, who must defend the faith whenever and wherever it comes under attack. As the world's remaining superpower and the embodiment of all that the Salafists hated, the United States is the primary enemy of Islam.

AFGHAN INTERLUDE

As the case of the Muslim Brotherhood in Egypt makes abundantly clear, ideology alone will not produce an effective extremist organization capable of waging global jihad. A confluence of events and circumstances allowed radical Islamism to crystalize into the world's most extensive and lethal terrorist network. Israel's stunning victory over four Arab armies in the Six-Day War of June 1967 seemed to confirm the moral bankruptcy of regimes that had emulated the West. God was punishing the Muslim world, the conservative theological argument went, for turning its back on traditional Islam. The Ayatollah Khomeini's Islamic revolution in Iran offered a promising contrast to the failure of the Arab states. The Shi'a cleric had succeeded in accomplishing what the Sunni Salafist movement had failed to do in countries like Egypt: establish an Islamic republic governed by sharia law. These events sparked an Islamic awakening, which moved Islamism from the margins to the center of the discussion of how Muslims were to live in the modern world.[12]

The transformative event in the life of bin Laden that led to the creation of his extremist movement did not, however, occur in the Middle East. In 1979, the Soviet Union invaded Afghanistan to prop up a communist regime threatened by a growing Islamist insurgency. Muslim regimes and wealthy individuals from the Middle East funded the foreign fighters, who also received aid from the United States. The conflict attracted young Arab men who wanted to wage jihad against the infidels invading a Muslim land. These *mujahideen* (holy warriors) never amounted to much either in numbers or fighting effectiveness. "Altogether, people who spent six years and people who spent six days, maybe the number will come up to ten thousand," concluded one Saudi journalist. "Because there was even jihad tour, jihad vacation."[13] The mujahideen never numbered more than a few thousand at any one time.[14] Sometime in the early 1980s, bin Laden invited Azzam to his home in Jedda, Saudi Arabia.[15] Azzam convinced bin Laden to join the jihad. He journeyed Afghanistan in 1984, not to create a terrorist organization but to become a martyr. He told a Syrian journalist that he felt guilty for putting his own well-being above the cause of Islam and that his delay in going to fight "requires my martyrdom in the name of God."[16]

Bin Laden, of course, did not die. For some time, he did not even fight. Instead, he used his personal wealth to fund other mujahideen. In late

1984 or early 1985, Azzam, bin Laden, and Bodejema Bounoua established the Afghan Services Office in Peshawar, Pakistan. The Services Office facilitated travel of foreign fighters to Afghanistan and funded their operations there. Its contribution to the war effort paled in comparison to the covert aid provided by the United States and Saudi Arabia. The Saudi government contributed $300–$500 million a year and encouraged private donors to contribute as well. None of this money, funneled through a Swiss bank account, went to the Services Office, which received only 20 percent of private donations.[17]

Bin Laden soon grew tired of playing a minor, supporting role in the war. He wanted to fight. In 1986, he built, at his own expense, a fortified camp just over the border in Afghanistan. He named it the Lion's Den and staffed it with Arab mujahideen, most of whom had little combat experience. In April 1987, bin Laden led 120 fighters in a disastrous raid on the town of Khost, which cost him what little credibility he may have had with the seasoned Afghan fighters.[18] A month later, he led a second, more effective raid, which nonetheless accomplished little beyond provoking the Soviets into bombarding the Lion's Den. By all accounts, bin Laden was personally brave but not a terribly effective battlefield commander. He proved very successful, however, at building his limited activities into a much bigger legend. "After *our* [emphasis added] victory in Afghanistan and the defeat of the oppressors who had killed millions of Muslims," he declared in 1998, "the legend about the invincibility of the superpowers vanished."[19] He even took credit for the collapse of the Soviet Union, "in which the U.S. has no mentionable role, but rather the credit goes to God, Praise and Glory be to Him, and the Mujahideen in Afghanistan."[20]

BIRTH OF AL-QAEDA

When the Soviet Union began its withdrawal from Afghanistan in May 1988, the Afghan Services Office appeared to have served its purpose. Emboldened by their success, however, its founders wished to keep the organization alive to further the cause of Islamist jihad. Azzam first articulated the idea of broadening the organization's purpose. In a 1988 article he declared every ideological movement needs a "vanguard that gives everything it possesses in order to achieve victory for the ideology. . . . That vanguard constitutes the solid base (*al-Qaeda Sulbah*) for the expected society."[21] The precise form and focus of the new group had yet to be determined, and a power struggle over that issue may have resulted in the death of Azzam, who was assassinated in Peshawar in November 1989.

Egyptian members of the Muslim Brotherhood (which had reformed as Egyptian Islamic Jihad), particularly Ayman al-Zawahiri, played a key role in the creation of al-Qaeda. A Saudi member of the organization claims to have been present at its birth and credits the Egyptians with a major role in shaping its mission. Hasan Abd-Rabbuh maintained that he "witnessed the birth of al-Qaeda" in bin Laden's Peshawar residence following the Soviet withdrawal. "The idea of al-Qaeda is an Egyptian one by the Islamic Jihad group."[22] In those early days, al-Qaeda had a limited focus. Another bin Laden associate described the leader's original intent: "Osama believed he could set up an army of men responding to the jihad call," Abu Mahmud stated. "When he presented the idea to us, he did not speak of jihad against Arab regimes, but of helping Muslims against the infidel governments oppressing them, as was the case in Palestine, the Philippines, and Kashmir, especially Central Asia, which was under Soviet rule then."[23]

ENEMIES NEAR AND FAR

Al-Qaeda's mission developed first into a regional and then a global jihad following bin Laden's return to Saudi Arabia in 1989. Once again, circumstances conspired with ideology to focus the jihadist cause. A civil war in Yemen attracted bin Laden's attention. This conflict seemed the perfect opportunity to deploy the mujahideen to support an insurgency against a communist regime, just as had been done in Afghanistan. Bin Laden approached the Saudi government for permission to deploy his fighters. What transpired remains unclear. According to Bruce Riedel, a former CIA Middle East specialist, the monarchy wanted the communist regime overthrown but may have been leery of entrusting the task to bin Laden's private army.[24] Clinton administration terrorism expert Richard Clarke, on the other hand, claimed that the head of Saudi intelligence liked the idea of using an unofficial force.[25] The issue became moot with the end of the Cold War and the resolution of the Yemen conflict in 1990. Bin Laden did not accept the peace settlement, however, because it gave the communists a share in power. He continued to fund the insurgents in defiance of the monarchy. The Saudi interior minister and brother of the king, Prince Nayif bin Abdul Aziz, called bin Laden into his office, ordered him to cease his activities in Yemen, and confiscated his passport.[26]

Bin Laden soon found himself embroiled in a bigger crisis. In August 1990, Saddam Hussein invaded neighboring Kuwait and threatened Saudi Arabia. Bin Laden saw this as an opportunity to deploy his Afghan mujahideen in defense of his homeland, which contained the holiest sites of Islam. No one in the Saudi government took him seriously. Instead, they turned to the United States, which had a powerful vested interest in protecting access to the region's oil. The United States led a coalition of half a million troops to expel Saddam. The air campaign lasted six weeks and the ground assault just four days. This stunning victory enraged bin Laden. Not only had the Saudi monarchy rebuffed him, it had invited infidels onto the sacred soil of the kingdom, where once the feet of the prophet Muhammad had trod.

Bin Laden's anger boiled over into antigovernment activities, and the Saudis expelled him from the kingdom in 1991 and later revoked his citizenship. He sought refuge in Sudan, where he continued to plot against the Saudi regime. During this period of exile, bin Laden reestablished ties with Zawahiri, who merged his Egyptian Islamic Jihad organization with al-Qaeda. Zawahiri was a strong proponent of fighting the "near enemy."[27] He sought to overthrow what he considered apostate regimes governing Muslim states. Egypt and Saudi Arabia ranked foremost on the list, but with the exception of Sudan, none of the states in the Middle East conformed to the ideal of an Islamist republic governed by strict sharia law. In 1995, Zawahiri's group mounted a failed attempt to overthrow Egyptian President Hosni Mubarak.

By the mid-1990s, it had become clear that the strategy of attacking the near enemy had failed. Not a single "apostate" regime had been overthrown.[28] The United States and Saudi Arabi were bringing pressure to bear on bin Laden's Sudanese hosts, who expelled him 1996. He relocated to Afghanistan, now under control of the ultraconservative Taliban. From there he issued a "Declaration of War against the Americans Occupying the Land of the Two Holy Places," namely, Saudi Arabia. Although most people identify the 1998 fatwa as the beginning of al-Qaeda's war on the United States because of its proximity to the East Africa embassy bombings, the 1996 declaration reflects the organization's shift to attacking the "far enemy." Bin Laden detailed the numerous acts of aggression and exploitation of Muslim lands by the "Zionist-Crusader alliance" and decried the sacrilege of the Saudi monarchy for inviting U.S. forces onto the sacred soil of the kingdom. He declared forcing the infidels out of Saudi Arabia a sacred duty incumbent upon all Muslims.[29] Interestingly, bin Laden did not call for the indiscriminate killing of any and all Americans wherever they could be found as he would do in his 1998 fatwa, issued on behalf of the Islamic front.

AL-QAEDA CENTRAL

In the same year that bin Laden arrived in Afghanistan, the Central Intelligence Agency created a unit tasked with monitoring his activities and those of his growing organization. In the late 1990s, al-Qaeda developed into a well-organized group with headquartered in Kandahar. Bin Laden led the group supported by a council (*shura*), which supervised five functional committees. The military committee ran a series of training camps in Afghanistan and procured weapons for operations. The finance committee raised money for the organization, and the travel committee made arrangements for travel. The Islamic study committee issued fatwas and rulings on various matters, and the media committee published newspaper articles and handled other media matters.[30]

Al-Qaeda could develop such a centralized organization because it had a safe haven from which to operate. The Taliban had won the civil war that followed Soviet withdrawal from Afghanistan. They imposed strict sharia law on the country and welcomed bin Laden and his followers, allowing them to establish training camps in the country. U.S. intelligence sources estimate that from 1996 to 2001, 10,000–20,000 fighters from all over the world received training in these camps.[31] Most of the trainees would return to their countries of origin. Until the U.S. invasion of 2001, al-Qaeda central used its safe haven to plan and conduct attacks, including the 1998 East Africa embassy bombings and the infamous 9/11 attacks on the Pentagon and the twin towers of the World Trade Center.

GLOBAL NETWORK

If al-Qaeda had been merely a one-dimensonal terrorist organization operating from a safe haven in a hostile country, its ability to hurt the United States would have been limited. Following the 9/11 attacks, the U.S.-led invasion of Afghanistan removed the Taliban from power and forced bin Laden and other al-Qaeda members to flee. Bin Laden narrowly escaped capture and had to move his base of operations to the Federally Administered Tribal Area of Pakistan, a loosely governed area on the Pakistan side of the border. Relentless pressure and decapitation strikes might have degraded the organization to the point where it no longer posed a serious threat to the United States or its allies. Unfortunately, al-Qaeda is a hybrid entity consisting of more than the core organization, al-Qaeda central.

Even before 9/11, U.S. intelligence officials recognized the presence of a global network of al-Qaeda cells and related groups. They did not, however, fully understand the nature and extent of the network or its capabilities. Contrary to popular perception, it is not a static collection of groups tightly tethered to the center, but a complex web of entities linked to the main organization and to one another by multiple, often shifting relationships. It also consists of cells directed from the center as well as self-constituted cells acting on its behalf without direction from al-Qaeda central. To further complicate matters, the network is adaptive and resilient. Relationships among components and between each of them and the center have evolved in response to changing circumstances.

Efforts to map member organizations, never mind the entire network, have proven challenging. Al-Qaeda has been described as a "brand" and its networks members "franchises." These labels, however, imply a greater degree of centralization than often exists. Karen Zimmerman has developed a comprehensive scheme for analyzing the al-Qaeda network. She distinguishes between "affiliates" and "associates" of the central organization. Affiliate groups have sworn allegiance to the leadership of al-Qaeda and sometimes taken direction from it, although they have also acted independently. Although they participate in the global jihad, affiliates also act based on purely local or regional agendas. Associate groups share common characteristics with al-Qaeda, including ideology, but are not officially part of its network. They may have functional but not command-and-control links with the central organization. A series of interpersonal connections crosses through the formal network, adding another layer of complexity.[32] In addition to affiliates and associates, the al-Qaeda network includes local cells. The central organization deployed some of these cells for specific operations. Al-Qaeda handpicked the 19 hijackers to carry out the 9/11 attacks. Other cells formed locally on their own and then linked back to the parent organization or simply acted on its behalf under a broad mandate.

As of 2013, the last year before ISIS eclipsed it, al-Qaeda had only six affiliates: al-Qaeda in the Land of the Two Rivers (commonly known as al-Qaeda in Iraq [AQI, which has evolved into ISIS], affiliated 2004); al-Qaeda in the Arabian Peninsula (AQAP, affiliated 2009); Jabhat al-Nusra (affiliated 2013); the Algerian Salafist Group for Call and Combat (which came to be known as al-Qaeda in the Islamic Maghreb (AQIM, affiliated 2006); al-Shabab in Somalia (affiliated 2012); and Jabhat al Nusra in Iraq (affiliated 2013).[33] Some affiliates like AQAP were created by mujahideen returning from the Afghan war. Others like al-Shabab received funding from al-Qaeda. Some like AQIM developed independently and then linked up with al-Qaeda central. Although willing to carry out attacks in support of the global jihad at al-Qaeda's behest, all the affiliates also have local agendas.

Another 12 groups, according to Zimmerman's classification, qualify as associates. These groups have not formally sworn allegiance to al-Qaeda, but they share its ideology and will occasionally cooperate with it when doing so is mutually beneficial. Among the associates is Boko Haram, the Nigerian extremist group infamous for the April 2014 kidnapping of 276 school girls, 110 of whom are still missing. The list also includes the Kashmiri separatist group Lashkar-e-Taiba, the Haqqani Network in the Pakistan-Afghan border region, and the Islamic Movement of Uzbekistan, as well as several less well-known groups.[34] Ideology notwithstanding, the associate groups are far more interested in local issues than global jihad. Some might be better classified as ethnic insurgencies. However, they have sometimes worked closely with al-Qaeda to deadly effect.

Another expert has eschewed categorizing groups by type in favor of a network analysis that measures the strength of ties between groups. Victoria Barber has constructed a model based upon shared objectives, location, activity, and level of affiliation with the al-Qaeda core group and mapped the links on a continuum. Her study reveals how the network has evolved over time in response to events. From 1996 to 2000, al-Qaeda had strong links with only three groups: al-Qaeda in Yemen (which evolved into al-Qaeda in the Arabian Peninsula), the Abu Sayyaf Group in the Philippines, and Egyptian Islamic Jihad (Zawahiri's group with which it eventually merged). The success of the 9/11 attacks, not surprisingly, led to a dramatic expansion of the al-Qaeda network. It formed moderate to strong links to seven additional groups and through them to more than a dozen others in Africa, the Middle East, and Asia. Over the next decade, however, the Global War on Terror took its toll. By 2013, links between al-Qaeda central and other groups had been broken or weakened.[35]

These and other models for mapping the al-Qaeda network are useful, but none completely captures its complexity and adaptability. As many as 56 organizations have had a relationship with al-Qaeda at one time or another.[36] Their relationships with the core and with one another have not remained static. Examining specific groups and how they have operated over time provides insight for supplemental network mapping. However, as no two groups are alike, and none is typical of the rest, conclusions must be tentative. Focusing on the most prominent groups reveals their similarities and differences. With the exception of al-Qaeda itself, all members of the network are first and foremost concerned with local issues. The global jihad is secondary.

Al-Qaeda in Iraq

Following the invasion of Iraq in the spring of 2003, the greatest terrorist threat to Americans came not from al-Qaeda itself, but from an affiliate raised to fight the invaders. "Al-Qaeda in the Land of the Two Rivers," commonly known as "al-Qaeda in Iraq (AQI)," conducted numerous successful attacks against U.S. forces in Iraq from 2004 through 2006. The death of its leader in 2006, the Anbar Awakening, and the surge of U.S. forces severely weakened it, but the remnants of its members went on to found ISIS. The evolution of AQI reveals a great deal about the complex relationship between al-Qaeda and its affiliates.

The Jordanian Abu Musab al-Zarqawi had operated on the fringes of al-Qaeda for more than a decade before founding AQI. Born Ahmad Fadhil Nazzal al-Khalaylah on October 20, 1966, in Zarqa, Jordon, al-Zarqawi had a history of violence and criminality long before he became radicalized. By his 23rd birthday, he had been the subject of 37 criminal investigations. At some point during his criminal career, he became radicalized and, in 1989, went to Pakistan, where he trained in an al-Qaeda camp. The Soviets had nearly completed their withdrawal from Afghanistan, so al-Zarqawi stayed to fight in the ensuing conflict for control of the country. He returned to Jordan in 1993, where he helped found "al-Tawhid" (divine unity), a small group of a dozen or so committed extremists. The group soon ran afoul of the Jordanian government, and al-Zarqawi spent five years in prison until being released under a general amnesty in 1999.

He went back to Afghanistan to meet bin Laden, who had learned of his activities in Jordan, and seek his help.[37]

By all accounts, their meeting in Kandahar did not go well. The well-educated bin Laden found the coarse commoner too extreme. Al-Zarqawi openly criticized the al-Qaeda leader and called for the execution of the Afghan Shi'a. Despite their differences, the al-Qaeda leadership agreed to fund establishment of a base for al-Zarqawi and his followers near Herat, a city close to the Iranian border. This marriage of convenience benefited both sides. The venture cost no more than $5,000 in seed money.[38] The al-Qaeda leadership saw the venture as an opportunity to build its Jihadist network in the Middle East.[39] For his part, al-Zarqawi retained his independence. His organization grew as more Arabs joined him over the next two years. The 2001 U.S.-led invasion forced him to flee to Iran with about 300 of his followers. For the next 14 months, al-Zarqawi operated in the Kurdish no-fly zone in northern Iraq, building his own organization and cooperating with the terrorist group Ansar al-Islam. He moved to the Sunni triangle to fight U.S. forces following the March 2003 U.S. invasion. Despite his openly avowed hatred of the Shi'a, al-Zarqawi received weapons and other equipment from the Iranians, who saw him as a tool for expelling the Americans.[40] In October 2004, Zarqawi declared himself emir of al-Qaeda in Iraq, and in December, he swore allegiance to bin Laden.[41]

Affiliation did not, however, bring harmony between the two groups. The alliance was a purely pragmatic one. Bin Laden wanted a presence in Iraq, and al-Zarqawi needed the status conveyed by the al-Qaeda brand name. Bin Laden objected to al-Zarqawi's extremism and brutality, but the Jordanian terrorist leader continued to do as he pleased. AQI unleashed a reign of terror in Iraq. In addition to targeting U.S. military personnel and other foreigners, al-Zarqawi and his followers killed anyone who opposed them. They employed torture and videotaped executions, including the beheading of an American by al-Zarqawi himself. They also fueled sectarian conflict by attacking Iraqi Shi'a. Their February 2006 bombing of the al-Askari Mosque in Samarra touched off a wave of sectarian violence that left more than 1,000 people dead.

In the end, AQI hurt the cause for which it was supposedly fighting. The brutality of al-Zarqawi's foreign mujahideen alienated Iraqis who wanted to regain control of their country, not see it become the cockpit of global jihad. In 2006, local sheiks decided to cooperate with the Americans to get rid of the extremists in what came to be called the Anbar Awakening. That cooperation, coupled with a surge of U.S. forces in the summer of 2007 and the death of al-Zarqawi in an airstrike on June 7, 2006, weakened AQI. The terrorist groups would no longer be a significant player in the Sunni insurgency, but after lying dormant for several years, it would reemerge as the far more dangerous ISIS.

The case of AQI reveals several lessons about the nature of the al-Qaeda network and Islamic extremism in general. First, alliances shift, and the network adapts. Al-Zarqawi received aid from bin Laden but retained his independence, swearing allegiance to al-Qaeda belatedly and, even then, reluctantly. Second, jihadist groups evolve. Al-Tawhid became AQI, which later morphed into ISIS. Third, terrorists often act on the precept that "the enemy of my enemy is my friend." The marriage between AQI and al-Qaeda was always an uneasy one of convenience based upon a shared hatred of the United States. Their common commitment to jihad was essential, but pragmatism dictated the level of their cooperation at any given time. Fourth, groups defy easy classification. AQI got aid from al-Qaeda during its formative days and swore allegiance to the central organization, but it acted independently. It was thus technically an affiliate but behaved more like an associate. Finally, in a loose network, individuals sometimes matter more than groups. The tortuous relationship between bin Laden and al-Zarqawi shaped the interaction between al-Qaeda and AQI.

Al-Qaeda in the Arabian Peninsula

With al-Qaeda under pressure from U.S. operations in Afghanistan and AQI waning in Iraq, a new threat emerged in the Arabian Peninsula. Formed in 2009 through a merger of al-Qaeda in Saudi Arabia and al-Qaeda in Yemen, al-Qaeda in the Arabian Peninsula (AQAP) became the most lethal international threat to the United States from its inception until the rise of ISIS. Yemen had long been a hotbed of jihadist activity. Yemeni mujahideen who had trained with bin Laden founded several Islamist groups, including Islamic Jihad in Yemen (1990–1994), Army of Aden Abyan (1994–1998), and al-Qaeda in Yemen (AQY) (1998–2003).[42] Al-Qaeda in Yemen came to the attention of the world on October 12, 2000, when it attacked the USS *Cole* in Aden Harbor, killing 17 sailors and wounding 39 others. These groups enjoyed tacit support, or at least acceptance, from the government of President Ali Abdullah Saleh, who found them a useful ally in his struggle with southern insurgents and northern separatists.[43] Following the attack on the Cole, the United States put pressure on the Saleh government to fight AQY. After 9/11, that pressure increased, and the United States sent Special Forces teams to Yemen to assist the government in attacking the terrorists.[44] A U.S. drone strike killed its leader in 2002, and membership in the group declined. The group revived after several of its members escaped from prison in 2006. Three years later, it combined with al-Qaeda in Saudi Arabia to form AQAP.

AQAP launched several attacks against foreign nationals in Yemen, including kidnappings followed by executions. It carried out attacks against the West. On Christmas Day 2009, Umar Farouk Abdulmutallab of Nigeria attempted to detonate a bomb concealed in his underwear on a Northwest Airlines flight as it prepared to land in Detroit. At his trial, he declared that the bomb was a "blessed weapon to save the lives of innocent Muslims" being killed by the United States and warned of more attacks to come. He admitted that he was acting on behalf of AQAP and had been inspired by and even met one of its leaders, the radical cleric Anwar al-Awlaki.[45] In October 2010, AQAP sent two parcel bombs hidden in printer cartridges to addresses in Chicago, but they were intercepted in Britain following a tip from Saudi intelligence.[46] AQAP also published a magazine in English, *Inspire*, which encouraged Muslims living the United States to carry out attacks on their own and provided instructions on how to do so. One of its issues explained how to convert an SUV into an impro- vised tank to run down pedestrians.[47]

Unfortunately, not all AQAP plots failed. On January 7, 2015, two gun- men entered the offices of the French satirical magazine *Charlie Hebdo* in Paris and killed 12 people with firearms. AQAP released a video claiming responsibility for the attack, which it said was carried out in response to cartoons defaming the Prophet Mohammed published by the magazine. The statement claimed that the gunmen had met with the radical cleric, Anwar al-Awlaki, who masterminded the plot before U.S. forces killed him in a 2011 drone strike.[48] Authorities in France and the United States have not been able to verify these claims. The terrorist attack, however, had all the hallmarks of a carefully planned operation, rather than the actions of an enraged lone wolf.

The case of AQAP confirms the lessons of AQI and provides additional insight into the Islamist extremist movement. Like AQI, AQAP has both a local and an international dimension, and which one it emphasizes has changed over time. It has carried out most of its attacks within Yemen, although several of these operations targeted foreigners. It has also oper- ated abroad. Since the outbreak of the Yemeni civil war in 2015, it has been increasingly preoccupied with that conflict. Several of its founders had been trained in al-Qaeda camps in Afghanistan. The group supported the global jihad and swore allegiance to al-Qaeda central but acted indepen- dently. *Inspire* represented its greatest innovation and foreshadowed the social media campaign of ISIS.

Al-Shabab

The East African Islamist extremist group al-Shabab ("the youth") has its origins in the chaos following the collapse of the Somali state in the 1990s. The group began as a youth movement under the umbrella of the Union of Islamic Courts (UIC). It rose to prominence in 2006, when the UIC gained control of Mogadishu and parts of southern Somalia and became the de facto government for about six months. Following the Ethiopian invasion and the deployment of an African Union force, al-Shabab launched an insurgency against the Transitional Federal Government, considered by many Somalis to be a puppet of the foreign occupiers. Al-Shabab thus capitalized on Somali nationalism, using it to gain support even from those leery of the group's radical Islamism.[49] By 2011, al-Shabab was the best-armed militant group in Somalia and controlled the largest stretch of its territory.[50]

While al-Shabab began as a local movement, it developed into a regional network with a presence throughout the horn of Africa. It retained power in Somalia through its ability to provide largely effective alternative governance in the areas it controlled. It ran courts based on sharia law, collected taxes, and provided a modicum of other services. Al-Shabab pays its fighters and compensates families of suicide bombers—powerful incentives for recruitment in a desperately poor country. Control of the lucrative charcoal trade, combined with contributions from the Somali diaspora and wealthy donors in Saudi Arabi and the Gulf States, has given it sufficient funding to operate. It has recruited foreign fighters from as far away as Minneapolis–St. Paul. Al-Shabab organized itself as a three-layer pyramid with the leadership at the top, followed by the foreign fighters and then the local Somalis.[51]

While al-Shabab resembles an insurgent movement more than it does a traditional terrorist organization, it has an international dimension. The group swore allegiance to al-Qaeda in 2012 and has carried out attacks against neighboring states. On July 11, 2010, al-Shabab operatives bombed venues in Kampala, Uganda, killing 76 people watching the final match of the World Cup soccer tournament. The group launched the attack to punish Uganda for participating in the African Union military mission in Somalia. When Kenya invaded Somalia in October 2011, al-Shabab vowed retaliation, a promise it has kept. In addition to minor attacks, it has conducted several major operations against its neighbor. On September 21, 2013, al-Shabab gunmen carried out an attack on the Westgate Shopping Mall in Nairobi, killing 68 people and wounding 175. In November 2014, its militants attacked 28 people on a bus traveling from Mandera to Nairobi. Then on December 2, 2014, the group massacred 36 Christian quarry workers in Koromei in northern Kenya. On April 2, 2018, the al-Shabab carried out a well-planned and executed attack on Garissa University in northern Kenya. The terrorists killed 142 students, 2 civilian guards, 1 police officer, and 2 Kenyan soldiers deployed to rescue student hostages.[52]

Continued pressure from Kenyan forces supporting the Transitional Federal Government of Somalia has weakened al-Shabab and reduced its area of control. However, it continues to conduct attacks within Somali. Al-Shabab illustrates the hybrid nature of terrorism. It began as a local militant group embracing Islamist extremism, gained territory through insurgency, created a regional network allowing it to carry out attacks abroad, and joined the global jihad movement.

Al-Qaeda Cells

Affiliate and associate groups make up key components in the global
network of terrorism, but al-Qaeda has also deployed cells to carry out
operations abroad. In some cases, the cells consisted of al-Qaeda members
who entered the target country to conduct the attack. In other cases, it
recruited operatives locally. Sometimes cells composed of local supporters constituted themselves to carry out an attack with little or no direction
from the center.

The 9/11 attacks represent the best example of a major terrorist operation planned by al-Qaeda central and carried out by a foreign cell deployed
for the purpose. Conceived by Khalid Sheik Mohammed and approved
by Osama bin Laden, the plot would be a bold strike at the U.S. homeland. Planning may have begun in late 1998 or early 1999, when the al-
Qaeda leader accepted the idea of using hijacked airplanes to attack U.S.
targets. Over the next two years, the group refined the plan. Fifteen of the
19 hijackers were Saudis, 1 was Egyptian (the tactical leader, Mohammed
Atta), 2 were from the United Arab Emirates, and 1 was Lebanese. Eigh-
teen of the terrorists entered the United States on tourist or business visas.
Only one came as a student. The four men who piloted the aircraft arrived
in 2000; the rest arrived the following year. They lived clandestinely in the
country while the pilots took flying lessons. Al-Qaeda funded the operation.[53] The plot cost between $400,000 and $500,000, with most of it depos-
ited in the terrorists' bank accounts via wire transfers but some brought in
as cash and travelers' checks by the men themselves.[54] For that investment
and the loss of the 19 hijackers, al-Qaeda killed almost 3,000 people and
imposed as much as $3.3 trillion in direct and indirect costs on the U.S.
economy.[55] The attack cost far more than most terrorist operations, but
never in the history of conflict has such a small investment yielded such a
large return.

The rapid conquest of Afghanistan and measures taken as part of the
Global War on Terrorism (GWOT) severely disrupted al-Qaeda's ability
to deploy terrorist cells composed of foreign fighters sent to target countries. Undeterred, the organization adopted a new approach. It used citizens of target countries to carry out its attacks. Some of these citizens had
been mujahideen trained in al-Qaeda's camps in Afghanistan. Others were
recruited locally by those with direct ties to al-Qaeda. Cells of this type
were often difficult to detect because their members lived and worked
within the society they attacked.

The four men who carried out the July 7, 2005, attack on the London
underground provide a good example of the locally recruited cell. All four
were British subjects, and all but one had been born in the United Kingdom.
The fourth, Germaine Lindsey, did not immigrate from a Muslim country.
He came as a child from Jamaica and converted to Islam in Britain. As with

most self-contained local cells, direct ties between al-Qaeda central and the London bombers have been difficult to establish. However, considerable evidence suggests such a link existed. Mohammed Siddique Khan, the ring leader, and Shehzad Tanweer, one of the operatives, had traveled to Pakistan in 2004–2005, and Khan traveled to a remote part of the Afghan-Pakistan border, where he is believed to have received training.[56] Hasib Hussein, the fourth bomber, probably traveled to Pakistan at an earlier date, but there is no clear evidence that he met with al-Qaeda leaders. Lindsey did not travel to the region.[57] Khan and Tanweer had also come to the attention of British intelligence prior to the attacks. In March 2014, MI5 (Military Intelligence 5, the domestic intelligence service) rolled up a terrorist bomb plot in "Operation Crevice." Five men have since been convicted for their role in the plot. MI5 identified 55 others who had had some relationship to the plotters as early as 2002, Khan and Tanweer among them, but it did not follow up this lead.[58] Given the number of potential suspects the agency had to surveil and the government's understanding of radicalization at the time, this oversight is less egregious than it seems.[59]

Whereas some cells took direction from al-Qaeda central, others acted on their own initiative. The men who carried out the March 2004 Madrid train bombings represent a good example of a self-constituted terrorist cell acting independently on behalf of the ideological cause. On March 11, 2004, 10 bombs detonated almost simultaneously on four trains headed for the city's central station, killing 193 people and injuring nearly 2,000 others. Police found another explosive device on a train track on April 2. On April 3, they cornered seven of the perpetrators in their Madrid apartment. During the raid, the terrorists committed suicide by detonating their remaining explosives. Subsequent investigations revealed a network of 27 people connected to the attack. Thirteen of the terrorists have been convicted in Spain, two in Morocco, and one in Italy; four committed suicide and seven are at still large.[60]

The Madrid group exemplifies what one analyst has called a "grassroots terrorist network." A grassroots network is "a group of individuals that accept the strategic objectives (top-level goals and aims) of the Global Jihad Movement and attempt to contribute to these from their country of residence." The members of such a group do not formally belong to the central organization or its affiliate or associate groups, but they may have links to these organizations.[61] Analysis of the Madrid cell reveals that some of its members did have ties to other jihadis, but the network was neither deployed nor directly controlled by al-Qaeda central.[62] The network formed due to the initiative of two leaders: Serhane ben Abdelmajid Fakhet, a Tunisian-born extremist with ties to al-Qaeda members, and Jamal Ahmidan, a Moroccan drug dealer radicalized in prison and influenced by Fakhet to plan and finance the operation in Spain using his drug profits.[63]

PROFILE OF AN AL-QAEDA TERRORIST

The question of who becomes a terrorist has vexed experts since al-Qaeda launched its first attack. Counterterrorism, like much law enforcement, relies on profiling, so everyone would like to know what an average al-Qaeda member looks like. The popular perception of the typical extremist group member being an impoverished, poorly educated young man has been discredited. Although poverty and lack of opportunity still play a role in motivating some recruits, many others join for a variety of reasons. Terrorist profiles differ by group, the location from which the recruit comes, and the role he or she plays in the organization.

Al-Qaeda leaders tend, with some notable exceptions, to be better educated than rank-and-file members. Osama bin Laden studied economics at Abdul Aziz University in Saudi Arabia but never earned a degree. Ayman al-Zawahiri is a medical doctor. Abdul Musab al-Zarqawi, on the other hand, dropped out of high school and became a petty criminal before he founded AQI. Cell and network leaders also tend to be older and better educated than their rank-and-file members. Mohammed Atta, leader of the 9/11 terrorist cell, had been a graduate student in urban planning at Hamburg University. Mohammed Siddique Khan, leader of the London bombing cell, attended Leeds Beckett University, and Serhane ben Abdelmajid Fakhet, leader of the Madrid bombing network, studied economics at the Autonomous University of Madrid. The other members of the Madrid network were generally poorly educated and held low-paying jobs.[64] The London bombers, by comparison, were better educated and comfortably well off. All but Jerome Lindsey had some postsecondary education.

Lack of data hinders profiling recruits who joined al-Qaeda central and most of its associated and affiliated groups. A treasure trove of documents captured near the town of Sinjar, Iraq, however, provide a rare look at the membership of AQI. The Sinjar records include personnel files for 700 foreign fighters who entered Iraq between August 2006 and August 2007. The West Point Center for Combatting Terrorism translated and analyzed these records. The analysis provides a snapshot of membership of one cadre in a single al-Qaeda affiliate in one country at a particular period of time. It cannot, thus, provide a profile applicable to the entire network. It does, however, allow for some useful, qualified deductions about who signed up for al-Qaeda's global jihad.

The files identify recruits by age, occupation, country of origin, and desired role within the terrorist organization. The foreign fighters ranged in age from 15 to 52. Their average age was 24–25 and their median age 22–23. All those whose country of origin could be identified came from the Middle East and North Africa, with 41 percent hailing from Saudi Arabia and 18.8 percent from Libya. Others came from Syria (8.2%), Yemen

(8.1%), Algeria (7.2%), Morocco (6.1%), and Jordan (1.9%). Only 157 of the fighters listed their occupations. Of these, the largest group (42.6%) were students. "Other," an ambiguous category to be sure, contained the next largest group of recruits (just under 20%). The rest came from a variety of occupations, including professions and skilled trades. Some of the files (389) also indicate what the volunteers hoped to do for the terrorist campaign. More than half (56.3%) volunteered to be suicide bombers. Most of the rest (41.9%) wanted to be fighters, with the remainder (1.8%) listing "other."[65]

Great care must be taken in drawing broad conclusions from so small a sample of recruits for a single terrorist group during a narrow period of time. The files certainly call into question the validity of simplistic terrorist profiles. Nonetheless, the high percentage of young people, many of them students, in the group does suggest that the angry-young-man image of terrorists has some validity. The Sinjar files do not support the common belief that most terrorists are economically disadvantaged and poorly educated. Instead, they have a variety of backgrounds and occupations. However, the role of poverty as a contributing factor to terrorist recruitment should not be ruled out, especially for recruits from poor countries or marginalized communities in more prosperous ones. As the membership of the Madrid network indicates, relative rather than absolute economic disadvantage may be a key variable. Finally, the Sinjar files indicate the strong regional basis of terrorist recruiting. Groups with a local focus tend to recruit foreign fighters from neighboring countries.

Although recruits may share some broad characteristics, motives for volunteering vary by country. Alienation seems to be the one constant in explaining why people become terrorists. While it often has objective causes, alienation is a profoundly subjective experience. Poverty, unequal opportunity, and discrimination may alienate people from the society in which they live, but the vast majority of alienated people never become violent. Individual experience usually combines with social circumstances to make a person susceptible to recruitment. Susceptibility alone, however, does not make one a terrorist. An agent in that individual's environment has to direct him or her to the extremist organization. That agent may be a friend, family member, or spiritual leader. Social media may have played a role in the recruitment of some members, but al-Qaeda has not made as extensive use of the Internet as ISIS.

FINANCING AND FUNDING

Like any organization, terrorist groups and networks need money to operate. A clear distinction must be made between funding a terrorist attack and financing the larger organization that carries it out. The cost of terrorist operations has actually declined since 9/11. The 9/11 Commission estimated the cost of the devastating attacks against the American homeland at $400,000–$500,000.[66] The group spent most of this money transporting the hijackers to the United States and supporting them for as a much as a year prior to the attack. The Madrid bombings cost approximately $10,000, most of which came from the drug proceeds of Jamal Ahmidan, and the London underground attacks cost less than $1,000.[67] The nature of the local terrorist cells explains the low cost of their operations. The perpetrators of the London attacks were U.K. subjects with jobs to support themselves, as were the 23 residents of the Madrid network. They required no external funds to pay their living expenses and could even afford to buy the materials to make the bombs they used.

Financing a complex organization like al-Qaeda requires not only considerably more money but also a steady stream of revenue. According to the 9/11 commission, prior to the attacks on the U.S. homeland, al-Qaeda had an annual operating budget of $30 million, $10–$20 million of which went to the Taliban in return for providing a safe haven in Afghanistan. Contrary to popular belief, money to finance the organization did not come from bin Laden's personal fortune, most of which had been spent or frozen by the mid-1990s, but from a complex network of revenue sources. Donors in Saudi Arabia and the Gulf States provided money, as did imams who diverted *Zakat* funds (money collected for the poor) from their mosques. Charities also provided a source of revenue, often without the knowledge of their donors.[68] Local al-Qaeda affiliates relied on a variety of activities, including narcotics trafficking and kidnapping for ransom, to finance their organizations. If they controlled territory, they could rely on taxing locals. Some groups, such as al-Shabab, profit from black market trade in commodities like charcoal.

Since 9/11, the international community has made a concerted effort to disrupt terrorist financing. Governments have seized and frozen millions of dollars in assets and closed down charities funneling money to extremist groups. New regulations have concentrated on making it more difficult to move illicit money through the international banking system. How much these efforts actually accomplish remains unclear. As part of a comprehensive counterterrorism strategy, reducing the flow of money to terrorist organizations may constrain, at least to some degree, their ability to operate. However, extremist organizations have been quite flexible, discovering new sources of revenue and using alternative means of moving money, such as the ancient *hawala* system of personal exchange through agents in different countries.

AL-QAEDA, DEFEATED OR DORMANT?

On May 2, 2011, U.S. Navy Seals killed Osama bin Laden at his compound in Abbottabad, Pakistan. Code-named Neptune Spear, the operation also netted a treasure trove of al-Qaeda documents. Crowds gathered at ground zero in New York City to cheer bin Laden's death as everyone wondered what his demise would mean for his terrorist organization. Al-Qaeda immediately acknowledged the death of its leader, and the group's second-in-command Ayman al-Zawahiri stepped in to take charge.

While the death of bin Laden did not put an end to al-Qaeda, it contributed to its decline. Relentless U.S. pressure had been degrading the terrorist organization in the years since 9/11. In the decade before the Abbottabad raid, most attacks had been carried out by al-Qaeda affiliates and associates rather than by the parent organization. Al-Qaeda central has not launched a major attack on its own since bin Laden's death. Down, however, does not mean out. The documents captured at the Abbottabad compound, some of which have been translated and released by the CIA, suggest that al-Qaeda may be rebuilding with the help of an unlikely ally: Iran. Following the U.S. invasion of Afghanistan, the Quds force, an elite unit of the Iranian Revolutionary Guard, offered sanctuary to al-Qaeda members. From that sanctuary, the al-Qaeda military committee planned the 2003 attack on the Khobar Towers in Saudi Arabia. The Quds Force also supplied Ayman al-Zawahiri with money and weapons, which helped him create AQI.[69] Al-Qaeda still exists. Whether it will rise again to its former prominence remains to be seen, but its ideology lives on and has given rise to an even more lethal successor: ISIS.

CHAPTER 3

ISIS

The "Islamic State in Iraq and Syria" (ISIS), also known as the "Islamic State in Iraq and the Levant" or the just the "Islamic State," evolved from al-Qaeda in the Land of the Two Rivers, commonly known as al-Qaeda in Iraq (AQI). In a broader sense, though, it is also the successor of the main al-Qaeda organization, whose ideology it shares—or, to be more precise, both are manifestations of a broader radical ideology, jihadi Salafism, or violent Islamist extremism. This belief system rejects secularism and Western democracy, considers the lesser (violent) jihad equal to the greater, and believes society should be governed by strict sharia law. In some respects, though, the ideology of ISIS differs from that of al-Qaeda. Osama bin Laden may have aimed at one day creating a global caliphate, but he never claimed to be the caliph, the leader of the entire community of Muslims (the Uma) and spiritual descendant of the Prophet Muhammad, as Abu Bakr al-Baghdadi, the leader of ISIS, has proclaimed himself to be. ISIS also emphasizes the need for territory as a source of legitimacy as well as a base for operations, concentrates on the near enemy (the Shi'a, apostate regimes, Christians, etc.) as well as the far (the United States and its allies), and offers a global caliphate as its vision of the future.[1]

Like AQI and unlike al-Qaeda, ISIS aggressively targets the near enemy, which it defines not only as apostate governments but also as the Shi'a, Christians, and minorities like the Yazidi. ISIS has also treated its captured enemies and people in the territories it occupies far more brutally than did its predecessor. Al-Qaeda did not use beheadings, immolation, or rape as instruments of terror. During the Iraq insurgency, bin Laden pressured Zarqawi to be less violent for fear of alienating Iraqi civilians. His admonitions fell on deaf ears. AQI brutality encouraged the Anbar Awakening, which contributed to the successful counterinsurgency campaign in Iraq. Iraqis found the reign of terror unleashed by al-Zarqawi and his foreign fighters so repugnant that they were willing to cooperate with the Americans to rid the country of the terrorists. ISIS did not learn from Zarqawi's failure. It has unleashed a reign of terror, not only on its enemies abroad but also on the people in the territory it controlled.

ISIS must be understood as a multilayered, hybrid phenomenon. The Islamic State consisted of the territory in Iraq and Syria that the organization controlled and governed (which has been liberated). It developed courts, a system of taxation, and an administrative structure. ISIS still exists as a global network of cells and members. The network provided recruits and resources for the state, and the leaders of the state directed operations by its cells. As the Islamic State came under increasing pressure and lost territory, it used the network to carry out a series of attacks abroad. The network can also operate on its own without direction from the center. Finally, ISIS exists as a manifestation of the radical Islamist ideology, motivating individuals as well as groups to act on its behalf. As will be discussed in Chapter 5, ISIS ideology has inspired many lone-wolf terrorists.

ORIGIN AND EVOLUTION OF ISIS

ISIS is a prime example of the law of unintended consequences. Had the United States not invaded Iraq in 2003, AQI would never have existed. Without AQI, ISIS would not have been formed. Even with the Iraq war, ISIS might never have gotten off the ground if the transition to self-rule had been handled better and the new Iraqi government had not treated the Sunni minority so badly. As previously noted, AQI had an uneasy marriage of convenience with al-Qaeda central. The main organization conveyed legitimacy on the new group, and AQI enabled al-Qaeda to strike at the United States after the central organization lost its safe haven in Afghanistan. Al-Zarqawi, however, continually resisted the efforts of bin Laden and al-Zawahiri to restrain him. In addition to alienating both Shi'a and Sunni Iraqis because of its brutality, AQI upset tribal leaders by appointing its own emirs and monopolizing economic resources in areas that it controlled.[2] In an effort to improve relations with local communities, AQI united at least six Sunni Islamist groups under a new Mujahideen Shura Council in January 2006.[3] Al-Zarqawi died in an airstrike in June, and in October, the Council created the Islamic State in Iraq (ISI). By then the Anbar Awakening was under way, and the United States had turned the tide of the insurgency. No one expected the new group to be much of a threat.

Severely weakened in its old base of Anbar Province, ISI moved and adapted. Driven out of predominantly Sunni regions, it found fertile ground in mixed areas racked by sectarian violence. In Baghdad and Dyala Province, Sunni communities turned to ISI for protection from Shi'a militias like Jaysh al-Mahdi.[4] ISI increased its strength in Dyala and neighboring Salah ad-Din Province in early 2007.[5] By 2008, the U.S.-led coalition and the Iraqi Security Forces turned their attention to these areas, and ISI had to retreat north to Ninawa Province, where it strengthened its hold on Sunni areas, including the key city of Mosul.[6] By the end of 2009, the counterinsurgency campaign had seriously weakened ISI's hold even in those areas. By the end of 2010, the government had only to consolidate its gains, win the trust of the local Sunni population, and continue to pacify Mosul.[7] Not only did the Iraqi government fail to take these necessary steps, but it also acted in a manner that encouraged a resurgence of ISI.

Had the new government in Baghdad tried to forge an Iraqi identity that transcended sectarian and ethnic divides, or at least treated members of all groups equally, ISI might never have evolved into ISIS. Instead, Prime Minister Nuri al-Maliki chose to govern in an authoritarian manner on behalf of the Shi'a majority. Corruption, cronyism, and inability to provide services alienated Iraqis. Al-Maliki stopped paying the Sunni sheiks to police their tribal areas. To make matters worse, he consolidated his own power and used the instruments of state security and the judiciary to persecute his opponents. This misgovernment had two disastrous effects. It encouraged ordinary Sunnis to support or at least tolerate ISI, which seemed to offer them some protection. It also weakened the armed forces. With officers promoted based upon loyalty to the prime minister rather than ability, the rank and file performed poorly.

Even with these abuses of power, however, ISI might not have been so successful were it not for a wave of change sweeping the Middle East. Beginning in Tunisia in 2010, democratic protests against authoritarian regimes and poor economic conditions spread rapidly and shook governments to their foundations. The "Arab Spring," as it came to be called, toppled Hosni Mubarak in Egypt and sparked a long, bloody civil war in Syria. It also inspired protests in Iraq. Government repression of these peaceful gatherings further strengthened support for ISI, drawing in many former Baathist Party members, who supported it as the only alternative to al-Maliki. ISI also exploited divisions within the Sunni community over the privileged position of the Awakening Councils set up by the Americans. At the same time, the group took advantage of the chaos in Syria to expand its network there, which in turn provided support for operations in Iraq. ISI thus triumphed due to the synergy of four factors: divisions within the Sunni community; Iraqi government corruption; its ability to attract resentful Sunnis, particularly former Baathists; and the Arab Spring.[8]

Outside Iraq, most people remained blissfully ignorant of the looming threat developing in the Middle East. The United States formally ended its occupation of Iraq in December 2011. The withdrawal date had been agreed by the Bush administration, and the Obama administration could not reach a satisfactory status-of-forces agreement to extend the large American deployment in the country. Al-Maliki also convinced President

Obama that repressive measures were necessary to prevent a resurgence of terrorism. Things went from bad to worse as violence increased throughout 2012 and 2013. In April 2013, ISI declared that the group would henceforth be called the "Islamic State in Iraq and the Levant" (ISIL) or the "Islamic State in Iraq and Syria (ISIS)," depending on the translation from Arabic ("al-dowla al-islaamiyya fii-il-i'raaq wa-ash-shaam").[9] It has also been referred to as "the Islamic State." Its Arabic detractors refer to the group as *daesh*, an Arabic acronym for ISIS that as a word can be translated "bigot."[10] Whatever one calls it, the group's success cannot be denied. It expanded operations in northern Syria, capturing Raqqa in January 2014. To the shock of everyone, Mosul fell to ISIS in June of that year.

The leader of ISIS marked the group's dramatic triumph with an equally dramatic proclamation. After the capture of Mosul, al-Baghdadi broke with al-Qaeda, declared a new caliphate, and proclaimed himself the caliph, the leader of the Uma and successor to the Prophet Muhammad. After World War I, the first president of modern Turkey, Kemal Ataturk, had abolished the position, which had been held by the Ottoman Sultans since the early sixteenth century. No contemporary Islamic scholar or state recognizes this outrageous claim, but it reveals the importance of both territory and leadership in the ISIS worldview. For such an infamous character, little is known about Ibrahim Awwad Ibrahim Ali al-Badri Samarrai, who took the nom de guerre "Abu Bakr al-Baghdadi." Born to a middle-class family in the Sunni Triangle north of Baghdad in 1971, he lived an unremarkable life before the U.S. invasion launched his meteoric rise to power. He helped found a minor insurgent group to oppose the invaders. Coalition forces apprehended him in early 2004 but considered him a "low-level threat" and released him in December. Incarceration contributed to al-Baghdadi's radicalization as it did to that of other ISIS top leaders, 17 out of 25 of whom spent time in U.S.-run detention facilities.[11] In 2006, he joined ISI, and he became the group's leader in 2010 after his predecessors had been killed. Al-Baghdadi shrouds himself in mystery as part of his leadership persona, so information on his early life and rise consists largely of self-propagated stories and a few truths. He claims to hold a doctorate in Islamic jurisprudence, but that claim has not been verified. To rise as rapidly as he did, al-Baghdadi must have leadership ability. He also knows how to inspire his followers.[12] He became the head of a de facto state, which he governed ruthlessly for five years, and will be remembered as a very successful extremist group leader.

GOVERNING THE ISLAMIC STATE

Once the Islamic State gained control of large swaths of Syria and Iraq, it faced a challenge encountered by many insurgent groups, albeit never on such a scale. It had to govern the people it controlled. Governance requires providing services, setting up and running a criminal justice system, collecting taxes, and creating an administrative system to oversee all these activities. Popular perceptions of ISIS portray the group as controlling people through coercion. Although it resorts to brutality on a regular basis, the Islamic State has also brought a degree of security and order to areas that have known war and chaos for some time. Under such turbulent circumstances, ISIS did not have to govern well; it merely had to govern adequately.[13] Considerable evidence suggests that it did so.

The Islamic State built upon existing institutions in the areas it occupied, co-opting and adapting them as needed. It ordered government officials to remain in their jobs. It demonstrated its ability to keep schools and hospitals running, maintain and even build infrastructure, provide water and electricity, and preserve law and order. It punished merchants who manipulated prices and cheated their customers. The department of Zakat even provided food and clothing to those in need.[14] ISIS authorities also ensured some quality control of consumer goods, for example, making sure that butchers did not adulterate beef with cheaper meat and did not water down gasoline. It paid its fighters, attracting unemployed youths to its cause.[15] The quality of ISIS governance remains unclear and probably varied considerably from place to place, but it was more than adequate to maintain control of the territory it held.[16]

Following the liberation of Mosul in 2017, reporters for the *New York Times* found more than 15,000 pages of ISIS documents that shed light on its administration of the city. The sources revealed that contrary to popular perception, the group financed its operations, not from foreign contributions or oil revenues alone but also from an efficient system of taxation. The Islamic State required government employees to remain at their posts, where many continued to receive salaries from the government in Baghdad. The ISIS bureaucrats expedited approval of property rentals, including property seized from members of religious minority communities. They doled out apartments and goods to their supporters. They collected fees for various services and made the Zakat, an annual asset tax of 2.5 percent required of devout Muslims, mandatory. The group's agricultural department offered a sharecropping arrangement to poor Sunnis unable to rent land a sharecropping arrangement. The Islamic State delivered some services such as trash collection more efficiently than had the Iraqi city government. Before the occupation, a worker who did not do his job properly could be suspended for a day; afterward, he could be imprisoned. Residents said that under the Islamic State, streets were cleaner, potholes repaired more quickly, sewers kept cleaner, and the water supply more reliable.[17]

Efficiency extended to the ruthless persecution of enemies. ISIS unleashed a reign of terror on the populations it ruled. One administrator recalled changing his route to work to avoid the sight of frequent executions in traffic circles and public squares and the sight of bodies hanging from bridges.[18] The dreaded *Husba*, known as the "morality police," enforced a strict code of conduct. They banned tobacco and alcohol and required women to wear hijab. Women could only go out with a male relative, and a man seen with a woman who was not his wife or a close female relative could be flogged.[19] Adultery and homosexuality carried the death penalty. The group used gruesome public executions as a form of social control. A teenage girl accused of adultery had a stone slab dropped on her head.[20] One analyst described use of such exemplary violence as "enforcement terror" because it aims to keep in line populations controlled by the extremists.[21] ISIS also beheaded captured Americans in retaliation for airstrikes and burned a Jordanian pilot alive. Most people living in the area it occupied viewed its ouster as liberation.

RECRUITS

While most ISIS fighters came from Iraq and Syria, the organization attracted recruits from all over the world. In 2016, an Islamic State defector provided NBC News with 4,600 ISIS personnel records from 2013 to 2014, which it passed on to the West Point Center for Combatting Terrorism for analysis. Analysts identified forms for 4,173 men, estimated to be approximately 30 percent of the foreign fighters who entered Iraq and Syria during this period.[22] Although ISIS attracted foreign fighters from 70 countries, more than half of these recruits came from 5 countries. Saudi Arabia contributed the largest number (797), followed by Tunisia (640), Morocco (260), Turkey (244), and Egypt (194). Most of the rest came from other countries in the Middle East, North Africa, Central Asia, and Southeast Asia. Even China contributed 138 recruits, probably from its disaffected Hui-Uyghur community.[23] Among those hailing from Europe, the majority came from Russia (210), but many of these people were probably guest workers from Muslim areas of the Caucasus and Central Asia. Among Western European nations, France contributed the largest number of recruits (128), followed by Germany (80) and the United Kingdom (57). From the Western Hemisphere, only Canada contributed recruits represented in the records (17).[24] This data supports what had been previously suspected: most foreign fighters came from the Islamic State's near neighbors.

The files revealed additional valuable information on the demographics of foreign fighters. The average age of recruits in the records was 26–27, but that varied by country of origin, with the average age of Westerners lower than that of non-Westerners. One man was 69, and 12 were in their 50s. There were 400 recruits under the age of 18, and 41 were under 15.[25] One file indicates that two brothers, ages 15 and 12, were being sent to a camp, suggesting they would be trained as future fighters and confirming ISIS's use of child soldiers.[26] This data conforms to the general pattern of terrorists being disproportionately young men. Unfortunately, the data set does not contain information on female recruits, even though women played an important role in the Islamic State.

The personnel records challenge the assumptions that terrorist recruits are unattached and poorly educated. Thirty percent of the recruits indicated that they were married, and 892 of the married men had at least one child.[27] The recruits were also better educated than generally believed. Among those in the data set, 1,371 had graduated high school, 1,028 had at least some university or post-high school education, and 36 had done some graduate work. Another 714 had gone as far as middle school, and 750 did not indicate their level of education. A small number (42) indicated that they had "religious or unspecified" education, and 199 marked "other." Only 33 indicated "none."[28] The Western recruits had a higher level of high school graduates and a significantly higher post-high school or university education rate.[29] Notably, 70 percent of recruits indicated that they had only a basic understanding of Sharia, suggesting that they did not come from ultraconservative communities.[30]

The ISIS recruitment files also challenge the notion that terrorist recruits are usually poor and often desperately so. Only 255 indicated that they were unemployed. The largest group indicated "unskilled/laborer" or low-skilled, 751 and 694 respectively. "Student" (656) and "business or self-employed" (640) made up the next two largest groups, followed by those who did not indicate their employment (455) and "other" (220). The remaining 574 had held skilled or professional jobs.[31] Poorer countries contributed a higher-than-average number of unemployed recruits, lending credence to the claim that financial incentives motivated some people to join ISIS.[32] The gathering of information on employment as well as education indicates that ISIS sought more than fighters among its foreign recruits. Commensurate with its need to govern territory, the Islamic State required people with a variety of skills.

The ISIS personnel forms also asked recruits to indicate what role they wanted to play in the organization. Of the nearly 4,000 who indicated a preference, only 12 percent volunteered for suicide missions. The rest wanted to be fighters. These numbers contrast markedly with the al-Qaeda Sinjar records, in which 56 percent of respondents volunteered for suicide missions.[33] The stunning success ISIS enjoyed in 2013 and 2014 probably inspired some to believe it might achieve its goal of expanding the caliphate. The group also changed its messaging from a guarantee of paradise in the hereafter to a vision of a pure Islamic state in the here and now.[34] Finally, the personnel forms asked recruits to identify the person who recommended them to the organization. While the sheer number of names listed, many of whom were unknown to authorities, impedes analysis, the mere fact that the information was requested indicates that whatever role the Internet and social media played, human vetting of recruits occurred.[35]

American readers may be surprised by the absence of U.S.-born jihadis in the ISIS files. The records, of course, are incomplete and limited to a single year. Nonetheless, very few Americans have joined the Islamic State. In a report published in February 2018, the George Washington University Project on Extremism found only 64 documented cases of recruits from the United States reaching Syria between 2011 and the beginning of 2018, as opposed to between 5,000 and 6,000 who came from Europe, although as many as 250–300 attempted the journey from the United States.[36] The vast majority of Americans joined ISIS, while a small percentage, especially of those who traveled during the early days, joined other groups like al Nusra. Despite the degree to which politicians hype the threat, the number of Americans being radicalized and joining ISIS was very low in both absolute and percentage terms. The degree to which American Muslims have been integrated into U.S. society, as evidenced by the near absence of exclusively Muslim neighborhoods and their degree of economic prosperity, explains why so few have been radicalized. The demographic data on those willing to support ISIS does, however, reveal some patterns that suggest ways of countering radicalization.

In 2017, the University of Chicago Counterterrorism Policy Center and the Australian Strategic Policy Institute coauthored *The American Face of ISIS: Analysis of ISIS-related Terrorism in the US March 2014–August 2016*.[37] The study examines 113 cases of Americans arrested for supporting ISIS by conspiring to attack U.S. targets, traveling or conspiring to travel to join ISIS, and helping others seeking to join ISIS.[38] Its findings challenged popular perceptions of who becomes a terrorist. The rates of marriage, level of education, and employment status of American recruits are close to those of the general population. The vast majority of those apprehended (83%) were U.S. citizens, and 63 percent were born in the United States. Of the non-U.S. citizens, 10 percent had a green card, and 3 percent had legal refugee status, but none of the refugees came from Syria. A significant number of those in the study (30%) were converts to Islam, and the vast majority (83%) indicated that online material, including lectures and execution videos, played a significant role in their radicalization.[39] Recent converts are often zealous and easier to deceive, as they often know far less about their new religion than those raised in it. The role of videos in the radicalization process suggests the importance of the Internet and social media in a country distant from the ISIS heartland.

The Americans do have some things in common with the ISIS foreign fighter recruits, however. Those from the United States had an average age of 27, roughly the same as that of the foreign fighters documented in the ISIS personnel records. The majority of the Americans were male (89%), although the number of females (11%) probably represents a new trend in jihadi recruiting. The ISIS foreign fighters were all men, but that fact reflects the limits of the data set rather than the reality on the ground.

However, 91 percent of the Americans arrested for attacking or conspiring to attack a U.S. target (as opposed to merely providing support to ISIS) were male.[40] The U.S. study had relationship data for 74 of its subjects, of whom 32 percent were married (comparable to the 30% rate among those in the ISIS recruitment files), 4 percent were engaged, and 5 percent had a partner.[41]

The George Washington University Program on Extremism study, *Travelers: American Jihadis in Syria and Iraq*, corroborates the findings of *The American Face of ISIS*. The 64 people examined in this study had an average age of 27, identical to that of the sample in the University of Chicago study. The gender mix of the two groups is also identical: 89 percent male, 11 percent female.[42] *Travelers* focuses less on demographics than on the manner in which would-be jihadists got to Syria. It groups them into three categories: pioneers, loners, and networked travelers. Pioneers went to Syria in small numbers ahead of the main movement and linked up with others from their ethnic communities when they arrived. A naturalized Bosnian American, for example, linked up with other Bosnian Muslims when he joined ISIS. Pioneers thus benefited from interpersonal relationships. Loners, on the other hand, represent a small group of individuals who made it to Syria on their own. Networked travelers comprise the largest group in the study. They cooperated with others through community clusters, friendship groups, and kinship ties; many were radicalized by "peer-to-peer" and "brother-to-brother" relationships.[43]

The evidence on Americans willing to follow ISIS allows for some tentative conclusions. They are of about the same average age as recruits from elsewhere (27), and the vast majority are male. Most are native-born or naturalized U.S. citizens. In terms of education, marital status, and economic background, they resemble the American mainstream, which makes them better off than the majority of ISIS foreign recruits from other countries. The most important takeaway from the data, however, is that very few Americans have been attracted by Islamist extremism. The threat posed to the United States by ISIS and its ideology is thus far lower than portrayed in the media and hyped by some politicians on the right.

The data from both the ISIS personnel records and the U.S. studies indicate that men make up the vast majority of ISIS recruits. However, some evidence suggests that women are underrepresented in the ISIS data. One report estimates that women make up 20 percent of Westerners who joined ISIS, which exceeds the figure for the University of Chicago Study (11%).[44] Women, of course, played constrained roles within ISIS because of the group's strict morality code and rigid understanding of gender roles, but they nonetheless made a valuable contribution to its operations. In addition to being wives and mothers, they participated in logistics, fund-raising, medical care, and intelligence gathering. In one study more than half (55%) of the women served as recruiters for the organization.[45] Women also staffed the all-female al-Khansa Brigade responsible for policing the strict female code of conduct in cities like Raqqa.[46] Some women went to Syria voluntarily, while others accompanied their husbands (perhaps involuntarily). In some cases, they were lured by romantic fantasies of marrying a fighter and living an exotic life.[47] When they arrived, women were taken to a guesthouse that served as a school and a matching service to provide brides for ISIS fighters, who found Western women, especially blondes, attractive.[48]

ISIS AND THE INTERNET

ISIS's use of Internet platforms has been the subject of some research and much conjecture. Everyone who studies terrorism recognizes that the group has a sophisticated social media strategy that makes extensive use of Facebook, Twitter, Instagram, YouTube, chat rooms, and static websites. Numerous studies have examined the nature of the ISIS media strategy as well as its goals, audience, and messaging. Another body of work examines how to identify extremist messages online and counter them.[49] Good studies of precisely how the Internet and social media contribute to radicalization and recruitment, however, are rare. The paucity of research on this important question stems in no small measure from the methodological challenges in carrying it out. A comprehensive study would require interviewing a significant number of ISIS foreign members to find to out how they had become radicalized and what role, if any, social media played in the process.

Available evidence allows for a few solid and many tentative conclusions. Studies of radicalization have generally tested one or more of five basic hypotheses about the Internet: (1) it creates more opportunities for radicalization; (2) it serves as an echo chamber, reinforcing what people already believe; (3) it accelerates radicalization; (4) it allows radicalization without contact in the physical world; and (5) it increases opportunities for self-radicalization.[50] One study based on European cases confirmed the validity of only the first two hypotheses. Websites, Twitter accounts, chat rooms, and other online resources do create more opportunities for radicalization. The Internet also creates echo chambers, virtual communities of people with the same worldview who reinforce one another's radical beliefs. The study found no conclusive evidence, however, that the Internet accelerated radicalization, perhaps because validating such a conclusion would require proving the negative. To fully test this hypothesis would require a control group of individuals who did not engage extremist ideology online to see how rapidly they radicalized compared to those engaged through social media. The study also found no clear evidence that people in the data set radicalized without human contact in the physical world or that the Internet encouraged self-radicalization.[51] Personal interaction and online activity may go hand in hand to such a degree that even the person being radicalized cannot sort out which mattered most. Individuals logging in to find like-minded people have already started down the path of radicalization. Many chat rooms are closed and require someone to introduce new members. The most widely believed—but hardest to support—hypothesis is that the Internet allows for "self-radicalization." The term conjures up images of people logging on and being persuaded to join terrorist groups. However, someone or something encouraged them to begin their online activity.

As with so many aspects of terrorism, the role of the Internet in radicalization cannot be reduced to broad generalizations. ISIS makes extensive use of the Internet, as do white nationalist groups, but it is only one of many tools available to them. Authorities in many countries have seen an increase in radicalization among prison inmates, who have no access to the Internet. Family, friends, and peer group members recruit followers, especially in countries whose Muslim populations remain concentrated in disadvantaged neighborhoods. Mosque and youth centers can also be sources of radicalization. The ISIS recruitment forms from 2013 to 2014 asked foreign fighters to identify the person who referred them or facilitated their travel to join the Islamic State, which indicates the importance of human interaction. However, in the United States, with its small, well-integrated Muslim population, the Internet does seem to play a greater role in radicalization of the small number of American ISIS recruits. The University of Chicago study did note the role of online content (lectures and videos) in radicalizing the people in its study. As will be examined in Chapter 5, the Internet also plays a significant role in the radicalization of lone wolves.

ISIS NETWORK

ISIS is not only an organization and, until recently, a quasi-state but also a terrorist network with affiliates and cells in many countries. Groups like Boko Haram, al-Shabab, and Abu Sayyaf have sworn allegiance to the caliphate, although it remains unclear what this association means. The interests of these groups continue to be predominantly local. They have essentially transferred their nominal allegiance from al-Qaeda to ISIS as the leader of the Islamist jihadi movement. A different situation exists in Libya, where the Islamic State has exploited the chaos caused by the overthrow of the Gaddafi regime.[52] A 2015 ISIS document reveals its plan for the country. In the document, ISIS asserted that eastern Libya should be seen as a new province of the caliphate and touted the strategic importance of the location at the crossroads of the Middle East and Africa.[53]

In addition to affiliates, ISIS also has a global network of cells. The difficulty of mapping networks, of course, lies in getting good intelligence on them. Unfortunately, extremist groups seek to keep the identity of members a secret, and law enforcement avoids revealing information on suspects for fear of alerting them. These factors result in a dearth of open-access information. The public usually does not learn about a terrorist cell until it strikes, and the authorities often form a complete picture of a cell's makeup and connections only after an incident. One study identified a sample of 1,000 ISIS supporters based on their Facebook posts. It found a pattern similar to that discernable among ISIS foreign recruits. Most of the supporters came from Iraq and Syria (17%) and South Asia (17%), followed by Southeast Asia (12%) and North Africa (10%). Europeans produced 6 percent of posts and North Americans just 3 percent.[54] Pro-ISIS Facebook posts do not, of course, equate to the presence of active terrorist cells. They do, however, provide a rough indicator of the degree of sympathy for the Islamic State in a particular area. To understand how ISIS has operated abroad requires examining a sample of terrorist incidents from around the world.

TERRORIST ATTACKS

ISIS has always used terror, both to reinforce control over people in its territory and strike its enemies. Most of its use of terror has focused on contested territory in the Middle East and thus supported its regional insurgency. As a coalition of nations increased pressure on the Islamic State, however, the group began to carry out attacks farther abroad in an effort to harm those attacking it and, perhaps, deter them from taking further military action. Planning for this global jihad may have begun as early as the fall of 2014, when the Islamic State created an overseas operations unit.[55] Led by senior ISIS member Abu Muhammad al-Adnani, the unit was subdivided into European, Asian, and Arab-world branches, each under the leadership of a lieutenant.[56]

At the same time that it created the operations unit, ISIS began screening foreign fighters as they arrived in Syria. No longer focused exclusively on the struggle in the Middle East, the Islamic State wanted recruits who could return to their countries of origin to carry out attacks. ISIS sent new recruits to dormitories just over the border from Turkey. Screeners interviewed and classified them based on a variety of factors that would determine their usefulness as assets in the international network and were especially interested in those with ties to organized crime.[57] They told one recruit from Germany that they no longer needed Europeans to come to Syria but did want them to carry out attacks in their own countries.[58] Recruits then received a short, intensive period of training before being sent back. Because they had not been abroad long, these recruits could plausibly claim that they had been vacationing in Turkey, the destination stamped on their passports.[59] The operations unit in Syria continued to provide direction and logistics support once the foreign fighters redeployed to their home countries.[60]

The network became fully operational in 2015. Beginning in the fall of that year, a spate of attacks struck Western nations. Some of these attacks were carried out by lone wolves, who will be discussed in Chapter 5. Others were the work of ISIS cells directed from the central organization. On October 31, 2015, the Russian airline Metrojet's Flight 9268 exploded shortly after takeoff from the airport in the resort city of Sharm El Sheikh, Egypt, killing all 224 passengers and crew. Most experts believed a bomb had been placed on the plane; ISIS claimed responsibility for the attack. Twelve days later, two suicide bombers struck a Shi'a suburb of Beirut, killing 43 people. Neither incident got the attention of the West like the one that would target France just three days later.

Paris and Brussels

Although they occurred five months apart and were viewed as distinct events at the time, subsequent investigation revealed that a single terrorist cell deployed by ISIS to the Brussels neighborhood of Molenbeek carried out the attacks in Paris and Brussels. The cell had plenty of time to carefully plan and conduct the Paris operation but had to rush the Brussels attack, which proved less effective. Investigation of the Paris attacks led authorities to Belgium. In cooperation with French authorities, the Belgians began closing in on the remnants of the cell operating in Molenbeek. The surviving members either accelerated plans for their operation in the city or improvised one as the authorities moved to apprehend them.

On the night of November 13, 2015, the ISIS cell carried out a series of near-simultaneous attacks in Paris, France. Over a period of just 20 minutes, they struck 4 restaurants, a sports stadium, and a concert venue using suicide bombs and assault rifles. The attacks killed 130 people and wounded 494. The worst carnage occurred at the Bataclan concert hall, where an American rock band was performing. At that venue alone, the gunmen killed 90 people.[61] France had suffered the worst terrorist attack in its history and Europe's worst since the 2004 Madrid train bombings. Two of the perpetrators were believed to be Iraqis who had entered Europe on false passports.[62] The rest were Belgian and French nationals of Moroccan descent. None was a recent immigrant. Nine of the 10 terrorists had been in Syria. Seven of them died during the attacks, but the cell leader, Abdel Hamid Abaaoud, along with Salah Abdeslam, the suspected logistics support person, and Chakib Akrouh, one of the shooters, escaped. On November 18, French police cornered Abaaoud and Akrouh in the Parisian suburb of St. Denis. During the ensuing shootout, Akrouh detonated his suicide vest. He and Abaaoud died in the raid. Abdeslam escaped to Brussels, where police captured him on March 18, 2016, three days before the attack on that city.[63]

The capture of Abdeslam and the raid on a cell safe house probably encouraged the remaining members to accelerate the timetable for a planned operation or to improvise one as the police closed in on them. Just before 8:00 a.m. on the morning of March 22, two suicide terrorists detonated bombs two minutes apart at the check-in area of Zaventem International Airport. The blasts killed 16 people. A third bomber fled the scene before detonating his device. About an hour later, another suicide bomber blew himself up on a train as it pulled out of Maalbeek station in downtown Brussels, killing another 16 people. A second terrorist assigned to bomb the underground failed to carry out his mission.[64] Mohamed Abrini, the airport bomber who had fled the scene before detonating his device, was arrested on April 9. For two attackers to back out of a suicide mission is highly unusual. The cell also sacrificed its bombmaker, Najim Laachraoui, in the suicide attack on the airport. Terrorists rarely waste such talent on a single mission. These facts provide further evidence that the cell carried out its operation before being fully prepared, realizing that it had one last chance of striking before being captured.

The Paris and Brussels attacks reveal a great deal about the pattern of terrorist recruitment in Europe. The cell that carried them out included two sets of brothers and three childhood friends. Some of the terrorists belonged to a network established in Molenbeek by ISIS recruiter Khalid Zerkani, including the cell leader, Abaaoud, the bomb maker, Laachraoui, and one of the Paris suicide bombers. Zerkani funded his operations through petty crime, which earned enough money to send at least 60 Belgian recruits to Syria.[65] The case of the Belgian cell indicates that, in Europe at least, kinship, friendships, and community ties played an instrumental role in radicalization. While the highest per capita number of recruits traveling to Syria from Europe came from Belgium, that country may be unique only in that radicalization began there at an earlier date.[66] "Clusters of likeminded militants emerged in Antwerp and Brussels and were drawn into the orbit of radical preachers," one analyst concluded.[67] Muslim ghettos like Molenbeek provide a fertile recruiting ground for jihadis.

Turkish Attacks

Most of Turkey lies in Asia, but it also belongs to NATO. The country has always looked East and West and has often had trouble balancing its interests in the two regions. Its borders with Syria and Bulgaria and the Aegean Sea, which it shares with Greece, have made it a transit country for refugees fleeing north and ISIS recruits headed south. Turkey was initially reluctant to oppose the Islamic State. It hated the Syrian regime of Bashir al-Assad more than it did ISIS, and it objected to U.S. cooperation with its historic adversaries, the Kurds. Under increasing pressure from its Western allies, Turkey began to stem the two-way flow of migrants in 2016. That policy, along with allowing the United States to launch airstrikes from bases in the country, put Turkey squarely in ISIS's crosshairs. ISIS has sympathizers among the Turkish population and has had no trouble inserting terrorists into the country.

Like Western Europe, Turkey has faced a spate of attacks since 2015. In July of that year, ISIS suicide bombers killed 32 people at a municipal center in Suruç in southeastern Turkey. In October, two suicide bombers killed 100 people at the main train station in the capital city of Ankara. On January 12, 2016, a suicide bomber killed 12 tourists in the historic peninsula in Istanbul. Then on June 28, terrorists tried to force their way into Ataturk International Airport, killing 45 people. On January 1, 2017, an ISIS terrorist killed 39 patrons and staff at an Istanbul nightclub. In addition to these major incidents, Turkey has faced a host of smaller-scale attacks. Besides killing foreigners and Turkish citizens, these attacks have damaged the country's once tourism industry.

Egypt

Modern Islamism has its origins in Egypt, although most of its adherents have not chosen the path of violence. Nonetheless, some of the most infamous extremists, including one of the 9/11 hijackers and al-Qaeda leader Ayman al-Zawahiri, hail from that country. While other states face a threat from ISIS cells, Egypt has had to contend with an affiliate organization. Since 2011, the terrorist group Ansar Bayt Al Maqdis, which swore allegiance to al-Baghdadi in November 2014 and changed its name to Wilayat Sinai (province of Sinai), has attacked the country. The group has 1,000 to 1,500 members and has carried out a low-level insurgency against the Egyptian army and a terrorist campaign in Egypt. In addition to killing soldiers, it has murdered foreign workers. It claimed credit for the bombing of Metrojet's Flight 9268, which exploded shortly after takeoff from the airport in the resort city of Sharm El Sheikh on October 31, 2015.[68]

In keeping with its Islamist extremist ideology, ISIS targets Egyptian Christians. On December 11, 2016, a suicide bomber killed 28 people at a Coptic church in Cairo. ISIS later posted a video of the bomber and referred to Christians as their "favorite prey." The following March, terrorists murdered a Christian man and then burned his son alive. Then on November 2, 2018, ISIS gunmen attacked a bus filled with Christians leaving a baptism at a monastery, killing 7 people and wounding 14 others.[69] The pattern of attacks reflects a blend of traditional insurgency and ideological extremism. Targeting military personnel has a strategic logic in a struggle for control of Sinai. Murdering people merely because of their religion serves no practical purpose but demonstrates the Islamic State's maniacal hatred of all who do not accept its beliefs.

United Kingdom

The United Kingdom has been no stranger to terrorism. It endured a 30-year campaign by the Provisional Irish Republican Army. No sooner had the Northern Ireland conflict ended than the country faced a new threat from al-Qaeda. On July 7, 2005, four suicide bombers killed 52 people on the London underground and a double-decker bus in Tavistock Square. Spared from the initial wave of ISIS terrorism that struck Europe in 2015 and 2016, Britain became a target in 2017. On March 22, 2017, 52-year-old Khalid Masood drove his car into pedestrians on Westminster Bridge, fatally injuring five people. He then rammed a barricade in front of the houses of parliament and stabbed a security guard to death before being shot dead by another security guard. He acted on behalf of ISIS but had no known connection to it.

While the Westminster attack was the work of a lone wolf acting spontaneously, the May 22, 2017, suicide bombing in Manchester revealed careful planning by someone known to MI5. Salman Abedi detonated a homemade bomb in the foyer of the city arena as people were leaving an Ariana Grande concert. The blast killed him and 22 others, including children and teenagers, and injured more than 800.[70] Authorities believe Abedi had been radicalized in prison as well as through online content. They also suspect he went to Libya, where he may have received training. MI5 had investigated him but did not believe he posed enough of a threat to warrant closer monitoring.[71] Whether Abedi acted under direct orders form ISIS remains unclear, but indirect evidence suggests that he did. He carefully chose and reconnoitered his target, deciding to strike at a time and place when security was most lax: in the foyer as people were leaving the concert. Less than 24 hours after the attack, ISIS claimed responsibility. "With Allah's grace and support, a soldier of the Khalifah managed to place explosive devices in the midst of the gatherings of the Crusaders in the British city of Manchester," its statement declared.[72] ISIS does sometimes take credit for lone wolf attacks carried out in its name, but it often takes longer to do so, withholding approval until it determines what transpired. With a plot it orchestrates, ISIS needs no such delay.

Less than two weeks after the Manchester bombing, terrorists struck again. On June 3, 2017, three men used their van to run down pedestrians on London Bridge. They then exited their vehicle and began attacking people with knives before police shot them dead. The terrorists killed eight people. MI5 had completed an investigation of one of the attackers and had an open investigation of a second, who had expressed terrorist aspirations, but they had found no evidence of an active plot.[73] While authorities believe the men accessed online jihadi content, there is no evidence that they had direct ties to ISIS, let alone acted on its orders. They appear to have been inspired by the success of the Manchester bomber to strike their own blow for the cause.

None of the attacks in the United Kingdom seems to have been carried out by anything resembling a cell. Three of the five perpetrators were British subjects, and one had dual Italian and Moroccan citizenship. Two were born in the United Kingdom to immigrant parents, one immigrated as a child and grew up in the UK, and one was a failed asylum seeker. One had a criminal background; another had been accused of domestic violence. Four of the five fit the pattern of the alienated young man who becomes a lone wolf. Only the Manchester bomber may have had ties to the extremist organization.

Spain

Like the United Kingdom, Spain has had its fill of terrorism. The decades-long struggle against the Bosque separatist group ETA (*Euskadi Ta Askatasuna*, "Bosque Homeland and Liberty") had barely ended when the conflict with al-Qaeda began. In March 2004, terrorists bombed trains headed for Madrid's central railway station, killing 193 people. Since then, Spain has been on the sidelines in the conflict with Islamist extremists. That changed in the summer of 2017 when a 10-man terrorist cell carried out two attacks, one in Barcelona and another in the neighboring town of Cambrils, killing 16 people. The worst terrorist incident since the Madrid train bombings did not come out of the blue. Catalonia had been a hotbed of Islamist extremism among its Muslim community, with 76 arrests of suspected terrorists and several foiled plots between 2013 and 2017.[74]

Horrible though the incidents were, they might have been much worse. The night before the attack, an explosion destroyed the cell's bomb factory in the town of Alcanar, killing two cell members and injuring a third. Evidence found in the debris suggested the terrorists were planning to deploy large car or van bombs that would have been devastating. With their "factory" gone and a cell member in custody, the survivors probably recognized that they might soon be apprehended and decided to improvise an attack. Around 4:30 p.m. on August 17, one of the terrorists drove a van down a crowded boulevard in Barcelona, killing 13 people. He then hijacked a car, stabbing its driver to death, and escaped. Police cornered him in a rural area four days later and shot him dead. Almost nine hours after the Barcelona attack, five of the remaining terrorists drove a car down another pedestrian thoroughfare in Cambrils and then exited the vehicle to go on a rampage with knives and an ax. They killed one woman before police shot them dead.

In their investigation following the attack, Spanish authorities gathered a great deal of information on the 10-man cell. Its members had all been radicalized by 45-year-old Moroccan Imam and possible cell leader Abdel-baki Es Satty in the town of Ripoll. All of Es Satty's recruits were in their 20s. One was a Spaniard; the other eight were Moroccan nationals with legal resident status who had grown up in Spain, the children of immigrants. There were four sets of brothers among them. By all accounts, the young men were well integrated into their community and showed no overt signs of radicalization. Seven of them had completed secondary education, and six of those were enrolled in professional training programs. Only three had criminal records—and only for petty crime.[75]

The precise relationship between the cell and the ISIS network remains unclear. An ISIS news outlet claimed responsibility for the Barcelona attack on the day it happened and before the attack in Cambrils. The suspicious travel pattern of Es Satty and some of the other cell members suggests they may have been in contact with extremists in Brussels and Paris.[76] A warning from the U.S. National Counterterrorism Center in May 2017 provides some of the strongest evidence of an ISIS link. The Americans warned Spanish authorities that ISIS "was planning to conduct unspecified terrorist attacks during the summer against crowded tourist sites in Barcelona."[77] It is difficult to see how U.S. intelligence sources could have gotten such accurate information if the Ripoll cell were not connected to the larger ISIS network. The cell probably acted autonomously under the broad Islamic State mandate to attack its enemies as opportunities presented themselves. The cell financed itself through selling stolen jewelry and purchased bomb-making materials within Spain.[78]

A GLOBAL NETWORK?

ISIS has certainly become an international threat, but to describe it as a global network of terror is misleading. Since the establishment of its caliphate in June 2014, the group has carried out or inspired 143 attacks in 29 countries (in addition to Syria and Iraq), killing a total of 2,043 people.[79] A closer look at precisely where these attacks have taken place, however, reveals a decidedly regional pattern to the violence. Most of the attacks occurred in the Middle East, the Islamic State's near abroad. A significant number occurred in areas where pre-ISIS groups operated, most notably Somalia (al-Shabab) and Nigeria (Boko Haram). The transit country of Turkey has experienced significant violence, as has Pakistan and Afghanistan, two hotbeds of violent extremism before ISIS came on the scene. Libya has also seen an increase in terrorism as ISIS established a foothold in its eastern provinces. Farther afield, the attacks have been fewer. One ISIS-directed attack has occurred in each of four European countries: France, Belgium, Spain, and the United Kingdom, although there have been several other ISIS-inspired attacks.[80]

Conspicuously absent from the list of countries in which ISIS has carried out an attack directed from the central organization is the United States. The Islamic state has had difficulty establishing cells in the U.S. homeland. This failure has more to do with the nature of the United States than it does with any ISIS limitations. American Muslims are generally prosperous and well-integrated into society. In contrast to the situation in Europe, they do not live in ghettos like Molenbeek. Their overall quality of life makes them more resistant to radicalization. The United States has experienced ISIS-inspired lone-wolf attacks, which will be discussed in Chapter 5, but even those have been few and far between. ISIS violence conforms to a pattern discernable over the past half century: most of what passes for "international terrorism" is in fact closely connected to local and regional conflicts.

THE FUTURE OF ISIS

The future of ISIS has been the subject of considerable discussion. The Islamic State as a territorial entity has been destroyed. By early February 2019, it had been reduced from 34,000 square miles at its height to just 20 square miles.[81] This remaining pocket was liberated in March. However, the ISIS network continues to pose a serious threat, particularly in those countries from which foreign fighters hailed. Thousands of ISIS recruits have already returned home. They could join existing cells or create new ones. They might also radicalize a new generation of terrorists. A similar development occurred with returning al-Qaeda fighters after the U.S. invasion of Afghanistan.

Far more worrisome is the persistence of ISIS ideology. Despite the differences between them, ISIS and al-Qaeda share a common belief system. They may disagree on priorities and methods, but they have common goals. Viewed from that perspective, ISIS might be considered "al-Qaeda 2.0," an improved, more lethal version of its predecessor. As long as the ideology persists, there will certainly be a "3.0," a revival of either or both organizations or the creation of a new one. The ability of extremists to spread their message via social media as well as through traditional forms of human interaction in mosques, prisons, families, and communities guarantees the persistence of Islamist extremism. ISIS has proven adaptable and creative in its use of online platforms. For example, it has made highly effective use of the new messaging application Telegram, "a cross-platform messaging service, which allows users to send chats, self-destructing messages (which disappear once they are read), photos, videos, and other documents without having to exit the platform and regardless of the size of message content."[82]

Even if nothing as formidable as ISIS rises again, Western nations will face a continued threat from lone wolves. Individuals with no direct connection to an extremist organization can adopt its ideology and strike a blow for the cause. In countries such as the United States, with no significant ISIS presence, the lone-wolf attack has become the most common form of Islamist terrorism. Considerable evidence suggests that such incidents will continue and may increase in frequency. The lone-wolf phenomenon will be examined in depth in Chapter 5.

CHAPTER 4

Domestic Extremism

The idea that the United States faces a serious threat from white, nominally Christian, homegrown extremists makes many people uncomfortable. The 9/11 attacks and the subsequent long struggle, first against al-Qaeda and then against ISIS, has conditioned Americans to view all terrorists as Muslims from faraway countries. Hard though the reality may be to accept, the United States has been plagued by a plethora of domestic extremist groups espousing an ideology based on racism, anti-Semitism, Islamophobia, misogyny, and homophobia that has inspired violence against other Americans. Most of these attacks have been perpetrated, not by the groups themselves or by individual members, but by fellow travelers, like minded individuals who have embraced the extremist ideology. Intentionally or not, these groups thus create a climate that encourages violence without engaging in violent activity themselves. The groups can even deny that they espouse an extremist ideology, let alone encourage violence. Calling for the U.S. to be an exclusively white nation, the logic goes, is not a call to arms. A group exercising its First Amendment right to free speech cannot be held responsible for the actions of nonmembers inspired to act violently by its rhetoric, they insist. These arguments may be true in a strictly legal sense, but they ignore the fact that stigmatizing racial, ethnic, and religious minorities encourages violence against them.

The plethora of groups espousing racist, Islamophobic, anti-Semitic, misogynist, and antigovernment beliefs represent a broad, amorphous ideological movement that provides a justification for violent action against people who do not fit a narrow definition of what it means to be American. Most of these organizations carefully avoid crossing the line between articulating a bigoted ideology and overtly inciting violence against minorities. Because their members do not perpetrate attacks, most of these groups cannot be classified as terrorist organizations or violent extremist groups. The FBI notes that "it is legal to have hateful or extremist beliefs as long as you don't commit crimes or violence based on those beliefs."[1] The Bureau defines categories of domestic extremist groups but does not maintain a list of them. Organizations that monitor hate groups, however, have developed functional definitions. The Southern Poverty Law Center defines a hate group as "an organization that—based on its official statements or principles, the statements of its leaders, or its activities—has beliefs or practices that attack or malign an entire class of people, typically for their immutable characteristics."[2] The Anti-Defamation League has a similar definition. It defines a hate group as "an organization whose goals and activities are primarily or substantially based on a shared antipathy towards people of one or more other different races, religions, ethnicities/ nationalities/national origins, genders, and/or sexual identities."[3] Useful though it may be, the term "hate group" does not situate these organizations on the political spectrum. For that reason, the term "far-right extremist group" seems more appropriate for this study.

Individually, far-right extremist groups may not engage in violence directly, but collectively, they constitute a dangerous ideological movement that poses a serious threat to the internal security of the United States. The fact that some of these groups and/or their members have armed themselves for an anticipated race war or a conflict with the government makes the threat more serious. A 2014 survey conducted by Duke University's Triangle Center on Terrorism and Homeland Security in cooperation with the Police Executive Research Forum found that most law enforcement members considered antigovernment violent extremists a greater threat than Islamist radicals.[4] From 1993 to 2017, there have been 150 right-wing terror incidents.[5] Between 2008 and 2016, people affiliated with far-right groups perpetrated 71 percent of murders committed by extremists.[6] White supremacists and others with exclusionary ideologies were responsible for 59 percent of extremist-related fatalities in 2017, an increase of 20 percent from 2016.[7]

This increase in violence correlates with a rise in the number of far-right extremist groups. Two political developments contribute to the proliferation of these groups in recent years. Election of the country's first African American president, Barak Obama, in 2008 spread fear among white supremacists, who were further emboldened by Donald Trump, whose call to "make America great again" resonated with their fear of lost white privilege. The number of hate groups increased from 917 in 2016 to 954 in 2017, with neo-Nazis increasing by 22 percent.[8] Understanding the growing threat from the radical right requires examination of the different types of extremist groups, analysis of the beliefs they hold in common, and discussion of the attacks carried out on behalf of the ideology they espouse. Examining all far-right extremist groups would be a daunting and largely fruitless task. Focusing on categories of extremists and representative organizations within them, however, reveals their common values. Each of the groups selected has been designated a hate group by the Southern Poverty Law Center and the Antidefamation League and stands at the far right of the political spectrum.

WHITE SUPREMACY

White supremacy (also known as "white nationalism" or "white power"), as the name suggests, is a belief in the inherent superiority of Caucasians. In its simplest form, that belief has been present from the founding of the republic. The framers of the constitution not only allowed slavery to continue, they counted each African American as three-fifths of a human being for purposes of allotting congressional seats by population. The belief was used to legitimize slavery and justify segregation during the era of Jim Crow (1877–1965). It persisted in opposition to the civil rights movement of the 1960s. The ideology experienced a resurgence in the aftermath of the Vietnam War as disgruntled veterans transferred hatred of the enemy in Southeast Asia to racial minorities at home.[9] A resurgence of white supremacy has occurred during the past decade and a half. A few prominent groups provide a general picture of the movement as a whole.

Ku Klux Klan

The most notorious white supremacist group, the Ku Klux Klan, was founded on December 24, 1865, by Confederate veterans to oppose reconstruction and reassert white supremacy in the occupied South. The group intimidated African Americans through lynching and other acts of violence. It remained active through the civil rights era of the 1960s. Changing social attitudes and persistent pressure by law enforcement degraded the organization. However, splinter groups such as the Knights of the Ku Klux Klan have continued its legacy of hatred and bigotry. As of 2015, KKK groups had a total of about 3,000 members. More than half of the splinter groups were formed during the last five years, suggesting that they are part of the revival of white supremacy currently plaguing the country.[10]

In recent years, white supremacy has tried to reinvent itself as a white pride movement. This effort gained traction as part of President Donald Trump's "make America great again" campaign, which many White supremacists understood to mean "make America white again."[11] "White nationalism," which holds that Caucasians are losing their privileged place in American society because of perceived preferential treatment given to minorities by federal, state, and local governments, became the movement's new brand name. In an April 10, 2018 interview with NPR, Jason Kessler, organizer of the 2017 "Unite the Right" rally in Charlottesville, Virginia, and a gathering in Washington, DC, on the first anniversary of that event, explained the movement's goals. "I'm not a white supremacist. I'm not even a white nationalist," he insisted. "I consider myself a civil and human rights advocate focusing on the under-represented Caucasian demographic." Pressed on the matter by host Noel King, Kessler could not clearly articulate how whites were "underrepresented." He also expressed his belief in Charles Murray's controversial and discredited book, *The Bell Curve*, which argues for the genetic, intellectual superiority of Caucasians.[12] Despite Kessler's insistence that he called for peaceful rallies, violence plagued the 2017 event in which a white nationalist drove his car into a group of counterdemonstrators, killing one woman and injuring several others. A closer look at particular groups reveals the nature of White supremacy/nationalism.

Stormfront

Founded in West Palm Beach Florida by Alabama Ku Klux Klan leader Don Black, Stormfront boasted 300,000 members in 2015, though their degrees of involvement varied widely.[13] The organization is an online community of like-minded individuals. It maintains an active website with blogs, a chat room, and a live-streaming radio program. While Stormfront does not itself appear to conduct public events, its site serves as a notice board for such activities.

Stormfront is an unabashedly racist website, but it couches its racism in the superficially polite language of white pride. "We are a community of racial realists and idealists," its welcoming statement boldly proclaims. "We are White Nationalists who support *true* diversity and a homeland for *all* peoples."[14] The group embraces a social-Darwinist worldview based on the presumed genetic superiority of Caucasians. "If Blacks or Mexicans or 'Browns' from the Middle East become a majority," its introductory statement warns, "then they will not be able to maintain the White man's social, cultural and economic systems because they do not have the minds needed to do so. Most Whites in the United States already know what happens when too many Blacks get together in a community, city or country—they 'pull themselves down.'"[15] Stormfront does not confine itself to racism. It is also anti-Semitic, decrying alleged Jewish conspiracies as well as the invasion of dark-skinned people. "The Jews have been working together behind the scenes to gain control of all the TV stations, schools, newspapers, radio stations, governments, movie studios, banks, etc.," the site warns, "—an all-encompassing 'Matrix' of lies—to destroy all potential rival groups and rule the world."[16] Stormfront considers separation as the solution to the "race problem": "We must secure the existence of our people and a future for White children," it demands. "We want an area(s) on the Earth (and/or perhaps states in the US) that are reserved for Whites, and Whites only, where we can live in peace apart from the horrors of the Third World and other races who would do us harm."[17] People have also posted Islamophobic, anti-LGBTQ, and anti-immigrant statements on the group's website, which Stormfront allows. Some participants are avowed National Socialists.

Stormfront and its members carefully avoid open incitements to violence. The group instructs bloggers, "*DO NOT* advocate or suggest any activity which is illegal under U.S. law,"[18] but posts by those who use its site suggest that many at least condone violence. One post praised a vigilante crowd for beating a Somali man in East London because they suspected him of an acid attack.[19] The real measure of the group's impact, however, lies not in its words but in the actions of those associated with it. A study conducted by the Southern Poverty Law Center found that between 1995 (the year the group was founded) and 2014, registered members on Stormfront committed close to 100 murders.[20] Some of the most infamous far-right terrorist attacks have been carried out by people active on the Stormfront website, including the July 2011 bombing and shooting rampage by Anders Breivik in Norway and the August 2012 murders of six people at a Sikh temple in Milwaukee by Wade Michael Page. After each of these high-profile incidents, activity on the Stormfront site increased.[21] Author Heidi Beirich aptly accuses Don Black and Stormfront of "motivational culpability" for encouraging the hatred that leads to such violence.[22]

American Freedom Party

Founded in 2009 as the successor to the American Third Position, this group presents itself as a legitimate alternative to the Republican Party, which it claims has abandoned true conservatism. The Freedom Party has much in common with other white nationalist groups as well as with similar parties in Europe. It purports to be a "party that represents the interests and issues of White Americans." The party's mission statement articulates its racist ideology, albeit in seemingly polite terms. The Freedom Party declares itself to be a "Nationalist party that shares the customs and heritage of the European American people. We need a Nationalist Party interested in defending our borders, preserving our language and promoting our culture."[23] Beneath this seemingly innocuous rhetoric, however, lies a racism as virulent as that of other hate groups.

Because it seeks to contest elections (at least in principle), the American Freedom Party has adopted a platform articulated as a list of "freedoms."

The party opposes racial mixing (labeled "freedom of association"), international organizations, immigration, and what it calls "foreign ideologies" ("liberalism, socialism, cultural Marxism, multi-racialism, feminism, neo-conservatism, fascism, and corporatism"). It rails against "militant feminism and radical homosexuality," which it claims are being "foisted" on the American people. The platform also advocates small government, supports gun rights, and calls for the abolition of the Internal Revenue Service. While the platform does not contain an overtly anti-Semitic plank, other documents on the party website express anti-Semitic views. A recent article declared that "Jews remain the biggest factor with the military-industrial complex."[24]

The American Freedom Party spouts the same rhetoric as other groups, although it does so in less crude terms. The Anti-Defamation League describes its members as "academic racists."[25] While there is no clear connection between the group and specific acts of violence, its racist ideology contributes to the general atmosphere of tension in the country. The very existence of the Freedom Party underscores how mainstream bigotry has become.

Council of Conservative Citizens

Founded in 1985, the Council of Conservative Citizens (CCC) boasted 15,000 dues-paying members at its peak.[26] The group developed from pro-segregationist "White Citizens Councils" of the civil rights era and has been reenergized by the xenophobia of the past decade. The CCC's statement of principles contains a litany of racist, anti-Semitic, and anti-government precepts common to such groups. It proclaims that the Unites States is a "Christian" and a "European [i.e., White]" nation and that those identities are being threatened by an influx of non-Caucasian immigrants and "racial mixing." The CCC considers the "traditional" family the basic unit of society and opposes efforts to weaken it "through toleration of sexual licentiousness, homosexuality and other perversions, mixture of the races, pornography in all forms, and subversion of the authority of parents."

Written in 2005, the statement of principles also contains the antigovernment and xenophobic precepts common to white nationalism. "We believe in States' Rights, the Right to Keep and Bear Arms, and the Bill of Rights," the statement declares. CCC defines these rights as freedom from "federal efforts to engineer or impose behavior and beliefs on citizens and communities." It rejects political correctness and opposes the concept of hate crimes and antibias legislation. The group also calls for the abolition of "the U.S. Departments of Education, Housing and Urban Development, Energy, Health and Human Services, and similar agencies." CCC also rejects internationalism, calling for the United States to withdraw from the United Nations, the North American Free Trade Agreement, and the World Trade organization.[27] The site contains links to other far-right groups; lists "news" items, which highlight crimes committed by African Americans against European Americans; and offers a bumper sticker, which reads, "Ban Muslims, not guns."[28]

The CCC does not openly advocate violence, but its rhetoric may have inspired one of the worst domestic terrorist attacks in recent history. Dylan Roof, the perpetrator of the June 2015 massacre of parishioners at the Emmanuel African Methodist Episcopal Church in Charleston, South Carolina, credited the group's website as awakening him to the alleged prevalence of black-on-white crime. Prominent conservative politicians, including former Arkansas governor Mike Huckabee have addressed the group, although he later condemned it.[29] CCC President Earl Holt III donated money to the campaigns of Rick Santorum, Ted Cruz, and Rand Paul. Following the Charleston shooting, Santorum, Cruz and Paul sought to return Holt's campaign contributions or donated them to charity.[30]

Identity Evropa

Founded in 2017, Identity Evropa presents itself as an "American Identarian Organization," committed to creating "a better world for people of European heritage—particularly in America—by peacefully effecting cultural change."[31] Given the group's high-profile role in the deadly Charlottesville Unite the Right Rally of 2017, Evropa's claim to being a peaceful organization seems disingenuous. The group claims to be "ethnopluralist" rather than white supremacist. It believes that "all ethnic and racial groups should have somewhere in the world to call home."[32] While this statement may sound innocuous, it glosses over the fact that the United States is already a diverse pluralistic society. The only way to make it a home for one racial group is to exclude the others. Evropa's strident anti-immigration stance makes clear its opposition to pluralism.

Evropa's "education" platform reveals its truly racist nature. This section of its website contains a report claiming that whites are the true victims of crime and blacks the primary perpetrators. The section attacks diversity, declares affirmative action a hoax, and proclaims the impossibility of reforming education to close performance gaps. The group has launched an aggressive leafletting and banner-hanging campaign, targeting colleges and universities it considers "bastions of cultural Marxism."[33] It hangs "No Sanctuary/Build the Wall" banners on buildings and bridges. It launched a "Save the Boer Campaign," a movement of solidarity with allegedly threatened white South Africans. It also convenes flash mobs to proclaim "European Roots/American Greatness."[34]

The Alt-Right

The alternative right, commonly called the "alt-right," is not an organization but a broad ideological movement, an umbrella under which many white nationalist groups easily fit. Richard Spencer, founder of the small white supremacist think tank National Policy Institute, coined the term in 2010 as the name of one of his online journals. He also maintains another online journal, *Radix*. The term "alt-right" has since been adopted by a broad range of people, some of whom belong to hate groups as well as many racists with no group affiliation who subscribe to white nationalism. As its name suggests, the movement claims to offer an alternative to conservative Republicans, whom it claims sold out by not defending white privilege. The movement has even adopted a name for these alleged turncoats. In July 2015, Radix republished an article by Alfred W. Clark, "'Cuckservative,' a Definition," to explain a term that had been recently coined to designate conservatives who do not subscribe to the alt-right's views. The term conflates two words: "cuckold," a derogatory term for a man whose wife is cheating on him, and "conservative." "Very basically, the cuckservative is a white gentile conservative (or libertarian) who thinks he's promoting his own interests but really isn't," Clark explains. "In fact, the cuckservative is an extreme universalist and seems often to suffer from ethnomasochism & pathological altruism. In short, a cuckservative is a white (non-Jewish) conservative who isn't racially aware."[35] The author uses polite language for the same message of hatred others express in cruder terms.

If the alt-right's official websites are at least somewhat restrained, its Facebook site contains downright vitriolic messages. The page contains links to inflammatory articles from Breitbart and other far-right sources, inviting members to join the hate fest. Distorted accounts of white peril and black crime affirm the convictions of its faithful followers, who weigh in with racist comments of their own. Two topic threads in particular illustrate the hate narrative of many alt-right followers. Since the end of Apartheid in 1994, South African governments have been seeking to address the issue of inequitable land ownership. An Afrikaner group known has AfriForum claims to be defending the rights of the white minority community. The group decries alleged widespread land seizures and suggests white South Africans may be targeted for genocide.[36] The alt-right has latched onto this false story, which fits its own racist narrative, viewing it as warning of what white Americans may face unless they remain vigilant. Fox News picked up the story and, based on its account, President Trump tweeted that his secretary of state would closely study "the South Africa land and farm seizures and expropriations and the large scale killing of farmers."[37] There has been no large-scale killing of white South African landowners.[38] Nonetheless, many alt-right supporters believe the story.

Another alt-right Facebook post drew even more inflammatory responses from followers. In November 2018, Ilhan Omar became the first Somali American woman elected to the U.S. House of Representatives. A post on the alt-right Facebook page showed a picture of her being sworn in to the Minnesota legislature on a "giant Koran" two years before.[39] In fact, she had held an optional ceremonial swearing in for family members after the official event. She used the *Quran* in the private ceremony, not the official one.[40] Nonetheless, the post unleashed a torrent of Islamophobic replies. "One nation under god. It's not one nation under allah [sic]," wrote one individual, apparently ignorant of the fact that Allah is just the Arabic word for "God." "Send her back to Somalia," wrote another. "Disgusting," added another. "This is a Christian country," wrote someone else.[41]

Articles published on altright.com provide further evidence of the group's racism. An opinion piece by Emmanuel Spraguer, "Antiracism Is Immoral," makes the convoluted argument that antiracism is worse than traditional racial discrimination:

Extreme discriminatory racism at least models nature. It at least promotes open competition between groups and celebrates the kinds of successes that nature itself customarily rewards. Anti-racism, on the other hand, is essentially just communism as applied to genes, race, and borders. It is anti-competitive, inherently dysgenic, not progress but anti-progress, and a way for the most worthless peoples on the Earth to gradually consume everything beautiful, precious and decent left on it.[42]

NEO-NAZI

While neo-Nazi groups share the racism of white nationalism, their anti-Semitic ideology and adoption of National Socialist (Nazi) symbols and iconography defines them. Neo-Nazis admire Adolf Hitler and tout the accomplishments of the Third Reich. They embrace social Darwinism, the idea that natural selection has created a racial hierarchy with Aryans at the top. These extremist groups subscribe to the Nazi concept of *Volksgemeinschaft* (loosely translated as "racial community"), the belief that one's identity depends on membership in a biologically determined community that must be kept pure. Most groups have explicit ethnic/racial membership guidelines, specifically excluding Jews and people of color. Like other far-right extremist groups, many neo-Nazis have reinvented themselves as "white civil rights" groups based on the disingenuous argument that Euro-Americans (whom they consider the only true Americans) are declining in relative numbers and being discriminated against. Like the original Nazis they admire, these hate groups see Jewish conspiracies everywhere, particularly in the media, corporate America, and the academy. They are also Holocaust deniers. Neo-Nazi ideology is often summed up in the

"14 words," code for the movement's slogan: "We must secure the existence of our people and a future for white children." A few representative groups illustrate the larger neo-Nazi phenomenon.

National Socialist Movement

Formed in 1974 as the "National Socialist Workers Freedom Party" and renamed in 1994 by its leader Jeff Schoep, the National Socialist Movement (NSM) is the largest neo-Nazi group in the United States. By 2009, NSM boasted 61 chapters in 35 states. The total membership is difficult to determine because the group does not release its membership rolls, but it probably numbers in the thousands, with a much larger group of sympathizers. In 2010, NSM's Southwest regional coordinator Jeff Hall ran for a seat on the board of the Western Riverside (California) Municipal Water District and garnered almost 28 percent of the vote (6,738), a clear indication of the movement's broad appeal.[43]

The NSM website contains a 25-point manifesto detailing its beliefs. "Only those of pure White blood, whatever their creed, may be members of the nation," the statement asserts. While this narrow definition clearly excludes all people of color, the manifesto also explicitly states that "no Jew or homosexual may be a member of the nation." NSM opposes immigration, calls for the union of white people into a "greater America," and demands "land and territory" to feed and settle its people. These demands echo the twin principles of "race and space" at the core of the original Nazis' ideology. Like their predecessors and unlike other white supremacists, NSM advocates an authoritarian government to ruthlessly implement its program for "the common good." It promotes a socialist agenda, promising universal health care, job creation, and education, just as the Nazis did. The group also supports the right to bear arms "for the purposes of personal, home, and national defense."[44] NSM demands withdrawing from the North American Free Trade Association, the International Monetary Fund, the World Trade Organization, and the United Nations.[45]

Vanguard America

Most Americans became aware of Vanguard America when James Fields Jr. used his car to run down counterdemonstrators at the "Unite the Right" rally in Charlottesville, Virginia, on August 12, 2017, killing Heather Heyer. Earlier in the day, Fields had been photographed marching with Vanguard members and carrying a shield bearing the group's logo. Vanguard denied Fields was a member and tried to distance itself from his actions. However, the Charlottesville attack reveals the link between hate groups and the violence they inspire. Clearly, the influence of far-right extremist groups extends far beyond their official membership rolls.

Founded in California in 2015, Vanguard America is a newcomer to the neo-Nazi movement, but it has capitalized on the wave of populist xenophobia sweeping the country in the last few years. The group espouses a classic National Socialist ideology based on racial and religious purity. "The racial stock of this nation was created for white Christian Anglo/Europeans by white Christian Anglo/Europeans," its platform maintains. "All other ethnicities, races, religions and demographics are absolutely not compatible with this nation's original culture." It advocates ethnic cleansing to include not only the deportation of illegal aliens but also "the repatriation of all African peoples back to their African nation of choice (to include some islands in the Caribbean)." It proposes giving these "repatriated citizens" some compensation and argues disingenuously that these deportations would benefit African economies. Vanguard also opposes religious pluralism. "Islam, Judaism and all other non-European or foreign religions, except for those whom [sic] are specifically peaceable and non-violent such as Buddhism and Taoism," the group declares, "should not have the freedom to practice in the United States due to their demeaning, conflicting and violent natures against the Christian faith." Vanguard uses the *Talmud* as an example of a book that allegedly mocks Christianity, thus revealing the group's anti-Semitism.[46]

ANTI-MUSLIM

While virtually all white nationalist and neo-Nazi groups are anti-Muslim as well as racist and anti-Semitic, some hate groups focus explicitly on Islam. These groups have appeared more recently in the history of American bigotry. Virtually all anti-Muslim groups formed in response to the 9/11 attacks. These organizations hype the terrorist threat posed by al-Qaeda and ISIS but go beyond condemning these groups to branding Islam a religion of hate and viewing all Muslims as at best a threat to American culture and at worst a threat to national security. Although these groups do not espouse racism or anti-Semitism, they attract people prone to those views. As the review of anti-Muslim hate groups, websites and social media reveals, bigots tend to be equal-opportunity haters. They may particular minorities, but they usually harbor a general prejudice toward all those different than themselves.

ACT for America

ACT for the America is one of the oldest and largest anti-Muslim groups in the United States. According to its website, ACT has more than one million members and a social media reach of 366 million (worldwide).[47] The Southern Poverty Law Center classifies ACT as a hate group because "it pushes wild anti-Muslim conspiracy theories, denigrates American

Muslims and deliberately conflates mainstream and radical Islam."[48] The group was founded in 2007 by Lebanese-American Brigette Gabriel. Born Hanan Qahwaji to Maronite Christian parents, she survived the Lebanese civil war and then immigrated to the United States. As the title of her first book (*Because they Hate: A Survivor of Islamic Terror Warns America*) indicates, her experience of that conflict shaped her attitude toward Muslims from an early age. Although she has only a high school diploma and one year of business school, Gabriel pans herself as "one of the leading terrorism experts in the world," a claim no scholar in the field recognizes.[49]

Gabriel founded ACT for America for the purpose of "educating, engaging, and mobilizing citizens and elected officials to impact legislative outcomes to keep America safe and secure."[50] The message sounds innocent enough, and the group has a strongly worded antidiscrimination, nonviolence policy statement. As hate websites go, ACT's is remarkably tame. One has to dig into the group's reports and the statements of its founder to find its Islamophobia. For example, the organization's 2011 report on grade 6–12 textbooks accuses publishers of "indoctrinating" students with an inaccurately positive view of Islam. "Islam has created and unleashed an uncontrollable wave of hatred and rage on the world, and we must brace ourselves for the consequences," Gabriel declared in her 2008 book *They Must Be Stopped*. "Going forward we must realize that the portent behind the terrorist attacks is the purest form of what the Prophet Mohammed created. It's not radical Islam. It's what Islam is at its core."[51] In 2011, she told a Tea Party gathering in Fort Worth, Texas, that "America has been infiltrated on all levels by radicals who wish to harm America. They have infiltrated us at the CIA, at the FBI, at the Pentagon, at the State Department. They're being radicalized in radical mosques, in our cities and communities within the United States."[52]

Although ACT is not overtly prejudiced against other minority groups, posts on its Facebook page suggest that many of its followers are. The site contains numerous anti-immigrant posts, including one in which multiple replies accuse Democrats of supporting the Salvadoran American gang MS-13. Another post rails against Nike for choosing as its spokesperson Colin Kaepernick, the African American NFL quarterback who initiated the practice of taking a knee during the playing of the national anthem at football games.[53] Local ACT chapter Facebook pages express prejudice even more stridently. ACT for Brandon, Missouri's, page features a post boldly proclaiming, "One Nation under God, not Allah," which argues that the United States is a Christian nation, not a Muslim one.[54]

Soldiers of Odin

The Soldiers of Odin is an American imitation of a Finnish anti-immigrant group that started to appear in the United States in 2015. By

2016, the group boasted chapters in 42 states. Chapters vary in size, and their total membership cannot be precisely determined because it does not make its rolls public. The group's official Facebook page, however, has 75,993 followers and has received 76,595 likes.[55]

"Soldiers of Odin USA" declares, "We will not bow down and submit to the Islamization of America."[56] While the site does not actively promote violence, some of its members clearly do. "Looks like Muslum [sic] hunting season is getting ready to open. No permit required, no bag limit, no sex restrictions," one individual posted. "Only requirement you have to inform law enforcement of how many, sex and age, and location of the kill." "Make it legal to shoot musilim [sic] men on site see how long takes them to leave country," another added.

Counter Jihad Coalition

The Counter Jihad Coalition bills itself as a "human rights and national organization."[57] The subtitle on its website home page, however, reveals its true intent and paranoia: "a coalition countering jihad on our streets."[58] The group specializes in distributing anti-Muslim hate literature. Its brochure, "Islam in a Nutshell: Peaceful or Violent?" declares that "Mohammed was a master of deceit. . . . Jihad is driven by the anti-Jewish and anti-Christian rhetoric of the Quran. . . . It is the political goal of Islam to annihilate all other civilizations."[59] Another publication proclaims, "ISIS is Islam," conflating the religion with radical Islamist extremist group, most of whose victims are other Muslims.[60]

American Freedom Defense Initiative

Founded in 2010 by Robert Spencer and Pamela Geller, American Freedom Defense Initiative (AFDI) is the successor to "Stop Islamization of America." The group espouses limited-government as well as an anti-Muslim ideology. "Our objective is to go on the offensive when legal, academic, legislative, cultural, sociological, and political actions are taken to dismantle our basic freedoms and values," its mission statement declares.[61] Though primarily anti-Muslim, the group has a broader agenda. "AFDI acts against the treason being committed by national, state, and local government officials, the mainstream media, and others in their capitulation to the global jihad and Islamic supremacism" it proclaims, the ever-encroaching and unconstitutional power of the federal government, and the rapidly moving attempts to impose socialism and Marxism upon the American people.[62]

To achieve its objectives, AFDI lays out a broad strategy. In addition to disseminating anti-Muslim propaganda, the group conducts demonstrations and counterdemonstrations, and it also holds conferences. It forms alliances with like-minded organizations and individuals abroad. It also promotes candidates who "understand state's rights and the necessity to limit the power of the federal government [as legal status permits]" and "fight against the march of Islamic supremacists [as legal status permits]." AFDI ideology contains an unhealthy dose of conspiracy theories and paranoia common to far-right extremist groups. It commits to "targeting infiltrators of our federal agencies and seeking their removal" and "defending the rights of the private citizen and opposing everything that increases his status of serfdom to the state."[63]

AFDI does not maintain a forum linked to its website, and the group's Facebook page consists primarily of posts by the organization with few comments. Both Geller and Spencer, though, maintain a substantial online presence. Their other sites suggest that their prejudice is not confined to Muslims. AFDI is not anti-Semitic. Indeed, Geller is herself Jewish, although her views have been consistently and stridently condemned by the Anti-Defamation League. "Geller exploits concern over terrorism to get an audience for her anti-immigrant and anti-Muslim agenda. She equates Muslim refugees with terrorism and promotes the idea that every Muslim wants to wage Jihad against the West," one ADL article stated.[64] In addition to demonizing Islam, she has attacked refugees fleeing to Europe and the Black Lives Matter movement.[65] Robert Spencer maintains the website Jihad Watch devoted to opposing what he sees as the threat of violent jihad, which he sees as a "central element of Islamic theology."[66]

CHRISTIAN IDENTITY

Members of the Christian identity movement share the racists and anti-Semitic beliefs of white nationalists and neo-Nazis. According to the Southern Poverty Law Center, "Christian Identity is a unique anti-Semitic and racist theology that rose to a position of commanding influence on the racist right in the 1980s."[67] They ground their racist beliefs not in social Darwinism but in the Bible. Based in Harrison, Arkansas, the Kingdom Identity Ministries is one of the oldest of these groups and the largest supplier of Christian Identity materials in the United States.[68] Kingdom Identity Ministries' doctrinal statement blends Christian fundamentalism with racism. The group believes that Adam was the "father of the White Race only" and that Caucasians are direct descendants of the 12 tribes of Israel and the true chosen people. They consider other races inferior and believe Jews to be the spawn of Satan. The group abhors interracial marriage (which it calls "race mixing"), supports traditional gender roles, and declares that homosexuality is "an abomination before God and should be punished by death."[69] The group distributes books and other materials espousing its views.

By some estimates as many as 50,000 Americans "practice some form of Christian Identity ministry," usually in their own homes or in small-group venues.[70] The boundary between members of the Christian Identity movement and other white supremacist groups is blurry at best. Although most white nationalists usually lack a detailed theology, they consider a conservative form of Christianity the only religion suitable for the United States and its citizens.

MILITIAS AND "PATRIOT" PARAMILITARY GROUPS

The militia movement consists of numerous groups formed around the two principles of the second amendment of the U.S. constitutions: (1) citizens have a right to bear arms and (2) the freedom and security of the republic depends upon a "well-regulated militia." These groups consider themselves the descendants of the Minutemen who fought at Lexington and Concord, the opening battles of the American Revolution. Despite their commitment to defending the Constitution, militia groups do not submit to state or federal authority. Most harbor a profound distrust of, if not open hostility to, the government. Many espouse conspiracy theories. They engage in paramilitary training in preparation for anticipated civil conflict. Their ideology is at best paranoid and at worst apocalyptic.

The modern militia movement took off in the 1990s, but it has roots in a long, ugly history of American vigilantism and antigovernment activism. From the Ku Klux Klan, which reinforced Jim Crow, through the Minutemen of the 1960s and the Posse Comitatus movement of the 1970s and 1980s, disaffected people have challenged the right of the federal government to "interfere" in their lives.[71] An increase in militia activity occurred in the 1990s as a result of several developments. In 1992, the FBI attempted to arrest Randy Weaver at his ranch in Ruby Ridge, Idaho. The ensuing shootout resulted in the deaths of Weaver's wife and son as well as an FBI agent. The following year, FBI and ATF agents besieged the Branch Davidian compound in Waco, Texas. After a 51-day standoff, agents moved to take the building. Fires broke out, perhaps deliberately set by the cult. Fifty-one people died in the conflagration. Antigovernment activists expressed outrage at what even the authorities had to admit were badly conducted operations. Militia groups sprang up all over the country, aided by the advent of the Internet. President Bill Clinton seemed iconic of the liberal elites whom militia members hated. Those who joined the new groups saw themselves as combatants in the "culture wars" of the era. They believed that any day, the government might come to take their guns and curtail their freedoms.[72]

Many armed anti-government groups today reject the term militia, describing themselves as "patriot groups." Because they engage in paramilitary training to combat a perceived government threat, they belong in the same category as groups that openly use the term "militia."

They reinvented themselves as a "patriot movement" to gain legitimacy. While militia organizations have much in common with other extremist groups, most do not (openly at least) embrace racism and anti-Semitism. They do take a strong anti-immigrant stand, though. Some groups even include antibias clauses in their mission statements. This apparent tolerance, however, is very misleading. By invoking a mythical colonial past, militia members make abundantly clear the sort of American society they want. White males make up the overwhelming majority of group members, and their posts show clear signs of racism and misogyny. A sampling of groups reveals a common ideology.

Three Percenters

On their website, Three Percenters (also designated as III-Percenters) insist that they are "NOT a militia" and "NOT antigovernment." They have been aptly described as a "patriot movement paramilitary group."[73] "We will be the last defense to protect the citizens of the United States if there ever comes a day when our government takes up arms against the American people," Three Percenters boldly proclaim. Founded in 2008, this "patriot militia" takes its name from the notion that only 3 percent of American colonists actually fought in the American War of Independence. Committed to defending their narrow interpretation of the Constitution, the movement has adopted a paramilitary structure outlined in its National Bylaws. It divides the country into operational areas, has a hierarchical system of command and control, and demands its followers take an oath similar to that sworn by serving members of the military. They ask members serving in the armed forces to swear a special oath in addition to the official one they take upon enlisting, promising not to obey orders the group considers unconstitutional, such as disarming U.S. citizens.[74]

Local groups engage in paramilitary training and political activism. Training includes rifle and pistol marksmanship and "advanced tactic/ shooting." Political activism requires members to vote and oppose laws the group considers unconstitutional. In keeping with others in the militia movement and, before them, the Posse Comitatus and Christian Patriot movements, Three Percenters oppose federal intervention in what they consider local affairs. "Keep in mind," the group's bylaws admonish members, "your Sheriff is the supreme law of the land and has the power to kick the Feds out if their actions are unconstitutional."[75]

On its official website, the group claims that it does not discriminate against anyone, but the posts on its Facebook page tell a different story. Following the unrest in Ferguson after the shooting of the young African American Michael Brown, the national organization shared a post titled "The Aftermath of Black Lives Matter." Supporters chimed in with a torrent of racist comments. "Rioters were most likely paid by the Obama administration," one person wrote, "& ok'd by DHS [Department of Homeland Security] that ran [sic] by the Muslim brotherhood." "Shutdown all the grocery stores and board them up," added another. "Let the animals starve or kill each other." "I think Black people resent having to obey laws," added a third.[76] The Three Percenters might argue that they merely provide a forum for free expression, but they clearly make no effort to remove such comments from their Facebook page.

Oath Keepers

Founded in 2009 by Steward Rhodes, a Yale Law School graduate and former Army paratrooper, Oath Keepers describes itself as "a nonpartisan association of current and formerly serving military, police, and first responders, who pledge to fulfill the oath all military and police take to 'defend the Constitution against all enemies, foreign and domestic.'"[77] It emphasizes that the oath taken by military personnel requires them to put defending the Constitution above obeying what it considers unlawful orders by the commander in chief. Like other paramilitary groups, it offers training, like its Spartan program, so that members and associates "will be trained to a high standard such that they may be called upon to protect our borders, or provide security for schools during active shooter situations, or serve on a Sheriff's posse under a constitutional Sheriff."[78] The stated goal of this training reveals the group's paranoia and potential for vigilante violence.

Despite having a strict nondiscrimination policy and even featuring videos of two African American members on its website, statements posted on its Facebook page reflect a broader bias. "The Black Lives Matter movement is just one of the social movements involved with the destabilization of the United States of America," it proclaims. "Others include La Raza, The Revolutionary Communist Party, the World Workers Party, the Muslim Brotherhood, ISIS and the Islamic Jihadist movements."[79] Statements of this sort also reveal the tendency of the group's followers to embrace conspiracy theories.

SOVEREIGN CITIZENS

The sovereign citizens movement consists of individuals rather than groups. Like militia members, sovereign citizens believe government has overstepped its bounds, but they go further, rejecting even local authority, claiming to obey nothing but common law as they understand it. They object to virtually all forms of regulation and oversight, including the requirement to get a license to operate a motor vehicle or own a dog. They refuse to pay taxes. Sovereign citizens often embrace the most extreme conspiracy theories, including the notion that government has monetized the value of each citizen for trade purposes and catalogued them using social security numbers. Although primarily an antigovernment movement, sovereign citizens often share the racist views of other far-right groups.

Sovereign citizens assert their unconditional right to own firearms of any kind. Fortunately, they rarely use them. Sometimes referred to as "paper terrorists," they oppose government through a variety of means, clogging up courts with bogus petitions and appeals. Sometimes this activity rises to the level of criminality, such as when they file false tax returns. Occasionally, an encounter between a sovereign citizen and the authorities turns deadly. On May 20, 2010, an Arkansas police car pulled over Jerry Kane and his son Joseph in a routine traffic stop. The elder Kane opened fire with an AK-47, killing two officers. Later that day police cornered the two suspects, who continued to engage them. Both sovereign citizens died in the ensuing gun battle. A more infamous sovereign citizen, Terry Nichols, carried out the Oklahoma City bombing with coconspirator Timothy McVeigh.[80]

UNAFFILIATED EXTREMISTS IN CYBERSPACE

Much extremist rhetoric does not come from recognized groups but from private sites, blogs, and posts. A few examples from the hundreds of online hate sites reveals the extent and nature of the threat. Fightwhitegenocide. com aims to "call out the anti-whites who push white genocide through mass non-white immigration and forced assimilation."[81] Newnation.org is a virulently racist site that highlights what it sees as an epidemic of black-on-white crime, often comparing perpetrators to animals, even referring to some as "monkeys" and to others as "black Negro Demons."[82] The Occidental Observer offers "original content touching on the themes of white identity, white interests, and the culture of the West." This relatively innocuous statement introduces a site committed to spreading stridently racist and anti-Semitic articles.[83] Offensive though the articles are, they pale in comparison to comments posted in response to the articles. One individual commenting on an article titled "Racism Is a Crime, Not an Opinion: Jewish Goyophobia and the War on White," claimed that Rosa Parks had worked for the NAACP as an agent provocateur when she refused to give up her seat to a white passenger on a bus in Montgomery, Alabama in, 1955. Another individual commenting on the same story accused her of being a tool of her "Jewish handlers."[84]

Although not specifically devoted to extremism, the online bulletin board "Reddit" has attracted hatemongers. The site has much more relaxed rules for posting than does Facebook or Twitter. Reddit allows communities known as "subreddits" to populate its site. Several racist subreddits have appeared in recent years. Many of these groups, such as the notoriously racist "Chimpire," limit access to registered members. Chimpire itself has spawned numerous subreddits whose names alone make clear the nature of their content: "CoonTown," "WatchNiggersDie," and "BlackGirls." By 2015, "CoonTown" alone boasted 3,287 subscribers. The ideology of white nationalism clearly has an extensive following online, with at least tens of thousands of people participating to varying degrees.[85]

COMMON BELIEFS OF FAR-RIGHT EXTREMISTS

This brief survey of representative groups reveals that beneath the surface of what seems like a diverse array of organizations lies a remarkably consistent set of core beliefs. White nationalists, neo-Nazis, militias, sovereign citizens, and other far-right extremist groups have so much in common that for practical purposes, they can be considered part of a single ideological movement. The newly formed "Proud Boys" actually embrace virtually the whole range of far-right beliefs. "How to make America great," the group's founder Gavin McInnes declares. "Abolish prison, give everyone a gun, legalize drugs, end welfare, close the borders, venerate the housewife, glorify the entrepreneur, shut down the government."[86] Different extremist groups might focus on different issues and have slightly different approaches, but they share a common worldview based on six broad tenets.

First, all far-right extremist groups espouse a narrow definition of national identity. Many insist that only Caucasians should have the full rights of citizenship. Some base their racism on pseudoscience, arguing for the inherent inequality of species. Others seek to preserve what they see as a unique Euro-American cultural identity. Both approaches would produce the same result: a whites-only America. Some far-right groups add religion as an additional criterion for being a "true" American. They would exclude all non-Christian people in general and Jews and Muslims in particular. While most groups implicitly exclude gays, lesbians, and transgender people, neo-Nazi groups specifically identify them as "pollutants" in the Aryan gene pool. Virtually all far-right extremist groups support deportation of illegal immigrants and oppose even legal immigration of people from "undesirable" groups. Far-right extremists are thus equal-opportunity haters. While they may gravitate toward an organization, forum, or blog that focuses on a specific group they particularly loathe, bigots usually abhor all marginalized people. This tendency explains the frequent presence of prominent racists on multiple sites that seem to have different goals.

Second, far-right extremist groups are atavistic. They seek to turn back the clock, not to a real period of American history, but to an imaginary past in which a homogenous white, Christian people supposedly lived in peace and harmony with one another. These racists dismiss the displacement of Native Americans and the institution of slavery not as terrible evils, but as inevitable consequences of the struggle for survival of the fittest. While few would reinstate slavery, many wish African Americans to be deported "back to Africa" or at least segregated in designated areas. These racists consider all progress in the United States as the accomplishments of the country's Caucasian citizens and blame what they see as national decline on the "mongrelizing" of the race through immigration and intermarriage. Many of them frame their atavism as a return to traditional values, the reestablishment of a society in which white men worked, their wives stayed home, and people of color "knew their place."

Third, far-right extremist groups have developed a powerful grievance narrative based upon a perceived loss of privilege. They lament that whites in general and white men in particular no longer seem to run things. The fact that Caucasian men continue to dominate politics and corporate America seems lost on them. White working-class, and even some middle-class men who accept this ideology, believe that they have lost their primacy of place to women and people of color through affirmative action and that immigrants have taken their high-paying manufacturing jobs, even though many of those jobs no longer exist. In this narrative, misogyny masquerades as a call for a revival of the traditional family in which men worked and women stayed home to raise the children.

Fourth, most far-right extremist groups harbor a deep distrust of government, which ranges from suspicion on the part of most white nationalist and neo-Nazi groups to open hostility on the part of sovereign citizens. Militias openly arm and train for the day when the government or the United Nations comes to take their guns. Far-right groups blame the government for affirmative action, which they claim discriminates against white men, and for regulations, which they see as undue interference in their lives. Some groups blend antigovernment rhetoric with conspiracy theories. Neo-Nazi groups, for example, insist that a cabal of Jews controls the federal government as well as the media and corporate America. Antipathy toward the existing state does not, however, prevent these groups supporting candidates for local, state, and federal office. The platforms of the Tea Party and the "Make America Great Again" campaign resonate with the rhetoric of many far-right extremist groups. The vast majority of those who voted for Donald Trump or Tea Party candidates do not, of course, support extremism of any kind, let alone espouse violence, but the striking similarity between some of the positions taken by these candidates and the ideas presented on hate group websites is no coincidence.

Fifth, far-right extremists believe the right to bear arms protects them against both the state and elements of the general population they perceive as threatening. Some groups fear that hordes of dark-skinned criminals will attack white people, who need to arm themselves for the coming race war. Others believe the government or some international organization will try to disarm them as a prelude to taking away their rights. While most groups advocate the right of individuals to bear arms, others have heeded the Second Amendment's call for "well-regulated militias," forming themselves into groups committed to defending their narrow interpretation of the Constitution. Virtually all far-right extremists consider gun ownership a necessity to preserve their way of life.

Sixth, paranoia characterizes all far-right extremist groups. These groups traffic in fear. They postulate a threat to straight, white Christian men and insist that the country is in imminent danger of being weakened, if not destroyed, by people of color, Jews, Muslims, immigrants, and liberals. They all present some variety of an "act-before-it-is-too-late" message. Many groups exaggerate the amount of crime perpetrated by people of color against Caucasians as evidence of the impending disaster. They also exaggerate the threat posed by Islamist terrorism, dismiss far-right violence as isolated crimes perpetrated by disturbed individuals, and dismiss hate crimes as a liberal hoax. Violence by illegal immigrants figures prominently in their grievance narrative. Paranoia manifests itself in demands for an end to immigration and secure borders.

PROFILE OF FAR-RIGHT EXTREMISTS

The sheer number and diversity of far-right extremist groups makes generalizing about their membership very difficult. Lack of access to membership rolls impedes analysis as does the reluctance of people to reveal their true feelings about race, religion, ethnicity, and gender in scientific surveys. One recent study does, however, shed light on the demographics of far-right extremist groups. Using data from the 2016 National Election Survey, George Hawley at the University of Alabama constructed a profile of those likely to be attracted to the alt-right, a broad umbrella movement under which most far-right extremist groups easily fit. The surveyors asked 3,038 non-Hispanic whites to express the intensity of their feelings towards the importance of race to their identity, the importance of white solidarity, and the degree of white "victimization" in American society. Approximately 28 percent of respondents expressed strong feelings of white racial identity, 38 percent felt strongly about the importance of white solidarity, and 27 percent believed whites suffered significant discrimination. Only 6 percent expressed strong positive feelings in all three areas.[87]

Hawley then examined the demographic characteristics of the 6 percent who felt strongly about white identity, solidarity, and victimization. He found that those without a college degree were twice as likely to express this constellation of racist attitudes. Income also correlated with adherence to attitudes espoused by the alt-right. As income declined, the percentage of respondents expressing strong feelings on all three issues increased.

Consistent with the income correlation, unemployed people were more likely than those with jobs to give strong positive answers to all three questions. More Republicans and Independents than Democrats gave strong positive answers to the three questions, as did more Southerners than those from other parts of the country.[88]

The study also yielded some surprises. Hawley found no significant gender gap in responses. Indeed, a slightly higher percentage of women indicated positive responses to each of the three racial identity questions.[89] Attitudes do not, however, always corelate with behavior. Based upon online activity and attendance at events, men seem to outnumber women, especially in militia groups. While both sexes may be equally prone to embracing racist ideology, men appear more likely to act on it. Hawley also found that a preference for alt-right ideology did not correlate with age. Every generation has about the same number of bigots. Hawley also found divorced respondents more like than married and single respondents to express strong feelings of white identity, solidarity, and victimization. He suggested that perhaps higher degrees of alienation explain the attraction to racial identity for divorces, or that holding racist beliefs increases the likelihood of divorce.[90]

In conjunction with other evidence, the Hawley study does allow for some tentative conclusions about those likely to join extremist groups. The members of all far-right extremist groups are overwhelming and, in many cases, exclusively white. In most groups, men outnumber women by a considerable margin, with the greatest disparity in neo-Nazi and militia groups with misogynist ideologies and often discriminatory membership requirements. The rank and file members of domestic extremist groups tend to be less educated than other Americans, although this may not be true of the leadership. Militias draw recruits more heavily from rural areas than do other hate groups. Anti-Muslim groups may or may not be anti-Semitic. Despite the official position of any far-right extremist group, however, its members and supporters frequently view all nonwhite Christians with the same antipathy. ACT for America may assert that it rejects racism, but judging by the posts on its Facebook page, many of its followers do not. While Hawley found that religion had no measurable effect on whether a person embraced racial ideology, that conclusion clearly does not apply to the Christian Identity movement. Beneath the demographic data lies a simple fact: whatever strengthens a person's grievance narrative attracts him or her to an ideology or group that offers empowerment. In that regard, members of far-right groups resemble their counterparts in ISIS.

NEXUS OF EXTREMIST IDEOLOGY AND VIOLENT ACTION

All the organizations described in this chapter would (and frequently do) take exception to being described as "hate groups" and would object vehemently to being characterized as extremist organizations. All avoid open incitement to violence, and most explicitly state their opposition to it. Many groups pay lip service to inclusivity. Some, like ACT for America and the Three Percenters, even have clear antibias statements. Their rhetoric is extreme, but their actions are not, and so they remain safely on the right side of the law, protected by the first amendment. Historically, few far-right extremist groups have engaged in overtly violent actions or plots, although those that have provide a clear warning of what well-armed, ideologically driven groups might attempt in future.

The connection between far-right extremism and violence is subtler and more insidious than it has been in the past. Around the turn of the twenty-first century, extremist groups began reinventing themselves to appear more acceptable to mainstream conservatives, particularly members of the white working class, some of whom have experienced a loss of economic and social status due to the decline in high-paying manufacturing jobs, and blame women and minorities for their situation. Many hate groups got rid of overtly racist symbols such as swastikas and SS thunderbolts. Some incorporated the American flag into their own iconography. They swapped overtly racist and anti-Semitic statements for declarations of white pride, celebrations of European American heritage, and assertions of patriotism. They committed themselves to protecting the rights of Caucasians allegedly threatened by liberal elites and discriminatory affirmative action policies. They repackaged Islamophobia and xenophobia as national security issues, disguising hostility to Latinos as a demand for secure borders and hatred of Muslims as a call to fight terrorism. Hostility to LGBTQ people turned into defense of the family and support for "traditional values." The marketing changed, but the message remained the same. Far-right groups also became skilled at using "coded racism," substituting seemingly innocuous terms for more offensive labels. For "banker," read "Jew"; for "criminal or looter," "black"; for "immigrant," "Hispanic or Muslim."

In addition to rebranding themselves, far-right extremist groups make skillful use of the Internet and social media. They keep the rhetoric on their official sites fairly restrained while providing forums in which people can express their bigotry more stridently. Many of these forums are password controlled, accessible only to registered group members. The Facebook pages of these organizations allow them to post provocative articles to which supporters can add even more inflammatory replies. These repliers may not even be members, so the groups can easily disavow them should they act violently. Because extremist groups guard their membership lists, it is impossible to determine how much crossover between groups, forums, and blogs occurs, but given that many of them post links to one another's sites, the number is probably significant. Much of the worst racist ranting occurs on Reddit and other sites on the dark web. Extremist groups can thus claim that they do not advocate violence or even hatred. When someone who frequents its site commits a murder or other violent crime in the name of its ideology, the extremist group can distance itself from the act by claiming that it not only does not condone such behavior, but it actively opposes it. The Council of Conservative Citizens took this approach after Dylan Roof said its site had inspired him. Far-right extremist groups thus contribute to a nexus of hatred and violence, which in aggregate amounts to domestic terrorism. Far-right extremist violence manifests itself in two forms: attacks by lone wolves who subscribe to the radical ideology and actual plots by members of extremist groups. Lone wolves will be discussed more fully in Chapter 5, but as already noted, many have been motivated by hate groups.

TERRORIST PLOTS

A number of abortive plots and a few successful ones have been hatched over the past few decades. The August 12, 2017, "Unite the Right" rally in Charlottesville, Virginia, produced a great deal of spontaneous violence, but at least some of the mayhem may have been planned. On October 2, 2018, four members of the white supremacist "Rise Above" movement were indicted on one count each of violating a federal riot statute and conspiring to violate it. FBI Assistant Special Agent in Charge Thomas Chadwick said that the four men "traveled from California to Charlottesville to incite a riot and to bring violence and harm to other Americans."[91] U.S. Attorney for the Western District of Virginia Thomas T. Cullen described the men as "serial rioters" and declared that Rise Above "organizes, trains and deploys to various political rallies not only to espouse" its ideology but also "to engage in acts of violence against folks who are taking a contrary point of view."[92] Careful analysis of video footage from the rally revealed the alleged perpetrators attacking counterdemonstrators, some of whom they injured.

The FBI foiled a more insidious plot in the fall of 2016. Three men belonging to a racist group known as the Crusaders conspired to bomb a housing complex occupied by Somali immigrants in Garden City, Kansas. The trio planned to detonate two cargo vans filled with ammonium nitrate. After the explosions, they intended to kill any survivors using firearms. "There's no leaving anyone behind, even if it's a one-year-old," one of the plotters declared. "I guarantee, if I go on a mission, those little fuckers are going bye-bye." The men referred to the Somalis as "cockroaches" and considered kidnapping and raping the wives and daughters of refugees. One of them, Patrick Stein, had been part of a Facebook group called "The III% Security Force of Kansas." Stein and fellow plotter Gavin Wright had tried to join the Kansas Flatlands Militia, an affiliate of the national III-Percenter movement, but the group supposedly turned them down, according to its commander Miles Evens.[93] Accepted into formal membership or not, the affinity between the III-Percenters' ideology and the terrorists' thinking is clear. On April 18, 2018, Stein, Wright, and Curtis Allen were convicted of conspiracy to use a weapon of mass destruction and conspiracy to violate the civil rights of their intended victims.

Unfortunately, the authorities have not always been able to catch extremists in time. In the spring of 2011, a gang of at least 10 young white men and women drove around Jackson, Mississippi, seeking homeless or intoxicated African Americans to assault. They assaulted one man near a golf course, attempted to hit another with their vehicle, hurled beer bottles at others, and fired metal balls from a slingshot at others, including a boy riding a bicycle. On the night of June 26, 2011, the assaults escalated to murder. A group of eight men and two women assaulted James Craig Anderson in a parking lot and then ran him over with the pickup truck in which they had been riding. He died of his injuries, and the perpetrators received prison sentences ranging from 4 to 50 years.[94] While the murderers did not belong to any specific hate group, their crimes occurred in the atmosphere of heightened racial tension following the election of the nation's first African American president. The crimes cannot be dismissed as lone-wolf terrorism. They were clearly premeditated, repeated, and perpetrated by a group of individuals with common beliefs.

These examples illustrate the potential for violence by far-right extremist groups and their supporters, especially those engaging in paramilitary training. Antigovernment plots abounded in the heyday of the Posse Comitatus and declined with the government crackdown that followed. The relative paucity of violent action by far-right extremist groups today may be due more to the success they have enjoyed in the mainstream political arena than to any newfound moderation. That could change if prevailing political winds shift. The Oath Keepers issued a call to members to aid in relief efforts following hurricane Florence. "Looting, armed robbery/car and truck jacking are an unfortunate reality in the wake of hurricanes," the appeal declared. "While we are focused on disaster relief, the need for protecting against violence is a reality and is part of what we do."[95] Fortunately, nothing bad happened, but given the tendency of these groups to equate "looter" with "African American," a tragedy might easily have occurred. A paramilitary group deploying armed members with a self-proclaimed law and order mandate is deeply troubling. Although lone wolves account for the majority of far-right violence, that could change very easily if armed groups perceive a threat to their vision of America.

CHAPTER 5

Lone Wolves on the Prowl

No study of violent extremism would be complete without in-depth consideration of lone-wolf terrorism. The phenomenon has become so prevalent that the term is bandied about with much imprecision. Anyone engaging in wanton violence is being called a "lone wolf." The increase in mass shootings at schools and venues perpetrated by disturbed individuals with no identifiable ideological agenda further complicates matters. Imprecise use of the term clouds objective analysis of this important phenomenon. Any discussion of lone wolves must, therefore, begin by considering what the term has meant historically, how it has evolved in recent years, and the threat it describes today.

The term derives its name from an aberration in nature. Wolves are social animals that live and hunt in packs. They seldom roam about alone. "Lone wolf" has a long history as a metaphor for any maverick operating outside the organization to which he/she nominally belongs. Law enforcement soon adopted the term to refer to criminals not associated with gangs.[1] In 1927, the journal *Dialect Notes* defined "lone wolf" as "a bandit or house breaker who works without confederates."[2] Substitute "terrorist" for "bandit or housebreaker," and you have the current definition of "lone wolf." Lone wolves do not belong to a terrorist group, network, or organization, although they may adopt the ideology of an active group. They carry out attacks on their own, usually to promote or at least publicize their agenda. Although they are not always on a suicide mission, they are usually willing to die while carrying out the attack. Unlike terrorist cells, they create no "communications chatter" and seldom leave the intelligence trail that helps law enforcement catch members of terrorist groups. Only friends, family members, and close associates have any chance of seeing the warning signs that a lone wolf is preparing to strike.

Lone-wolf attacks are becoming much more common and more lethal. The decade of the 1980s saw just seven lone-wolf attacks. During the 1990s, the number doubled to 15. For the first decade of the 2000s, it reached 23, and during the next five and a half years, it hit 35.[3] The number of people who died in these attacks also increased. During the 1980s, lone-wolf attacks killed 49 people. The number who died in the 1990s shot up to 180, 168 of whom perished in single attack, the 1995 Oklahoma City bombing. The first decade of the new century saw 98 people killed by lone wolves, and from January 2010 to July 2016, 160 people died, 49 of them in the Pulse Night Club shooting in June 2016.[4] Beneath the increase in frequency and lethality of terrorist attacks lies another disturbing trend: the nature of lone-wolf terrorism is changing.

TRADITIONAL LONE WOLVES

Until the last few decades, most lone wolves belonged to a category one author describes as "idiosyncratic."[5] Perpetrators who carried out attacks were motivated not by terrorist ideology but by their own agenda and/ or a deeply personal sense of grievance. These lone wolves often suffered from mental illness and/or exhibited antisocial behavior. They sometimes provided a statement of what they wanted, however bizarre and unattainable. In other cases, especially those in which the perpetrator died in the attack, the lone wolf left no evidence of intent. The absence of an ideological motive means that these lone wolves are better understood as disturbed individuals rather than terrorists.

Muharem Kurbegovic

Decades before lone-wolf terrorism became a household word, Yugoslav immigrant Muharem Kurbegovic carried out a deadly attack as the first step in a planned wave of terror. On August 6, 1974, he detonated a bomb in a locker across from the check-in counter of Pan American Airlines at Los Angeles International Airport (LAX). The blast killed 3 people and injured 36. That evening, Kurbegovic called the *Los Angeles Herald Tribune*, identifying himself as "Muharem Kurbegovic, Chief Military Officer of Aliens of America," the terrorist group he said he represented, and claiming responsibility for the blast. Three days later, he telephoned the local CBS station with information on the location of a tape-recorded message explaining the attack. On the tape, Kurbegovic explained that the LAX bombing was the first in a series of attacks to occur at locations across the United States. The name of each location would begin with a letter from "Aliens of America," and the attacks would continue until the words had been spelled out or until the group's demands had been met. The first target had been an airport, providing the letter "A."[6] As it turned out, Kurbegovic was acting alone; his alleged terrorist group did not exist.

Although he did not progress far before being caught, Kurbegovic planned a sophisticated series of attacks. Three days after the first attack, he placed a bomb in a locker (L) at the Greyhound bus station. This time, however, he warned the authorities in time for them to find and disarm the device. Satisfied with the publicity he had received from the media, Kurbegovic said he did not need to make his point by detonating another device. By this time, the "alphabet bomber," as he came to be called, had left enough clues for the authorities to close in on him. A combination of tips from his acquaintances and voice analysis of the tape recording led authorities to Kurbegovic, whom they arrested on August 20. In his apartment, they found bomb-making materials, sodium cyanide, and literature on chemical and biological warfare.[7]

The tape Kurbegovic left for police reveals a bizarre agenda. He wanted to create a country free of communism, nationalism, religion, fascism, and racism.[8] He claimed to be the Messiah. His belief system conformed to the ideology of no known group or movement. Psychiatrists diagnosed Kurbegovic as paranoid schizophrenic, but a judge deemed him fit to stand trial. He was convicted on multiple counts and is currently serving a life sentence without the possibility of parole.

Theodore Kaczynski

Theodore ("Ted") Kaczynski is the quintessential example of the traditional, idiosyncratic lone wolf. Born to Polish American parents in Chicago in 1942, Kaczynski demonstrated a genius for mathematics that got him admitted to Harvard University with a scholarship at the age of 16. He earned his doctorate from Michigan in 1967 and then accepted a teaching position at the University of California, Berkeley. His promising academic career ended two years later when he abruptly resigned his assistant professorship and moved to Montana. In 1978, he returned to Chicago to work in a factory at which his brother was a supervisor. His employer fired him for sending crude limericks to a coworker after she broke up with him. He returned to Montana to live off the grid.

Over the next 18 years, Kaczynski carried out a series of bomb attacks that baffled the FBI. In May 1978, he left a homemade bomb at the University of Chicago with the return address of a Northwestern University professor, who was the intended target. Returned to its purported sender, the bomb injured a security guard at Northwestern when he opened it. In May 1979, Kaczynski left another package bomb at Northwestern's Technology Institute, which injured the graduate student who opened it. That November, he mailed a parcel bomb, which did not explode but caught fire on American Airlines Flight 444, forcing it to make an emergency landing. On June 10, 1980, the president of United Airlines suffered cuts and burns opening another parcel bomb, which fortunately did not detonate at his Lake Forest, Illinois, home. By this time, the FBI had figured out that the same individual had produced all four devices, though they saw no clear connection between the targets. They dubbed the unknown perpe-trator the "Unabomber" (Una for "university and airline"). Over the next 16 years, Kaczynski deployed more than a dozen homemade bombs to a variety of academic and industrial targets, resulting in several injuries and two fatalities.

The Unabomber continued to confound the FBI, which could neither see any clear pattern in his choice of targets nor discern his motives. That situation changed in April 1995, when Kaczynski sent a letter to the *New York Times* promising to stop the attacks if a major periodical published his personal manifesto. On April 18, the *Washington Post* printed it as an eight-page supplement. When he recognized the writing as similar to his brother's, David Kaczynski notified the FBI. They arrested Ted on April 3, 1996. Without that tip, they might never have found the Unabomber.

The Unabomber's manifesto is a rambling diatribe against industrial-ization and modern society. He also railed against "leftism" and claimed people were "over-socialized."[9] Some forensic psychiatrists diagnosed Kaczynski with paranoid schizophrenia, although others disputed that diagnosis. A judge declared him fit to stand trial, and he always insisted he was sane. He was convicted on multiple counts and is currently serving a life sentence without the possibility of parole at the federal maximum-security prison in Colorado. Despite his antigovernment attitude, Kac-zynski had no association with any radical group, and his beliefs did not conform to those of any extremist ideology.

Stephen Paddock

While most traditional lone wolves leave some evidence of their motives, even writing lengthy, if rambling, manifestos, some leave little evidence to explain their behavior. The deadliest mass shooting in U.S. history remains the most puzzling lone-wolf attack. On October 1, 2017, 64-year-old Stephen Paddock opened fire on a crowd of concertgoers from the 32nd floor of the Mandalay Bay Hotel in Las Vegas, Nevada. Using 14 different rifles, he fired more than 1,000 rounds, killing 58 people and wounding 413 others. As police closed in on him, Paddock committed sui-cide by shooting himself in the head.

Although he planned his attack meticulously, Paddock left no clue as to his motive. He reconnoitered several other venues, including the Lol-lapalooza music festival in Chicago, and did thorough reconnaissance of the Las Vegas target site. He spent a year stockpiling weapons and ammunition. The Las Vegas police closed his case a year after they began their investigation, no closer to identifying a motive than when they had started. They concluded that Paddock acted alone using legally purchased weapons and had no criminal record. He had shown no signs of ideologi-cal racialization. He seems to have chosen his target, a country-western music concert, because it would yield a large body count, not because of any symbolic value. "In reference to the 2,000 investigated leads, 22,000 hours of video, 252,000 images obtained and approximately 1,000 served legal processes," the report concluded, "nothing was found to indicate motive on the part of Paddock or that he acted with anyone else."[10]

School Shooters

Although not usually classified as terrorists, the active shooters who have threatened U.S. schools in recent years have much in common with traditional lone wolves. They usually act out of an intensely personal motive, such as being bullied. Despite displaying evidence of asocial behavior or even mental illness, they often plan their attacks meticulously, surveilling their targets and collecting weapons and ammunition. As a result, they usually strike with deadly affect, and they often take their own lives at the end of their rampage. On April 20, 1999, Dylan Klebold and Eric Harris murdered 12 students and a teacher at Columbine High School in Colorado. On March 21, 2005, Jeffrey Weise killed five students, a teacher, and a security guard at Red Lake Senior High School in Minnesota. On February 14, 2008, Steven Kazmierczak killed five students at Northern Illinois University, in DeKalb.

The school shooter who most closely resembles the profile of the traditional lone wolf committed one of the most heinous mass shootings in U.S. history. On December 14, 2012, Adam Lanza entered Sandy Hook Elementary School in Newtown, Connecticut, and murdered 20 children, ages six and seven, and six staff members. Like Kurbegovic and Kaczynski, Lanza had been diagnosed with mental disabilities: Asperger's syndrome, obsessive-compulsive disorder, and sensory integrative disorder. His father also claimed Lanza may have suffered from schizophrenia. Like other lone wolves, he developed and eventually acted upon a bizarre ideology. He joined the online forum "Shocked beyond Belief," where members freely discussed mass killings. He railed against society and declared that public education indoctrinated students. Matt Lysiak, author of *Newtown, An American Tragedy*, concluded, based upon Lanza's posts and other evidence, that he may have attacked the children to spare them what he believed he suffered in school.[11] The discussion forum seems to have reinforced his beliefs and, thus, may have facilitated his plot.

Another school shooter who conforms to the lone-wolf pattern had ties to a white supremacist group. On February 14, 2018, Nikolas Cruz entered Marjorie Stoneman Douglas High School in Parkland, Florida, and shot dead 17 students with an AR-15, a civilian version of the M16 assault rifle. Cruz had a personal motive, having been expelled from the school the year before. He also had a history of behavioral problems. However, he had also participated in paramilitary training offered by the Republic of

Florida, a white supremacist group.[12] To what degree, if any, the group's ideology motivated him remains unclear.

NEW LONE WOLVES

In recent years, the lone-wolf phenomenon has taken a new, more sinister turn. While traditional lone wolves acted out of profoundly personal, idiosyncratic motives, the new lone wolves carry out violent attacks on behalf of broader ideological movements. They usually do not belong to any particular group but ascribe to an ideology that extremist groups articulate. Some of these groups tacitly or even actively encourage sympathizers unaffiliated with the group to strike a blow for its cause. Bin Laden's 1998 fatwa called on all Muslims to kill Americans. AQAP's *Inspire* magazine provides specific information on how lone wolves can carry out an attack. In other cases, the groups contribute to a poisonous atmosphere that inspires violence, even if they do not openly incite it. Ideologically motivated lone-wolf attacks are becoming the most common form of contemporary terrorism. To distinguish between these lone wolves and their predecessors, the FBI has adopted the term "homegrown violent extremists."[13] However, because the term "lone wolf" enjoys such widespread currency, it makes sense to continue using it, provided the phenomenon is precisely defined.

ISLAMIST LONE WOLVES

The Islamic State has made the most sophisticated use of the Internet and social media to recruit lone wolves. It has enticed followers to not only to leave their homes and journey to Syria to die for the cause but also to strike a blow whenever and wherever possible in their home countries. In a September 2014 statement, ISIS spokesman Abū Muhammad al-'Adnānī ash-Shāmī called upon supporters around the world to carry out attacks on behalf of the Islamic state: "If you can kill a disbelieving American or European—especially the spiteful and filthy French—or an Australian, or a Canadian, or any other disbeliever from the disbelievers waging war, including the citizens of the countries that entered into a coalition against the Islamic State," he admonished Muslims, "then rely upon Allah, and kill him in any manner or way however it may be."[14]

Al-Qaeda, ISIS, and their associates have inspired lone wolves. These individuals sometimes become radicalized through direct personal contact, but more often they do so via the Internet and Social media. They plan and carry out an attack, usually with firearms and/or bombs but also with motor vehicles. The Islamist organization then blesses the lone-wolf attack after the fact, granting martyrdom status to anyone who dies in such an operation.

Unlike traditional lone wolves, these terrorists usually do not show signs of mental illness, though they are often socially maladjusted. They seldom provide an elaborate statement of their beliefs but rather simply acknowledge their allegiance to a particular group. Acting alone makes them much harder to identify before they strike, although after the fact, friends and family members often report changes in behavior that occurred leading up to an incident. The number of lone-wolf attacks has increased dramatically in Europe and the United States. The truck driver who killed 87 people on Bastille Day in Nice, France, in 2016, appears to have been a lone wolf as was the man who killed 12 people at the Berlin Christmas market in December 2016. As it has lost ground in the Middle East, ISIS in particular has lashed out abroad by launching carefully planned attacks by using its network, but also by encouraging lone-wolf terrorism. Examining some cases reveals not only the diversity of Islamist lone wolves but also their common characteristics.

Nadal Hasan

On November 9, 2009, 40-year-old Major Hasan Nadal walked into the Soldier Readiness Center at Fort Hood, Texas, yelled "Allahu Akbar" (Arabic for "God is great") and opened fire with a semiautomatic pistol. He killed 13 soldiers and wounded 32 others. Born in the United States to Palestinian immigrant parents, Nadal grew up in Arlington, Virginia, and earned a degree in biochemistry (with honors) from Virginia Technical Institute in 1995 and a medical degree from the Uniformed Services University of Health and Sciences in 2003. He later added a master of public health degree to his impressive list of credentials. Not only did Nadal not fit the profile of a terrorist, he appeared to be living the American dream: the child of immigrants who became a successful professional.

In the aftermath of the attack, authorities traced Hasan's path to radicalization. After the death of his parents in 2000, he became more religiously observant. That in and of itself should have been no cause for concern, but his later behavior was. In 2001, he began attending the Dar Al-Hijrah Islamic Center in Falls Church, Virginia. The radical cleric and future leader of Al-Qaeda in the Arabian Peninsula, Anwar al-Awlaki, was serving as Imam at the center, but it remains unclear whether he and Hasan interacted. In 2008, Hasan emailed al-Awlaki, who by this time had moved to Yemen, asking if American soldiers who killed their comrades in the interest of Islam would be considered martyrs. Over the period of about a year, Hasan exchanged 16 emails with al-Awlaki.[15] At his trial, Hasan admitted that he was the shooter but claimed to be a warrior who had switched from the wrong to the right side.[16] No evidence has been found to suggest that al-Awlaki ordered Hasan to carry out his deadly attack, although the cleric clearly played a role in his radicalization.

Tsarnaev Brothers

On April 15, 2013, Tamerlan Tsarnaev (age 26) and his brother Dzhokhar (19) planted two homemade pressure-cooker bombs hidden in backpacks near the finish line at the Boston Marathon. They exploded, killing 3 people, including an 8-year-old boy, and wounding 261 others, 16 of whom lost legs. The brothers fled the scene, and a manhunt for them ensued. On April 18, they murdered a Massachusetts Institute of Technology police officer, hijacked a car, and drove to Watertown, Massachusetts, where police cornered them. Early on the morning of April 19, they shot Tamerlan in a gun battle in which he was also struck by a vehicle. He died in the hospital a few hours later. Later that day, police found his brother hiding in a boat parked in a backyard nearby. A jury found Dzhokhar guilty on multiple counts, including murder and use of weapons of mass destruction, and recommended a death sentence, which the presiding judge imposed. He is currently awaiting execution during the lengthy appeals process.

The Tsarnaev brothers were Chechens, born in Kyrgyzstan, who immigrated to the United States in 2003 when Tamerlan was 17 and Dzhokhar 9. Tamerlan masterminded the plot and probably radicalized his younger brother. The FBI report on the bombing paints a vivid picture of Tamerlan as personally frustrated and ideologically driven. His family struggled, his parents separated, and he failed in his dream to become an Olympic boxer. He was arrested for domestic abuse. In June 2010, he married his pregnant girlfriend, who delivered their daughter in October. Despite his ethnic ties to the Caucasus, a region in which Islamist extremists have been active, Tamerlan appears to have begun his radicalization after moving to the United States, probably online. In 2011, the Russian Federal Security Service (FSB) notified the FBI of its concern that he might return to Russia to join an extremist group and asked the FBI to notify it if he did. The FBI also investigated Tamerlan to see if he posed a threat to the United States and determined that he did not. He did travel to the Russian Federation in January 2012, visiting Dagestan and Chechnya during his stay. Although the FBI found no unequivocal evidence that Tamerlan met with terrorist leaders, the trip does seem to have contributed to his radicalization, as he carried out the bombing shortly after his return.[17]

Dzhokhar Tsarnaev adapted much better than his brother to life in the United States. He attended high school at the Cambridge Rindge and Latin School, where he became cocaptain of the wrestling team and did well enough to earn a small college scholarship. He went on to the University of Massachusetts, Dartmouth. Even though he did not do well academically, he appears to have been well liked and socially well-adapted, drinking and smoking marijuana, like many college students his age. He was close to his brother, who probably radicalized him.[18]

The FBI found no evidence of a link between the Tsarnaev brothers and any known terrorist organization. Claims that Tamerlan met with extremists during his trip to the Caucasus have not been substantiated. A search of his computer after the attack did turn up a YouTube account set up after his return from Russia with links to videos on Islam in Russian, one of which dealt with a jihadist prophecy.[19] Dzhokhar told authorities that he and his brother learned to make the bombs they used by reading *Inspire*, the online magazine published in English by AQAP.[20] The amateur nature of the attacks supports the conclusion that the brothers acted alone. Their bombs were crude, and they did not deploy them to maximum effect.

Muhammad Abdulazeez

On July 16, 2015, Muhammad Youssef Abdulazeez drove to a military recruiting station in Chattanooga, Tennessee, and fired through the window but did not hit anyone. He then traveled to a nearby U.S. Navy operational support center, where he opened fire again, killing four Marines and mortally wounding a sailor. Police responding to the attack shot and killed Abdulazeez.

A combination of personal issues and Islamist radicalization motivated Abdulazeez, just as they had Tamerlan Tsarnaev. Born in Kuwait in 1990 to Palestinian parents, he immigrated with his family to the United States in 1996. Abdulazeez grew up in a comfortable American home, got into the University of Tennessee, Chattanooga, and graduated with an engineering degree in 2012. He struggled with substance abuse and depression. He got a job at the Perry Nuclear Power plant, but his employer fired him after just 10 days in 2013 because he failed a drug test. He was arrested in April 2015 for driving under the influence of alcohol, which embarrassed his family. He was also in debt and considered declaring bankruptcy.[21]

Because Abdulazeez died in the attack, determining his path to radicalization has been difficult. His father had twice been investigated by the FBI for donating money to Palestinian groups believed to support terrorism. Abdulazeez made five trips to Jordan, staying with an uncle whom U.S. authorities considered radical. A search of his home and computer after the attack revealed that he had CDs and downloads of lectures by Anwar al-Awlaki and had researched whether martyrdom would absolve him from his sins. Two days before his death, Abdulazeez wrote a revealing blog post. "Brothers and sisters don't be fooled by your desire, this life is short and bitter and the opportunity to submit to Allah might pass you by," he declared. "If you make the intention to follow Allah's way 100 percent and put your desires to the side, Allah will guide you to do what is right."[22] This message, however, could have been an admonition to live a devout life rather than carry out a terrorist attack. Its ominous meaning became clear only in retrospect. The FBI found no definite link between Abdulazeez and any known terrorist group. In many ways, he seems to have been a suicidal young man looking for a religiously justifiable way to kill himself.

Rizwan Farook and Tashfeen Malik

On the morning of December 2, 2015, Rizwan Farook and Tashfeen Malik, a married couple, left their infant daughter with Farook's mother and drove to his place of employment, the office of the San Bernardino County health department at the Inland Regional Center. There they opened fire with AR-15 rifles and semiautomatic pistols on the office holiday party, killing 14 people and injuring 24 others. The two fled the scene and died in a gun battle when police surrounded their SUV. The attackers surprised many terrorism analysts who had never expected a suicide attack to be carried out by a married couple, let alone a couple with a child. The incident also raised the question of whether Malik radicalized Farook, he radicalized her, or the two journeyed down the path of extremism together. Their choice of target suggests that, once again, personal motives were mixed with ideological convictions.

Born to Pakistani immigrant parents in Chicago, Illinois on June 14, 1987, Rizwan Farook grew up in what court documents described as a troubled home. According to those records, his mother, Rafia, accused his father of being physically and verbally abusive, describing him as "negligent and an alcoholic."[23] The couple separated in October 2008. How precisely this turmoil contributed to Farook's radicalization remains unclear, but it probably traumatized him. The young man earned a bachelor's degree and had worked for the San Bernardino Health Department for about five years prior to the attack.

Tashfeen Malik was born in Pakistan in 1986 but moved to Saudi Arabia with her parents in 1990. She was studying the Quran at the al-Huda Institute for women in 2013 and 2014 when she began corresponding with Farook via the Internet. According to then–FBI director James Comey, they expressed their "joint commitment to jihad and to martyrdom."[24] In October 2013, the two met in Saudi Arabia while Farook was making the Haj pilgrimage. In July of the following year, she got a fiancée visa to enter the United States, and they married in August. Their daughter was born the following May.

The authorities have found no evidence indicating that the couple received help from any extremist organization. The neighbor who sold Farook weapons sought to make money but did not know of their plans. Their choice of target and its timing were personal as well as ideological. Farook had complained to his father that people at work had made fun of him for his beard and that he had quarreled with a Jewish coworker on the day of the attack.[25] Malik had also stated in an online post that she did not think Muslims should have to attend a non-Muslim holiday event.[26] Some evidence suggests that Malik was the dominant partner in their relationship. Coworkers noticed a change in Farook's behavior after he married her. He became more religiously observant and critical of Muslims who were not. Survivors of the massacre said that Malik fired first and that Farook hesitated. She was also the one who pledged allegiance online to ISIS for both of them before the attack.[27]

Omar Mateen

The deadliest terrorist attack on U.S. soil since 9/11 occurred in the early hours of June 12, 2016. Omar Mateen entered the Pulse nightclub in Orlando, Florida, and opened fire with a SIG Sauer MCX semiautomatic rifle and a Glock 17 semiautomatic pistol, killing 49 people and wounding 53 others. Mateen took hostages and held the police off for several hours before a SWAT team breached the building wall and killed him. After the attack began, he called 911 and swore allegiance to the Islamic State. During the hostage situation, he called a local news station to say he was acting on behalf of ISIS. He also posted on Facebook during the attack. "You kill innocent women and children by doing us [sic] airstrikes," he wrote. "Now taste the Islamic state vengeance."[28] Despite his pledge of allegiance to the Islamic State, authorities found no evidence of a connection between him and the extremist group. He acted alone.

Like many lone wolves, Mateen had lived a troubled life before his shooting rampage. The child of Afghan immigrants, he was born in New York City on November 16, 1986, but spent most of his childhood in Port St. Lucie, Florida. He earned an associate's degree in criminal justice technology in 2006, held a job as a security guard at the time of the attack, and hoped to become a police officer. Nonetheless, he had had difficulty fitting in for most of his life. An elementary school report described him as "constantly moving, verbally abusive, rude, aggressive," and prone to talking about violence.[29] He married an Uzbek immigrant in 2009, but she divorced him on the grounds of domestic abuse.[30] At her trial as an accomplice, the lawyers for his second wife Noor Salman claimed that he physically and sexually assaulted. A jury acquitted her on all counts.

Mateen seemed to have had radical leanings in his early teens when he joked about the 9/11 attacks. The FBI investigated him in 2013 after he made statements claiming connections to al-Qaeda and Hezbollah but found these claims not credible. The following year, the Bureau investigated him again when one of his acquaintances from a local mosque carried out a suicide bombing in Syria, but the FBI found that the two knew each other only casually.[31]

Evidence suggests that Mateen had been radicalized online. Because he targeted a nightclub frequented by LGBTQ people, authorities speculated that he might have been a closeted homosexual who carried out the attack to expiate his own guilt. In the immediate aftermath of the massacre, rumors about him attending Pulse and other clubs and using a gay dating application abounded, but these allegations proved to be baseless. Mateen was looking for a crowded venue to produce a mass casualty event. He may not even have known that the Pulse served a gay clientele.[32]

Sayfullo Habibullaevic Saipov

On October 31, 2017, Sayfullo Saipov drove a rental truck down a bike path in New York City, killing 8 people and injuring 11 others. Police shot him in the abdomen before apprehending him. He is currently awaiting trial. Prior to the attack, the 29-year-old Uzbek immigrant appeared to be well adapted to life in the United States. He immigrated in 2010, married another Uzbek-American, and had three children. He had worked as a truck driver and had owned two trucking businesses in Ohio before moving to Florida, where, according to some reports, he had trouble finding work and had financial difficulties.[33] In March 2017, he moved to Paterson, New Jersey, where he worked as an Uber driver. Other than speeding tickets and an arrest for failing to appear in court for one of them, Saipov had a clean record. He does not appear to have had the serious personal problems characteristic of other lone wolves.

Despite coming from a region of the world with a strong jihadist presence, Saipov was radicalized in the United States. Saipov waived his Miranda rights and admitted during interrogation that he had been inspired to carry out the attack by watching videos on his cell phone. A search of his phone found 90 ISIS videos stored. He also stated that he had begun planning the attack about a year prior to carrying it out. Another cell phone Saipov owned contained searches for truck rentals and Halloween festivities in New York City, indicating he deliberately chose both the time and place of the attack. Finally, the defendant asked that the ISIS flag be hung in hospital room and stated that he "felt good" about what he had done.[34]

Profiles and Patterns

The six cases and eight perpetrators examined here demonstrate the difficulty of developing a precise profile of the typical Islamist lone wolf, but they also reveal some suggestive patterns. With the exception of Nidal Hassan, all the perpetrators were under the age of 30, conforming to the pattern of terrorist attackers who belong to groups. All but one, Tashfeen Malik, were male, which also fits the pattern. Surprisingly, marital status was not an indicator of propensity for violence. Five were married at the time of the attack, and three had children. The perpetrators also call into question the claim that immigrants pose a serious security risk. Only two were recent immigrants, and, with the possible exception of Tashfeen Malik, all seem to have been radicalized in the United States, including Saipov, who like Malik came to the United States as an adult. Although some had financial difficulties, none could be considered poor, and several were comfortably middle-class. Lack of education does not explain their radicalization. Hassan had a medical degree, Farook and Malik had bachelor's degrees, and Mateen had an associate's degree.

Most of the perpetrators had two striking characteristics in common. First, all but two (Malik and Saipov) were generation 1.5 or 2—people who immigrated as children or those born to immigrant parents. These groups seem to be particularly vulnerable to radicalization. Often they neither identify with the culture from which their parents came nor feel welcome in their new home. Desire for purpose, validation, and belonging may attract them to extremist groups. Second, all but two of the perpetrators had serious personal problems, including violent and/or asocial behavior. Again, Malik and Saipov are the outliers; however, little is known about these two before they came to the United States, so they may not be as different as they appear. Personal issues usually mingle with ideological motives to inspire lone wolves.

RADICAL-RIGHT LONE WOLVES

The ideology of far-right extremist groups has inspired more lone-wolf terrorism than has Islamist jihadism. Because violent acts by people espousing white nationalist and other racist ideologies are usually classified as hate crimes, their cumulative effect can easily be missed. Two treatises written by far-right extremists articulated how lone wolves acting on behalf of white supremacist ideology could bring about the political change they desired: William Pierce's 1978 dystopian novel *The Turner Diaries* and Louis Beam's 1983 essay, "Leaderless Resistance."

Published by Pierce under the pen name "Andrew Macdonald," *The Turner Diaries* documents through the eyes of one of its leaders, Earl Turner, an insurgency against the U.S. government following its systematic effort to confiscate all guns owned by private citizens as the first step in creating a totalitarian state. A group known as the Organization fights back, eventually carving out a white republic in southern California, from which it expands to control first the country and then the world. It "ethnically cleanses" Jews and people of color from the area it controls. The Organization is a clandestine network of cells capable of operating independently and in cooperation with one another.

The underground units consist of members who are known to the authorities and have been marked for arrest. Their function is to destroy the System [government] through direct action. The "legal" units consist of members not presently known to the System [i.e., the government]. (Indeed, it would be impossible to prove that most of them are members. In this we have taken a page from the communists' book.) Their role is to provide us with intelligence, funding, legal defense, and other support.[35]

Louis Beam echoes some of the ideas espoused by *The Turner Diaries* in his succinct blueprint for armed resistance to what he sees as government tyranny. He built upon the work of Colonel Ulius Louis Amos, who in 1962 wrote about how Americans might respond to a communist takeover of the United States by waging a campaign of "leaderless resistance." Beam explained how Amos's strategy could be used against the U.S. government. He argued that resistance groups organized in a hierarchical pyramid were too vulnerable to penetration and disruption by government agents. A communist-style, linked-cell system, on the other hand, required resources that the antigovernment resistance movement in the United States did not have. He advocated instead a "phantom cell" organization in which small groups and individuals could act without direction as opportunity permitted on behalf of a common ideology. "No one need issue any order," he declared. "Those idealists committed to the cause of freedom will act when they feel the time is ripe, or will take their cue from others who precede them."[36] Beam's essay on "leaderless" resistance became a blueprint for domestic lone-wolf terrorism.

The connection between these treatises and attacks by lone wolves is hard to determine. Most perpetrators did not read either publication. However, the ideas these works contain have percolated through the white supremacist and other far-right movements to such a degree that many people have been exposed to the ideas they contain without even knowing it. Lone wolves engage in leaderless resistance, whether or not they realize it. An examination of some of these individuals reveals common characteristics as well as individual differences.

Eric Rudolph

In some ways, Eric Rudolph resembled the traditional lone wolf in that he developed his own rather idiosyncratic worldview. He formed his ideology, however, out of the whole cloth of views common among people on the radical right. "He had borrowed ideas from a lot of different places and formed his own personal ideology," concluded Chris Swecker, head of the Charlotte, North Carolina, FBI office at the time of Rudolph's arrest in that jurisdiction. "He clearly was anti-government and anti-abortion, anti-gay, 'anti' a lot of things. The bombings really sprang from his own unique biases and prejudices. He had his own way of looking at the world and didn't get along with a lot of people."[37] Viewed from a different perspective, Rudolph fits the pattern of the leaderless resister, which explains the support he enjoyed from like-minded people, some of whom probably aided him during his years on the run.

Between 1996 and 1998, Rudolph planted four bombs. He detonated the first on July 27, 1996, at the Centennial Olympic Park during the Summer Olympics in Atlanta, Georgia, killing two people. On January 6, 1997, he bombed an abortion clinic in the Atlanta suburb of Sandy Springs, injuring seven people. A month later, he detonated another device at a lesbian night-club in Atlanta, injuring four people. Police deactivated a second device at the site before it exploded. Finally, on January 29, 1998, he bombed a wom-en's health clinic, killing a security guard and seriously injuring a nurse. The FBI put Rudolph on its "Ten Most Wanted Fugitives" list in May 1998. He eluded capture for five years, using his survival skills to hide in wilder-ness areas of North Carolina, perhaps with some help from sympathetic locals. Captured in May 2003, he pled guilty to all charges and is serving multiple life sentences without the possibility of parole.

Rudolph displayed the same blend of asocial behavior and ideological conviction common among Islamist lone wolves. He had a turbulent child-hood. His father died when he was a teenager, and his mother moved Eric and an older brother to a Christian Identity compound in Missouri, where they lived for less than a year. The impressionable and isolated young man may have acquired some of his views at this location. In an interview after his sentencing, Rudolph's mother Pat denied sharing the group's racist and anti-Semitic views but voiced her own distrust of government.[38] Rudolph dropped out of high school after ninth grade and joined the Army in 1987. He was discharged in 1989 for marijuana use. He decided upon his violent course of action sometime over the next few years.

During his trial and in subsequent statements, including an autobiogra-phy published with the help of his brother, Rudolph explained his motives. He justified the clinic bombings as moral acts designed to save the lives of the unborn. He claimed that he intended the Olympic Park bombing as the first in a series of attacks designed to force closing the games and thus embarrass the government for allowing abortions. He claimed that he had intended to issue a warning prior to detonation and apologized for the deaths he caused. Rudolph also railed against homosexuality and feminism, which he deemed inimical to the family and traditional values, themes popular among far-right extremist groups. He denied being rac-ist but asserted that "institutional racism today targets primarily whites, through discriminatory policies such as Affirmative Action, racial quotas, 'hate crimes' laws, sensitivity training, and speech codes," an argument frequently made by white supremacists.[39]

Timothy McVeigh

On April 19, 1995, Timothy McVeigh parked a rental truck filled with fertilizer laced with accelerant next to the Alfred P. Murrah Federal Build-ing in Oklahoma City. When he detonated his homemade bomb, the blast tore the side off the building, killing 168 people, 19 of them children at a day care center, and injuring more than 700 others. With the help of Terry Nichols, McVeigh had carried out the deadliest terrorist attack in the United States to date and the second deadliest in American history, surpassed only by 9/11. Police apprehended him a few hours later in a traffic stop. On June 2, 1997, a jury convicted McVeigh on federal charges and sentenced him to death. He was executed on June 11, 2001. His accomplice, Terry Nichols, is serving a life sentence without the possibility of parole in the supermax federal prison in Colorado.

McVeigh fits the pattern of the lone wolf engaged in leaderless resistance to a T. He read and enthusiastically endorsed *The Turner Diaries*, distributing copies of the book at gun shows. His attack mimicked Earl Turner's bombing of the FBI building in the novel. Police found a page from the book in his car when they arrested him. It read:

The real value of our attacks today lies in the psychological impact, not in the immediate casualties. For one thing, our efforts against the System gained immeasurably in credibility. More important, though, is what we taught the politicians and the bureaucrats. They learned today that not one of them is beyond our reach. They can huddle behind barbed wire and tanks in the city, or they can hide behind the concrete walls and alarm systems of their country estates, but we can still find them and kill them.[40]

As he waited on death row, McVeigh sent a letter to FOX News reporter Rita Crosby, explaining his motives for the terrorist attack. He said that he bombed the Murrah Federal Building to make a statement. "Foremost, the bombing was a retaliatory strike," he stated, "a counter attack, for the cumulative raids (and subsequent violence and damage) that federal agents had participated in over the preceding years (including, but not limited to, Waco)." He added that he had also carried out the attack as a preemptive strike against federal agents behaving like soldiers attacking the American people. Finally, he declared his actions "morally and strategically equivalent to the U.S. hitting a government building in Serbia, Iraq, or other nations. . . . Based on observations of the policies of my own government, I viewed this action as an acceptable option."[41] Like virtually all such perpetrators, he died remorseless.

McVeigh showed some of the same signs of dysfunction exhibited by other lone wolves. His parents separated twice before divorcing, and on one occasion, he lived with his father after his mother left with his two sisters. After graduating high school, he entered a two-year business college but dropped out. He joined the Army and fought in the Gulf War, but he later left the service, as a sergeant. In 1993, he began traveling the country, distributing antigovernment literature. He did not hold any long-term job or seem to have formed any close relationships.

Anders Breivik

Anders Breivik is Norwegian. However, he embraced an ideology popular with far-right extremist groups in the United States and was active on the American white nationalist website Stormfront. His case illustrates not only the extremist ideology prevalent in many Western countries but also the international links between groups and individuals. On July 22, 2011, the 32-year-old disguised himself as a policeman and planted a van filled with explosives in the government districts of Oslo, Norway. The blast killed eight people. Before anyone figured out what had occurred, Breivik took a boat to the nearby island of Utøya and shot dead 69 teens and young adults attending a Norwegian Labor Party youth camp.

Breivik wrote a rambling 1,500-page manifesto detailing preparations for the attack and explaining his reasons for carrying it out. The document predicts a race war in Europe culminating in 2083, the date that also serves as the document's title, with a genocide against Muslims. Breivik decried the purported Islamization of Europe and claimed to have been personally victimized by Muslim immigrants. His manifesto also protested multiculturalism, Marxism, and feminism. He blamed the Norwegian Labor Party for promoting these movements and ideas and for indoctrinating youth to support them. Breivik claimed that his radicalization began with the 1999 NATO bombing of Serbia on behalf of Muslim Kosovars. The document also contains a detailed account of his preparations for the bombing and the camp massacre and a daily journal ending on the day of the attack.[42]

An initial psychiatric evaluation declared Breivik to be a paranoid schizophrenic and, therefore, unable to stand trial, but a subsequent evaluation contradicted that conclusion, declaring him sane at the time of the attack and sane at the time of the evaluation.[43] Conflicting diagnoses suggest that whatever his precise state of mind, Breivik was hardly normal. He had had a troubled youth. His parents divorced within a year of his birth, and his manifesto/journal complained of his father's absence and his mother's upbringing of him. "I do not approve of the super-liberal, matriarchal upbringing as it completely lacked discipline and has contributed to feminize [sic] me to a certain degree," he wrote.[44] He described his mother's new husband as a "primitive sexual beast."[45] He admitted to using steroids and in his July 2, 2011, entry said that going off them made him more aggressive.[46] His chaotic manifesto is more reminiscent of Ted Kaczynski than Dylan Roof, no matter what his clinical diagnosis. Nonetheless, the rhetoric of the right helped focus his anger on a group of innocent victims.

Dylan Roof

On the evening of June 17, 2015, 21-year-old Dylan Roof went to the African Methodist Episcopal Church in Charleston, South Carolina. About an hour into a Bible study he was attending, Roof pulled out a Glock 45 pistol and opened fire on the group. He killed nine people and injured one before leaving the church. Security footage of Roof allowed law enforcement to distribute his photo. Acting on a tip from a woman who recognized him, police arrested Roof in Shelby, North Carolina, the following day. A jury convicted him on 33 federal counts and recommended the death penalty, which the judge handed down on January 10, 2017. Roof later pled guilty to state charges, accepting a life sentence in lieu of another death sentence. He is currently awaiting execution at the Federal Prison in Terre Haute, Indiana, where Timothy McVeigh was executed.

Roof left ample evidence of his motive and his path to radicalization. He said that he intended his attack to start a race war that would result in the reassertion of white power. Before opening fire, he declared his intent to "shoot black people," and when asked by one of his victims to stop, he replied, "No, you've raped our women and are taking over our country. . . . I have to do what I have to do."[47] In a written statement found after the shooting, Roof explained how he became convinced he had to act, as he saw it, in defense of his race. After looking up the Trayvon Martin case, he said he Googled "black on white crime" and had "never been the same since that day."[48] According to his manifesto, the "first website" he came to was the "Council of Conservative Citizens," where he found "pages upon pages of the brutal black upon white murders."[49] For the rest of the document, Roof ranted about African Americans, Jews, Latinos, and Asians and the need to take back the country from them. He concluded that someone had to act, "to take it to the real world, and I guess that has to be me."[50]

Dylan Roof did not suffer from a diagnosable mental illness. Like most lone wolves, however, he had a troubled past. Born in 1994 to a couple that had divorced and temporarily reconciled, Roof moved back and forth between the homes of his parents throughout his childhood. Both his parents struggled financially, and his stepmother claimed Roof's father was abusive. Roof dropped out of high school and, according to several reports, abused drugs and alcohol.[51] Despite his turbulent life, Roof never showed signs of violence. His first run-in with the law occurred in February 2015, when police arrested him at a shopping mall for possession of suboxone, a controlled painkiller. Store employees called police, concerned that the young man came in dressed in black and asked suspicious questions about staffing and store hours.[52] He may have been casing the mall as a possible target.

The most perplexing aspect of Roof's childhood is the apparent absence of racial animosity. He lived in middle-class neighborhoods, attended integrated schools, and had African American friends.[53] He appears to have been radicalized online, and his case reveals the role that sites like that of Council of Conservative Citizens play in inspiring terrorists, even if they do not openly encourage violence or even condone it. The group's disavowal of Roof after the shooting does not undo the influence its ideology had on him. Maladjusted though he may have been, Roof might never have acted violently were his discontent not focused on a suitable scapegoat.

James Alex Fields

Twenty-year-old James Alex Fields Jr. went to Charlottesville, Virginia, to attend the Unite the Right rally on August 11–12, 2017. He was photographed wearing a white polo shirt like those sported by members of the far-right extremist group Vanguard America and holding one of its shields on Saturday. That afternoon, he drove his car into a crowd of counter demonstrators, killing Heather Heyer and injuring 19 others. He fled the scene, but police apprehended him soon after. He was convicted of a state murder charge in December 2018, and plead guilty to Federal hate crimes in March 2019. He is serving a life sentence without possibility of parole.

Of all the lone wolves examined here, Fields has the most pathological background. At his court appearance, he admitted to suffering from bipolar and attention deficit–hyperactivity disorders, depression, and anxiety and to taking medication for some of these conditions.[54] Raised by his widowed single mother, he had a history of violence. Police records indicate that she had called 911 at least nine times because she feared her violent son, who on one occasion, she said, threatened her with a knife, hit her, and locked her in a washroom.[55] Fields's high school history teacher claimed the boy had shown an unhealthy interest in the Nazis and said another teacher had filed a report about him over disturbing views expressed in an assignment.[56] Fields enlisted in the army in 2015 but was released four months later for "failing to make training standards."[57]

As with Roof, the case of James Alex Fields Jr. illustrates the deadly synergy between hate groups and lone wolves who act based upon on the extremist ideology of those groups. Vanguard America is a white nationalist group whose motto is "blood and soil," which clearly invokes Nazi ideology. After the Charlottesville attack, the group tweeted a disclaimer. "The driver who hit the counter-protestors today was in no way a member of Vanguard America," it declared. "The shields seen do not denote members, nor does the white shirt. The shields were freely handed out to anyone in attendance."[58] Despite its denial, the group's ideology and iconography clearly influenced Fields.

Brenton Tarrant

New Zealand authorities have charged Brenton Tarrant for murder in a shooting rampage at two mosques in Christchurch, New Zealand, on

March 15, 2019, that killed 50 people during Friday prayers. Before the deadly attack, the 28-year-old Australian immigrant sent a rambling 74-page manifesto to government officials. He espoused a white supremacist ideology, declared himself a fascist, and expressed admiration for Anders Breivik and Dylan Roof.[59] Authorities believe that Tarrant acted alone and have found no evidence of ties to any extremist group. He appears to have been radicalized online.

Investigations into Tarrant's background revealed an unremarkable childhood, although his parents divorced when he was young and his father died in 2010. These events may have had a traumatizing effect on him. After his father's death Tarrant appears to have lived a rootless existence, traveling the world, before settling in New Zealand. He expressed anger at what he saw as the invasion of western countries by Muslim immigrants and was apparently upset by the series of terrorist attacks in Europe during 2016–2017.[60] Tarrant claimed he had been planning the attack for two years.

Profiles and Patterns

The six perpetrators discussed in this section represent a small sample of the hundreds of people who engage in violence on behalf of far-right ideologies. Most incidents are prosecuted as assaults or murders. Some rise to the level of a hate crime. In aggregate, these ideologically motivated attacks amount to domestic terrorism. While six individuals hardly constitute a large enough sample from which to develop a profile, the perpetrators had certain characteristics in common with one another. All six were young men between the ages of 20 and 32. None had every been married. While they seemed to be of above-average intelligence, none did particularly well in school. Only McVeigh had any postsecondary education, and he dropped out of business college. Rudolph, Roof, and Fields all dropped out of high school. On average, the domestic lone wolves were less educated and less able to form relationships than their Islamist counterparts. Although all demonstrated asocial behavior, only Fields had been diagnosed with mental illness, although some clinicians considered that Breivik may also have been mentally ill.

CONCLUSION

Islamist and far-right-extremist lone wolves have two things in common. First, the majority of perpetrators in both groups had suffered some personal trauma that may have made them vulnerable to radicalization. Divorced parents alone do not explain their propensity for violence. Domestic violence, being frequently moved, substance abuse, insecurity, and other factors left these individuals with a profound sense of personal grievance and isolation that, combined with an extremist ideology, produced deadly results. The Internet and social media played a significant role in radicalizing them. ISIS, of course, openly calls for lone wolves to strike and even provides them instructions on how to do so. Far-right extremist groups in the United States usually avoid such incitement and sometimes even condemn violence. Nonetheless, their rhetoric has inspired some people to carry out lone-wolf attacks. Their views contribute to legitimatizing an ideology that promotes terrorism.

The frequency and intensity of lone-wolf attacks on behalf of both radical Islamist and far-right ideologies suggests that this style of attack is likely to continue and perhaps become more prevalent. As the cases considered here suggest, firearms have become the most common and most effective weapons used by lone wolves. In the years since Oklahoma City, and particularly after 9/11, it has become more difficult to get materials necessary to make truck bombs and even harder to park close enough to large public building to do serious damage. Almost anyone, however, can easily obtain semiautomatic rifles and pistols. Roof, Mateen, Tarrant and Breivik demonstrated how these weapons can be employed with relative ease to carry out a mass-casualty attack. Breivik killed far more people with his guns than he did with his bomb. The 2016 Bastille Day attack in Nice, France, and the 2017 Christmas Market attack in Berlin, Germany, as well as the Halloween 2017 attack in New York City, illustrate that vehicles can also be turned into lethal terrorist weapons. Combining the two could prove devastating. Finally, the lone-wolf attacks examined in this chapter illustrate that ideology matters more than groups. None of the perpetrators belonged to an extremist organization, but all espoused an extremist ideology held by such groups.

CHAPTER 6

Nightmare Scenarios

For more than a century, the bomb and the gun have been the weapons of choice for terrorists. In recent years, these weapons have been augmented by the motor vehicle as improvised tank used to run down pedestrians. The ease with which firearms can be obtained in the United States and increasingly in Europe ensures that extremists will continue to use them. Despite efforts to restrict access to them, bomb-making materials can still be obtained, and information on how to make an improvised explosive device can be found online. Anyone can get access to a motor vehicle. In the deadliest terrorist attack to date, 19 hijackers used airplanes as flying bombs to take down the Twin Towers and damage the Pentagon on 9/11. Dramatically increased airport security has reduced the likelihood of such a catastrophic attack recurring.

Despite the persistent use of conventional weapons as instruments of terror, experts continue to worry about extremists employing even deadlier means to accomplish their goals. The thought of extremists using chemical, biological, nuclear, and radiological weapons, known as weapons of mass destruction (WMD), has long worried law enforcement authorities. Recently, WMD has been joined by cyberattacks as the new terrorist nightmare scenarios. For the most part, however, such attacks have been confined to the pages of science-fiction novels and the scripts of grade B movies, but the possibility of their occurring in the real world must be taken seriously. At the same time, fear of these threats should not be exaggerated.

WEAPONS OF MASS DESTRUCTION

The U.S. Department of Defense defines "weapons of mass destruction (WMD)" as "Chemical, biological, radiological, or nuclear weapons capable of a high order of destruction or causing mass casualties."[1] The thought of such weapons falling into the hands of violent extremists has been a cause for great concern. Fortunately, the acquisition/creation and deployment of such weapons poses serious challenges that have thus far prevented terrorist groups or lone wolves from using them successfully. Governments must, however, plan for the possibility that a WMD attack could occur in the future. Each class of WMD has its own unique characteristics and must be considered separately.

Chemical

The belligerents in World War I were the first to use chemicals as weapons on a large scale. They fired shells filled with chlorine, phosgene, or sulfur (mustard) to create a poisonous gas, which acted as a blister agent, irritating moist membranes in the eyes, nose, throat, and lung. These gases blinded soldiers and caused death through asphyxiation. The heavier-than-air gases proved effective against troops in trenches but could be countered by gas masks. Because it caused tremendous pain and suffering without affecting the outcome of hostilities, poison gas was banned by the Geneva Protocol in 1925.

Despite its being outlawed, poison gas has been used in recent history. On March 16, 1988, Saddam Hussain used poison gas against the Kurdish town of Halabja in northern Iraq, killing at least 5,000 men, women, and children. Airplanes dropped canisters containing mustard gas and nerve agents such as sarin, tabun, and VX.[2] Nerve agents attack the central nervous system, causing the failure of vital bodily functions such as breathing. During the Syrian Civil War, the regime of Bashir Asaad used chlorine and sarin against rebel-held areas on numerous occasions. Despite an outcry from the international community, little action was taken against the regime, other than limited U.S. airstrikes in April 2018. Bashir's father Hafez had begun developing the country's chemical weapons program in the 1970s, and the regime still has a significant stockpile of chemical agents.[3]

Fortunately, there has been only one confirmed chemical attack by an extremist group. On March 20, 1995, the Aum Shinrikyo cult released sarin nerve gas on Tokyo subway trains during morning rush hour. The attack killed 12 people and injured approximately 5,000. Such a potent chemical released into the confined space of subway cars should have been more lethal. The liquid mixture appears to have been too diluted and the delivery system (plastic bags punctured by umbrellas) not very effective.[4] Manufacturing sarin requires industrial facilities and technical expertise, which Aum Shinrikyo could acquire because of its protected status as a religious organization and years of preparation. Even with that advantage, the cult did not produce weaponized-grade gas or deliver it effectively. Most extremist groups do not have the resources the Japanese cult did. Nonetheless, terrorists might acquire weaponized nerve gas by being given or stealing it from a state with a chemical weapons program. In the chaotic environment of Syria, such a threat must be taken seriously.

The highest death toll from a chemical agent in a single incident resulted not from a terrorist attack but from an industrial accident. On December 2, 1984, 30 tons of methyl isocyanate leaked from the Union Carbide pesticide plant in Bhopal, India. Approximately 15,000 people living in surrounding shantytowns died from exposure to the toxic chemical—some immediately, others as a result of longer-term health effects of exposure.[5] Manufacturing such a large quantity of pesticide is beyond the capability of most extremist organizations, but acquiring enough commercial-grade material to conduct a smaller-scale attack probably is not.

In addition to gases, other toxic chemicals could be used by violent extremists. The Russian government has been blamed for the 2006 fatal poisoning of Alexander Litvinenko using polonium 210 and the 2018 poisoning of Sergei Skripal and his daughter using the Novichok nerve agent A-234, from which the two recovered. Litvinenko and Skripal had been given asylum in Britain, where the attacks occurred. The use of ingestible poisons may be effective for assassinations, but they do not make good weapons for terrorist attacks because of the difficulty of delivering them in large enough quantities to produce mass casualties. Poisoning a city's water supply, for example, would require such a large amount of chemical that the perpetrators would almost certainly be caught in the act. Even if they succeeded in deploying enough poison, filtration systems and the filters in many homes would remove most toxins.

Biological

The 1919 influenza outbreak illustrates the lethality of naturally occurring pathogens. Lasting just 15 months, the pandemic killed 3–5 percent of the entire world population, including 195,000 Americans.[6] The first recorded use of a biological agent as a weapon of war occurred during the 1346 siege of Caffa in Crimea. The Tatar and Saracen attackers hurled the bodies of plague victims over the city walls to spread disease among the defenders.

Modern states developed biological warfare capabilities during the twentieth century. Both the United States and the Soviet Union weaponized bacillus anthracis (anthrax), milling naturally occurring spores so that they could be easily dispersed over a wide area, kill their victims quickly, and then settle to the ground, allowing troops to occupy cleared territory. Some weaponized anthrax still exists, but acquiring it and finding a suitable distribution mechanism would not be easy. In October 2001, an emotionally disturbed scientist at the Fort Detrick Biodefense Laboratory in Fredrick, Maryland, sent anthrax to politicians and the media in a bizarre plot to preserve funding for the anthrax vaccine project on which he was working. Five people died in the attack, and 17 others became ill. The suspect, Bruce E. Ivins, committed suicide while awaiting trial.[7] Although cleanup proved expensive, the anthrax attacks paled in comparison to those of 9/11 just over a month earlier. If a trained scientist had difficulty conducting an effective anthrax attack, how much more difficult would it be for an extremist organization without such expertise?

Another nightmare scenario has terrorists spreading disease by deploying infected individuals to populated areas or contaminating food supplies. An effective pathogen would have to be very lethal and easily transmittable. With a mortality rate of 30 percent and easy aerosol transmission via contact with an infected person, smallpox has the desired characteristics. Following eradication in the country, the United States stopped routine vaccination against the disease in 1972.[8] Those born after that date are vulnerable to infection. Using smallpox as a weapon would not, however, be easy. In 2005, scientists created a computer simulation of a smallpox attack on Portland, Oregon, population 536,000 (approximate at the time). They found that with no government response, 380,582 people would be in infected by day 70, of whom 12,499 would die. A program of "targeted vaccination and quarantine" beginning on day 14, however, would reduce the number infected to 2,564, reduce the death toll to just 312, and contain the outbreak by day 35.[9] The authorities would thus have two weeks to identify and contain the outbreak, well within the capability of the U.S. health care system. The risk of the contagion to the terrorists, however, especially those living in less developed parts of the world with poorer healthcare systems, would be considerable.

The limitations of pathogens as instruments of terror may also be seen in the one case in which extremists used them for an attack within the United States. In the fall of 1984, the Rajneesh cult in Wasco County, Oregon, tried to influence the election of county commissioners by poisoning voters. They deployed two-person teams with bottles of liquid containing salmonella (a principal cause of food poisoning) to contaminate salad bars in local restaurants. The attack made 751 people ill, but no one died. Authorities deported the cult leader to India after fining him $400,000 for other offenses and sent three of his deputies, including the woman responsible for planning the attack, to prison. She served 29 months and was then deported. The plot not only failed but also led to the destruction of the cult's community in Oregon.[10]

Frightening though the prospects of bioterrorism may be, the difficulty of implementing an attack explains why so few have been attempted and none has been particularly successful. "To deploy a disease—a natural killer—as a weapon of war is theoretically an alarmingly straightforward concept," concluded a report by the Chemical and Biological Weapons Non-proliferation Project. "However, effectively harnessing Mother Nature's killing capacity is, according to many an expert, easier said than done."[11] Because extremists have proven to be quite creative and adaptable, the United States and its allies must continue to study and prepare for a biological attack. Barring a technological breakthrough, however, such an attack remains far less improbable than one using conventional weapons.

Nuclear

Osama bin Laden made no secret of his desire to get a nuclear bomb, which he would certainly have used. Even without al-Qaeda's sworn intent to obtain such a WMD, security experts pondered the likelihood of an extremist group getting hold of even a small nuclear device. They envisioned three ways terrorists might acquire such a weapon: they could steal a bomb, be given a functioning device by a state, or obtain the materials and expertise necessary to build one of their own. The probability of any of these scenarios occurring is considerably lower than popularly imagined.

The odds of a nuclear power, even a rogue state like North Korea, being foolish enough to give a nuclear bomb to an extremist group are low, and stealing one would be very difficult. All arsenals are well guarded, and the weight of bombs and warheads would make them difficult to move. The Soviet Union allegedly had portable nuclear devices, popularly known as "suitcase nukes." In 1997, former Russian Security Council secretary, General (Ret.) Alexander Lebed, told the television exposé *60 Minutes* that the Russian Federation could not account for some of these devices. In the aftermath of 9/11, the fear of such a weapon falling into the hands of al-Qaeda gained credence. Subsequent investigations have, however, cast doubt on this threat. First, experts have not been able to verify that the Soviets even had such devices in the first place. Second, they maintain that if the Soviets did have suitcase nukes, there is no evidence that they lost control of any of them. Third, without maintenance, the nuclear material in such devices would have decayed in the years since the end of the Cold War and become less effective.[12]

Obtaining the materials necessary to make a nuclear device would be considerably easier than obtaining a fully operational one, but the challenges in building a bomb might prove insurmountable. Terrorists would first have to steal the plutonium or uranium-232 necessary to construct a bomb. Plenty of nuclear material exists, and unfortunately, not all of it has been adequately secured. If they acquired enough to make a bomb, the extremists would need to produce a suitable trigger. The technical details of such an endeavor are beyond the scope of this work. Suffice it to say that experts have concluded that it would require a variety of skills a single individual would probably not possess as well as requisite facilities in a secure location to make a bomb. Kidnapping a single nuclear scientist would not provide the extremists the expertise necessary to make a bomb. The risk of an accidental detonation—which would not, incidentally, result in a nuclear blast—would be quite high. If the bomb makers in Barcelona blew themselves up making conventional IEDs, how much more likely would amateurs be to destroy their work assembling a far more sophisticated nuclear device? Without the help of a state providing material and expertise, a terrorist group would be unlikely to build even a small nuclear device.[13]

Radiological

Another nightmare scenario involves the use of a radiological disbursement device, commonly known as a dirty bomb. Such a weapon uses a conventional explosive to disperse radioactive material over a wide area. The idea appears simple enough: get some radioactive material and attach it to a bomb. In the popular imagination, such a device would cause thousands of deaths and render large areas uninhabitable for decades. The reality is far less threatening. The effectiveness of a radiological dispersal device depends on exposing victims to a sufficient concentration of radioactive material long enough to kill them immediately or make them sick over a period of time. Given the types of isotopes most available to terrorists, the radioactive material would have to be ingested or inhaled. Unlike a nuclear blast, a conventional detonation would affect a very limited area, probably no more than a few city blocks. Unless the radioactive material were aerosoled (no easy task), it would fall to the ground. The concentration of aerosol material would diminish with distance from the epicenter. Most experts conclude that only those too injured to flee the initial blast area would be exposed to a lethal dose of radiation. Far more people would be killed by the conventional explosion. The fear caused by the attack could, however, have serious economic consequences as people might be afraid to return to an area, even if it had been decontaminated.[14]

While a dirty bomb would be far less effective than generally imagined, a radiological weapon delivered by other means might be deadlier. As the poisoning of Litvinenko illustrates, contaminating food or water can have lethal effects, although irradiating a large population by this means would be much more difficult than assassinating a single individual. A more effective means of delivery would be to douse a group of people with contaminated water, causing them to ingest a lethal or at least an illness-inducing dose of radioactive material.[15] The effects of such an attack would not, however, be apparent for some time, thus depriving the extremists of the drama that bombs and bullets provide.

CYBERATTACKS

In 1966, Dennis Feltham Jones published *Colossus*, a science fiction novel about supercomputers created by the United States and the Soviet Union to control their respective nuclear arsenals. The computers become sentient, link up with one another, and rule humanity. Ever since then, people have been awed by—and anxious about—the role computers play in their lives. Those feelings have only intensified since the creation of the Internet. Computers have made life easier in many ways and have enormous potential for good. They have also created vulnerabilities that extremists can exploit. Thus far, however, cyberterrorism exists as a potential threat rather than an existing reality. Once again, science fiction and Hollywood have conjured up nightmare scenarios of terrorists hacking the controls of airplanes and the Scada systems controlling traffic signals to wreak havoc on defenseless populations. A more sober assessment of potential cyber-threats and actual attacks as well as an understanding of those who perpetrate them reveals a less frightening picture.

Cyber Incidents

A clear distinction must be made between cyberattacks that have occurred and potential threats that have yet to materialize. To date, cyber-attacks have been launched by criminals and states. Criminals have used a variety of means to steal information in order to profit. They use malware designed to capture valuable data, such as account numbers and passwords. Phishing deceives users into providing such information voluntarily. In denial-of-service attacks, the attackers disrupt access to web-based services. Distributed denial-of-service acts have achieved the same purpose more effectively by flooding a site with traffic from multiple sources, making it harder to block the attack. Cyber-attacks can be as minor as blocking a viewer from watching the Superbowl or as serious as stealing hospital patient records and holding those records for ransom. Hackers can also steal proprietary information (a form of corporate espionage). China, Russia, and Iran have been accused of stealing proprietary information from the government and U.S. companies.[16]

States have also used cyberweapons in international conflict. In 2005, the computers controlling the Iranian centrifuges used to enrich the country's weapons-grade uranium were infected with malicious software known as the Stuxnet virus. The virus caused the motors driving the centrifuges to run too fast and too long, burning them out. Experts have concluded that the United States developed Stuxnet in cooperation with Israel to disrupt the Iranian nuclear program.[17]

In 2007, Estonia experienced a massive cyberattack that was organized, many experts believe, by the Kremlin. Following the relocation of a Soviet war memorial and rioting by ethnic Russians, the country experienced a massive disruption of services. Spam launched by botnets and a flood of online requests overwhelmed servers, disrupting government communications and banking services. The attack lasted weeks and rendered ATMs sporadically inoperable.[18] In response to the attack, Estonia has developed a state-of-the-art cybersecurity program. The year following the Estonian incident Russian hackers conducted denial-of-service and website-defacement attacks against Georgia during the invasion of South Ossetia, although the cyber-attacks did not affect the outcome of the conflict.[19]

Potential Cyberthreats

No one has yet been killed by a cyberterrorism attack. Even the sophisticated state-on-state incidents have been expensive to the county targeted but not lethal to its people. The possibility of that situation changing must be considered. Most scenarios envision hackers gaining access to computer systems that control critical infrastructure to produce catastrophic disruptions that would cause mass casualties. A few examples illustrate what—theoretically at least—might be done.

The notion that terrorists could gain access to air traffic control systems and crash airplanes remains in the realm of science fiction. These systems are not completely autonomous. They rely on human-computer interaction, with ample opportunity to detect and counter external interference. A more likely scenario has been proposed in which hackers would exploit a vulnerability in the new Automatic Dependent Surveillance system to be implemented at airports throughout the United States by 2020. Some experts believe hackers could flood the system with radio signals from phantom planes, thus creating panic among pilots and controllers, which could lead to fatal accidents. They warn that the system lacks the necessary encryption to prevent such false signals from being transmitted. The Federal Aviation Administration insists that it is taking steps to mitigate such risk.[20]

Another cyberterrorism scenario has extremists interfering with a nation's power grid. In December 2015, Ukraine experienced a temporary blackout attributed to Russian hacking. Between 2011 and 2017, a worldwide series of intrusions into industrial and energy firms, dubbed "Dragonfly 2," have been documented by the American software company Symantec. Each time the attackers have gone deeper into the system, suggesting they may have some ability to interrupt service. However, once again, Russia, not some extremist group, appears to have been behind the hacking. The ability to disrupt, or even shut down a power grid, would adversely affect economic activity and government services. Security experts note that, although such intervention is worrying, it does not herald the threat of an imminent attack. The U.S. system is sophisticated and resilient. Hospitals and other critical institutions have the ability to generate their own power. Finally, the attacks on power grids that have occurred appear to be the work of a foreign government with capabilities far beyond those of any extremist group.[21]

Action-film aficionados have witnessed the chaos portrayed in *Live Free or Die Hard* in which criminals hacked a city's traffic lights. Could such a thing be done in real life by terrorists armed with a laptop, as some experts have claimed? In August 2006, two Los Angeles traffic engineers hacked into the city's traffic lights at key intersections, programing them to stay red longer and cause significant traffic jams in support of a strike.[22] This episode inconvenienced commuters and imposed costs on the city but did not result in a single accident. Researchers have also succeeded in hacking into a specific traffic signal, changing it from red to green. These breeches, however, do not mean a terrorist could tamper with an entire system to produce widespread disruption, let alone lethal results. Signals have safeguards to prevent all lights from turning green simultaneously. For the time being at least, widespread traffic attacks will be confined to the silver screen.[23]

The vulnerability of computer-controlled devices to hacking must, however, be taken seriously. In 2015, researchers disabled the brakes and steering of a Jeep Cherokee by taking control of its "Uconnect" and entertainment dashboard. This experiment led to the recall of 1.4 million vehicles vulnerable to hacking due to a design flaw.[24] The experiment also revealed the need to build security into all systems that allow remote access. Designers must constantly be looking for vulnerabilities and ways to remedy them.

These examples illustrate a few of the ways extremists could, theoretically at least, launch cyberattacks. In reality, how likely are they to actually do so? The nearest terrorists came to using cybertools to lethal effect occurred in March 2015. ISIS posted names, addresses, and photographs of 100 service personnel in 23 states, calling on its followers to kill them.[25] The group claimed to have hacked data sources to obtain the information, but unsuspecting soldiers might have made it available on their Facebook pages and other social media sites. So far, extremists have employed cybertools as instruments of soft power. They use the Internet to recruit, fund-raise, communicate with one another, and disseminate their ideology. Experts doubt that at present, extremist groups have the expertise necessary to conduct a sophisticated attack similar to those mounted by Russia. Al-Qaeda, for example, has called upon its supporters with the requisite skills to launch cyberattacks but has been unable to do so itself.[26] Neither has ISIS nor any domestic extremist group been able to carry out a cyberterrorist attack. A 2016 report by the Australian Cyber Security Centre aptly describes current extremist cyber capabilities:

Apart from demonstrating a savvy understanding of social media and exploiting the internet for propaganda purposes, terrorist cyber capabilities generally remain rudimentary and show few signs of improving significantly in the near future. They will continue to focus on DDoS [distributed denial-of-service] activities, hijacking social media accounts, defacing websites, the hack and release of personal infor-mation and compromising poorly secured internet-connected services.[27]

In other words, extremist hackers will behave similarly to criminal and nuisance hackers.

FROM NIGHTMARE TO REALITY

The nightmare scenarios examined here are just that—bad dreams, worst-case scenarios of what extremists might be able to do in the future. Although governments must consider every possible threat, they should also keep those threats in a healthy perspective and educate the public to do the same. Extremists have shown an ability to be flexible and adaptive, so few tactics can be ruled out. On the other hand, little can be accom-plished by fretting over worst-case scenarios while ignoring clearer, more immediate threats. The international community must continue to secure nuclear materials. Nations should prepare for every sort of pandemic, even a human-created one, and cybersecurity efforts must continue. At the same time, governments must be vigilant for the immediate threat of the low-tech attack. The bomb, the gun, and the vehicle will continue to be the terrorists' weapons of choice because they are so easy to obtain and use and have proven so effective.

Conclusions and Responses

The diversity of groups, organizations, and ideologies considered in this study reveal that violent extremism is a complex phenomenon. VEOs defy easy categorization. Groups have proven adaptable and resilient. No simple profile fits all terrorist recruits. Extremist ideologies have proven very difficult to counter. Experts are struggling to understand the process by which people become radicalized. Identifying those prone to radicalization has been difficult. Programs to counter radicalization and rehabilitate VEO members have enjoyed only limited success. Protecting free, open, democratic societies from attack while preserving the freedoms their residents hold dear continues to challenge those responsible for national security. These challenges notwithstanding, this study does yield some important conclusions, which can aid in countering violent extremism.

TERRORISM IS A CHRONIC PROBLEM, NOT AN EXISTENTIAL THREAT

Terrorism has been a preoccupation for Americans since 9/11. The shock of the attack on the Twin Towers and the Pentagon makes this reaction understandable. Almost 20 years after that terrible event, however, the nation should take a sober look at the reality of the situation. Terrorism, like organized crime, is a chronic problem but not an existential threat. From the founding of the Caliphate in June 2014 to the end of July 2016, ISIS killed 2,043 people in 29 countries.[1] By comparison, 17,284 people were murdered in the United States alone in just one year (2017).[2] During that same year an estimated 72,000 Americans died from drug overdoses, and 40,100 died in traffic accidents.[3] Islamist extremists have killed 89 people in the United States since 2009. During the same period, school shooters have murdered 288 of our children.[4] The lifetime odds of being killed by a foreign-born terrorist are 1 in 45,785, while those for being killed in an ordinary assault with a firearm are 1 in 315.[5]

Looked at from the societal rather than the individual level, terrorism pales in comparison to other threats facing the United States and the world. Extreme weather caused by climate change has cost the United States at least $240 billion a year over the past decade.[6] Many scientists consider climate change the "biggest global health threat of the 21st century."[7] In addition to the catastrophic effect of global warming, a host of other threats rank far ahead of terrorism. A global pandemic like the flu of 1919 would kill millions of people. Resource depletion and environmental degradation threaten the very existence of human life. Overpopulation is already producing widespread hunger and even starvation. International conflict still poses a greater threat than attacks by VEOs. A nuclear attack by a rogue state such as North Korea on its neighbors would be catastrophic.

Why then does terrorism loom so large in the popular imagination? The 9/11 attacks have, of course, left their indelible mark on the collective psyche, but in recent years, fear of Islamist terrorism has been deliberately manipulated for political gain. On June 14, 2016, then-candidate Donald Trump addressed a rally in North Carolina and spoke of the Orlando nightclub shooting. "The children of Muslim American parents, they're responsible for a growing number, for whatever reason, a growing number of terrorist attacks."[8] Since 2015, there have been only four ISIS attacks in the U.S. resulting in fatalities. An average of one attack per year over a four-year period hardly amounts to a "growing number." Exaggerating the international threat and linking it to fear of immigration does, however, make for rhetoric that appeals to a certain segment of the electorate.

DOMESTIC EXTREMISM IS MORE DANGEROUS THAN INTERNATIONAL EXTREMISM

Whatever the threat posed by terrorism in general, that from domestic extremist groups and individuals is more serious than that from international ones. The number of hate groups and the much larger number of followers they attract far exceed the number of Americans espousing radical Islamist ideology. The vast majority of group members and fellow travelers will never commit a violent act, but their ideology will continue to inspire a significant number people who will. Since 2001, 119 people have been killed by terrorists, whereas at least 121 have been murdered by far-right extremists.[9] However, considerable evidence suggests that the number of victims of far-right extremists may be much higher. Neither the FBI nor state and local law enforcement agencies label such violence terrorism, and so they do not track it as such. A relatively small number of violent acts are prosecuted as "hate crimes," while the rest are treated as ordinary state or federal crimes. This approach suggests violence committed by far-right extremists may be seriously underreported.[10] Nonetheless, the number of hate crimes has been increasing. The FBI report for 2017 indicated that 7,175 hate incidents had been reported, a 17 percent increase from the previous year.[11]

In recent years, there has been a tendency in some circles to downplay hate crimes, dismissing them as the work of lone wolves or deranged individuals rather than seeing them as the result of a larger ideological movement. According to the Southern Poverty Law Center, 954 hate groups were active in the United States in 2017, an increase of 4 percent over the previous year. All but 233 of these groups espoused far-right ideologies. The largest growth occurred among neo-Nazi groups, which increased 22 percent.[12] Because extremist groups do not make public their membership rolls, determining precisely how many members they have is difficult. Indirect evidence suggests tens of thousands belong to one organization or another, while many more people support or at least sympathize with far-right ideology. A *Washington Post-ABC News* poll conducted after the 2017 "Unite the Right" rally in Charlottesville, Virginia, found that 9 percent of those surveyed felt that it was acceptable to hold "neo-Nazi or White supremacist views."[13] Extrapolated for the entire U.S. population at the time of the survey, that equates to 22 million people.[14] By comparison, in January 2018, the FBI was investigating 1,000 ISIS-related threats as well as an unspecified number of lone wolf-threats from those sympathetic to the group.[15]

Among far-right extremist groups, the 273 armed, antigovernment militias may be the most worrisome.[16] These groups vow to defend their narrow interpretation of the Constitution and to resist what they consider encroachments on local autonomy by the federal government. Many engage in paramilitary training and encourage members to stockpile arms, ammunition, and survival gear. These groups have yet to engage in overt violence against the government, but the 2017 occupation of the Malheur Wildlife Refuge in Oregon and the deployment of armed Oath Keepers to provide "security" after Hurricane Florence is worrisome. These incidents may be harbingers of worse things to come.

The rise in the number of far-right extremist groups has been spurred by two political developments. The 2008 election of the nation's first African American president, Barack Obama, sent shock waves through the white supremacist community. Eight years later, the election of Donald Trump, whose "Make America Great Again" message resonated with those now identifying as "white nationalists," emboldened far-right extremist groups. Both fear and empowerment serve as effective recruitment tools. Whether the recent spike in hate groups is temporary or part of a long-term trend remains to be seen.

Far-right extremist groups seldom engage directly in violence and may even condemn it. Some organizations have antidiscrimination statements on their websites and Facebook pages. They hide behind innocuous language, using terms such as "white pride," "European heritage," and "Christian morality." They disguise xenophobia as "national security" and cloak homophobia and misogyny with the veil of "traditional values." While they go by different names, the various extremist groups share a common ideology, which demonizes foreigners and people of color. Equal-opportunity haters, they differ only as to the marginalized group upon which they focus their animosity. The ideology these groups espouse inspires a great deal of violence. In aggregate, that violence rises to the level of domestic terrorism and should be treated as such. Based upon the number of adherents this broad ideological movement claims, the violence it has inspired and the weapons many of its followers possess, far-right extremism poses a greater threat to the United States than does international terrorism.

VIOLENT EXTREMISM IS A MULTIDIMENSIONAL, HYBRID PHENOMENON

Contemporary terrorism, both international and domestic, is a hybrid phenomenon. Violent extremist groups have always been manifestations of ideologies, but in the past, terrorism tended to be a one-dimensional phenomenon. Often the group itself represented the only real problem. In the 1970s and 1980s, Europe experienced a wave of leftist terrorism. Destroying the Red Army Faction (Baader-Meinhof Gang) did not eliminate Marxism, but it did remove the violent far-left threat from Germany. Destroying the Red Brigades had the same effect in Italy. Many Northern Irish Catholics still desire union with the Irish Republic, but the Good Friday Accords put a stop to PIRA and Protestant paramilitary violence. Both the radical Islamist and domestic extremist threats today exist on three levels: organized groups, networks of cells and affiliates, and a broad ideological movement that inspires violence perpetrated by people who have no formal affiliation with any organization.

ISIS began as an indigenous terrorist group in occupied Iraq, evolved into an insurgency, and became a protostate. It created a network with cells and affiliate groups around the world. It is also the latest manifestation of a radical Islamist movement going back at least 60 years. The idea of restoring the Muslim world to its alleged historic roots by violent means extends at least as far back as the Egyptian Muslim brotherhood in the 1950s. The Internet allows groups and individuals to disseminate the ideology widely and rapidly. Adherents need not have direct contact with a person in the physical world to become radicalized. Joining an extremist organization seems to require some human interaction, but adopting an ideology and becoming a lone wolf may be done entirely online.

Far-right extremism in the United States is also a hybrid phenomenon. A plethora of groups espouse a broad, exclusivist ideology that is easier to describe than name. "White nationalism" or "white supremacy" comes closest to capturing the constellation of beliefs espoused by these groups. Adherents to this ideology wish to make America a white, Christian (meaning evangelical) nation. Their worldview includes anti-Semitism, Islamophobia, racism, misogyny, and xenophobia. Not every group formally espouses each of these ideas, but their followers frequently do. Racists tend to be equal-opportunity haters. The commonality among far-right extremist groups became abundantly clear at the August 2017 "Unite the Right" rally, which attracted numerous hate groups and unaffiliated followers. Vanguard America, KKK, Identity Evropa, Proud Boys, Traditional Workers' Party, and the League of the South participated in the event at which prominent white nationalists, including David Duke, Richard Spencer, and Jason Kessler, spoke.[17] Cooperation among these groups and individuals reveals that hate groups network with one another. A great deal of crossover activity by members and fellow travelers occurs online, although mapping this activity requires access to membership rolls the groups do not make public.

IDEOLOGY MATTERS MOST

The U.S. government and its allies have done a good job combating terrorist groups and degrading networks. Working with its allies, the United States has severely weakened al-Qaeda and effectively targeted its leadership. It has enjoyed similar success against the Islamic State. U.S. law enforcement successfully prosecuted individuals within the antigovernment movement and destroyed the posse comitatus groups of the 1970s and 1980s. While counterterrorism strategy must continue to target groups and networks, this approach will not be sufficient. Ideology, not organizations or networks, is the center of gravity for extremist movements. As long as it exists, it will give rise to new extremist groups or revive old ones.

Countering a complex ideology is, of course, far more difficult than combatting groups and networks. Groups have leaders and require funds to operate, which makes them vulnerable. Target the leaders and cut off the flow of money, and the organization fails. Ideas, on the other hand, must be countered with ideas. In the case of religiously motivated extremists, members of their own faith communities are best able to counter the radical message. Only good theology can counter bad theology. Muslim scholars can fight Islamist extremism far more effectively than anyone else. Christian theologians and clerics have the knowledge to counter the perversion of their religion by the Christian Identity movement. One such effort is the "Living Islam" website run by Shaykh Abdallah bin Bayyah, president of the Forum for Promoting Peace in Muslim Societies. The site rebuts ISIS theology based upon the *Quran*, the *Hadiths* (sayings of the Prophet Mohammed), and the teachings of great Islamic scholars.[18] Mainstream Christian denominations have spoken out against the misuse of their religion in the service of hatred and bigotry. In 2013, the ADL published a letter from two rabbis criticizing Pamela Geller for her long track record of hateful and virulently anti-Muslim views."[19] Following the Tree of Life Synagogue massacre in October 2018, the leaders of many Christian denominations issued statements condemning intolerance and standing in solidarity with the American Jewish community. Interfaith dialogue and solidarity are powerful antidotes to religious extremism.

A more generic response to the ideological threat would be to restrict and, if possible, curtail its dissemination of extremist material online. Prior to the advent of the Internet, hate groups had a much harder time spreading their message. Today, anyone can access extremist ideology through the Internet. Twitter and Facebook have made some effort to ban the most extreme content, but with limited success. Much Islamist material comes from abroad. Domestic extremist groups hide behind the first amendment guarantee of free speech. They also avoid using the most offensive racist slurs that might violate the user agreements of online platforms. In any case, censorship may not be the best approach to countering extremism. Allowing groups to operate in the open, where they can be more easily monitored and perhaps infiltrated, may be preferable to driving them deeper underground. Perhaps, though, the time has come for a more serious conversation on the difference between free speech and hate speech.

LONE WOLVES WILL CONTINUE TO PROWL

The number, frequency, and lethality of lone wolf attacks has been increasing. The Internet allows individuals to participate in a terrorist campaign without formally joining any group. The availability of semi-automatic pistols and rifles as well as high-capacity magazines makes it possible for a single individual to carry out mass shootings. Omar Mateen managed to kill 49 people before being stopped. Rizwan Farook and Tashfeen Malik murdered 14 people at Farook's workplace. Had they chosen a target-rich environment, such as a crowded shopping mall on a busy day, the body count would have been much higher. In September 2013, gunmen struck the Westgate Shopping Mall in Nairobi, Kenya, with rifles and grenades, killing 67. The San Bernardino shooters could easily have achieved the same result.

Virtually all recent terrorist attacks on behalf of far-right ideology in the United States have been carried out by lone wolves. Some perpetrators have been charged with federal hate crimes, but many others have faced only state murder charges. Consequences, including the death penalty for hate crimes, however, do not deter such attacks, which have been on the increase. Ironically, hate groups use the "lone-wolf" label to disavow the violence their ideology inspires, even when a perpetrator specifically names them, as Dylan Roof named the Council of Conservative Citizens. A group will claim, rather disingenuously, that because the perpetrator did not formally belong to the organization, it is not responsible for that person's actions inspired them. As long as the nexus of hate and violence exists, lone-wolf terrorist attacks will continue.

NO SIMPLE TERRORIST PROFILE

The broad range of groups, cells, and lone wolves examined in this study make abundantly clear the difficulty of categorizing extremists and the danger of simplistic profiling. Nonetheless, recruits do have some things in common. Outlining broad characteristics can be useful in identifying at-risk populations, but conclusions must be qualified and variations by country and organization taken into account. White supremacists differ in some respects from jihadists. Lone wolves have some characteristics that distinguish them from those who belong to a group. Leaders of extremist groups differ from their members. Any profile must, therefore, be tentative. The dangers of racial or ethnic profiling must always be kept in mind. Treating someone as a suspected extremist can help to make him or her become one.

Members of VEOs share some common characteristics. With some notable exceptions, they tend to be disproportionately young (under the age of 30) and male. The latest research on cognitive development suggests that consequential thinking does not fully develop until at least the mid-20s (possibly later) and takes longer to mature in young men than in young women.[20] Failure to appreciate consequences makes young men good soldiers; it also makes them good terrorists. The relationship between economic status and radicalization is more complex. Outside the West, poverty still plays a role in recruitment. In some cases, the promise of pay lured people to join ISIS. In Western Europe, poverty is less an issue than inequality. Recruits from the ghettos of France and Belgium do not lack for the necessities of life, but they are less well off than their non-Muslim counterparts, and that reality fuels the grievance narrative. ISIS recruits from the United States, on the other hand, do as well economically as average Americans. Far-right extremist groups seem to attract recruits from across the economic spectrum, though a disproportionate number of militia members come from the working classes. ISIS recruits from the United

States and Europe tend to be better educated than those from elsewhere. American far-right extremists have fewer college graduates among their ranks. In all extremist groups, no matter their ideology, leaders are usually better off and better educated than their followers.

Despite the political hype over the security threat posed by immigrants, little evidence supports the argument that they are more likely than others to become terrorists. Refugees and asylum seekers want to be accepted by their host countries and tend to avoid illegal activity. They are also busy struggling to make a new life for themselves. Their children, on the other hand, are more prone to radicalization. Unable to identify with the culture from which their parents came and finding it difficult to be accepted in their new society, these young people are vulnerable to recruitment by a group that gives them a sense of belonging. Ethnocentric societies that do not welcome newcomers, such as many countries in Europe, exacerbate this problem.

Whether they support ISIS or white nationalism, lone wolves have a strikingly similar set of characteristics. Of the cases examined, all but Tashfeen Malik were male. Although none had a conclusive diagnosis of mental illness, most had either experienced some childhood psychological trauma or showed signs of being socially maladjusted, such as spousal abuse or a problem with drugs and alcohol. A dysfunctional background was a remarkably consistent characteristic of perpetrators in Europe and the United States, both in adherents of Islamist and far-right extremist ideology. None of the lone wolves was poor, and many were well educated. Some were solidly middle class and held good jobs. There was no evidence that any of them had personally suffered a wrong at the hands of people from the groups they targeted. Dylan Roof, for example, went to integrated schools and had African American friends, but that did not stop him from murdering nine African Americans at church in Charleston in order to start a race war. Their grievance narratives were not based upon personal experience.

RADICALIZATION OCCURS THROUGH MANY MEANS

Closely related to the question of who becomes a terrorist is the issue of how recruits adopt extremist ideology. Experts are still struggling to understand the radicalization process. As with profiling, a one-size-fits-all approach does not work in determining how individuals become radicalized. Recruits follow many paths to violent extremism. In much of the world, recruitment occurs through interpersonal contact. That contact may occur in a variety of venues. Prison has been one source of recruits. The Moroccan drug dealer Jamal Amidine entered prison as a criminal and emerged as a jihadist. He funded and helped organize the 2004 Madrid train bombings. Anis Amri, who attacked the Christmas Market in Berlin,

Germany, on December 23, 2016, may have been radicalized in an Italian prison. White supremacists have long had a strong presence in U.S. prisons. Mosques, youth centers, and bookstores in Europe have also been fertile recruiting grounds.

Family ties and friendship continue to figure prominently in terrorist recruitment. The cell that carried out both the Paris and Brussels bombings had two set of brothers and two childhood friends. The Barcelona cell had four sets of brothers, and all of its members attended the same mosque, where a radical imam recruited them. ISIS personnel records indicate that foreign fighters were asked to indicate who facilitated their travel to Syria, suggesting the importance of direct interpersonal contact. The unavailability of membership rolls makes analyzing recruiting patterns for far-right extremist groups in the United States very difficult. The regional concentration of many groups, however, suggests that personal networks do play a role. Given the past success of the FBI in infiltrating them, far-right groups may try to vet those they admit.

Online radicalization has been the subject of much hype and speculation but far less good research. Everyone agrees that the Internet plays a crucial role in spreading extremist ideology for both Islamist jihadis and the far right, but experts struggle to determine precisely how it contributes to recruitment. Social media (Twitter, Instagram, Facebook, etc.) certainly feeds both the grievance and empowerment narratives. Investigators frequently find extremist content on the computers of perpetrators. That, however, only demonstrates that social media played a role in their radicalization, not that it caused it. If recruiters use the Internet to conduct interviews via Skype or Facetime, that does not constitute online radicalization. One has to ask, what motivated the recruit to look for radical content on the Internet in the first place? In the case of lone wolves, however, considerable evidence suggests that the Internet may be the primary and perhaps even the sole source of radicalization. As the term suggests, lone wolves tend to have trouble socializing, so they do not make good group members. Islamist VEOs, particularly ISIS, have been effective at providing an opportunity for these loners to focus their anger on a target that the movement identifies. Far-right extremist groups prefer to denounce violence and disavow those who perpetrate it, even though their ideology inspires lone wolves to kill.

COUNTER-RADICALIZATION AND DERADICALIZATION MATTER

Identifying vulnerable populations and at-risk individuals along with understanding the radicalization process can help authorities prevent recruiting and rehabilitate those who have already joined. Both Saudi Arabia and Singapore have deradicalization programs that have enjoyed mixed success. The most hardened terrorists probably cannot be rehabilitated, whereas some less committed ones have been. One of the leaders of the al-Qaeda franchise in Yemen graduated from the Saudi rehabilitation program and reverted to terrorism. He had probably pretended to reform to win his freedom. The United States has captured few recruits trying to join ISIS. The U.S. Justice System also has a strong preference for retributive rather than restorative justice. As a result, the United States has little experience with rehabilitation.

One case, however, stands out. In 2015, nine Somali American men from Minneapolis-St. Paul were arrested as they began their journeys to Syria to join ISIS. They were charged with providing material support for terrorism. One of the defendants, Abdullah Yusuf, became the first American to go through a rehabilitation program for ISIS recruits. While he awaited trial, Yusuf worked with Heartland Democracy, a not-for-profit group that helps at-risk youth in the Twin Cities. The group did not try to talk the 20-year-old man out of his beliefs. Instead, they focused on strengthening his critical thinking skills by having him read works such as Mr. Luther King Jr.'s "Letters from a Birmingham Jail," the *Autobiography of Malcolm X*, and the writings of the French philosopher Michel Foucault. Yusuf pled guilty and testified against the former friends, who had helped radicalize him. The judge sentenced him to time served and 20 years' probation.[21] It must be noted that only one other defendant received a reduced sentence of two and a half years for cooperating with authorities. The others received sentences ranging from 10 to 35 years. All the defendants had been evaluated by the German deradicalization expert Daniel Koehler to determine their suitability for rehabilitation.[22]

The Heartland project was thus a labor-intensive effort with limited success. It does, however, suggest an approach to reintegrating former extremists back into society. Given the difficulty of talking anyone out of his or her beliefs, some experts advocate focusing on disengagement rather than deradicalization.[23] A participant does not have to disavow his or her ideology, just agree not to engage in violent behavior or support those who do. The British authorities developed a furlough program for members of PIRA incarcerated in the Maze Prison. The program enjoyed considerable success, although it took place when the conflict in Northern Ireland was winding down.

Far less attention has been devoted to deradicalization of far-right extremists. One not-for-profit group, however, devotes itself to that difficult task. Cofounded in 2011 by former white supremacist Angela King and former neo-Nazi Christian Picciolini, Life after Hate seeks to help people disengage from hate groups. Since its founding, the organization has helped more than 150 people make this difficult transition. Life after Hate also conducts research and runs education programs.[24] Participation in the program is voluntary, and the number of people it has impacted is low relative to the number of people who espouse far-right ideologies. Like the Minnesota program, Life after Hate offers a promising start and an indication of what might be accomplished with more resources. With sufficient political will and more funding, mandatory participation in such programs might be offered to people convicted of hate crimes as an alternative to lengthy prison sentences.

Necessary though rehabilitation programs are, they are no substitute for prevention. Governments have thus shown more interest in counter-radicalization than in deradicalization. Deradicalization programs aim to identify at-risk individuals within vulnerable populations and reach out to them before they get radicalized. To be effective, these programs require cooperation from teachers, clergy, community leaders, and even parents who can spot signs of disturbing behavior in their young people. As with drug and alcohol abuse and suicide, people can be trained to spot warning signs. As long as the country clings to a justice system that seeks to punish rather than help offenders, however, parents will be extremely reluctant to report their children, no matter how worrying their behavior becomes. Great care must also be taken not to overreact to changes in behavior. Just because a young Muslim man becomes more devout does not mean he is poised to become a terrorist. Prevention programs require trust between the authorities and the community in which vulnerable individuals live. In places like Molenbeek in Brussels, the Muslim *neighborhoods* of Paris, and poor areas of London, for example, trust is very low. In the United States, where Muslims are well integrated, trust is higher and cooperation better. Nonetheless, no one reported warning signs exhibited by the lone wolves who struck U.S. targets over the past decade.

Governments and not-for-profit organizations have increasingly invested in counter-radicalization programs. Two examples from the United Kingdom illustrate common approaches to counter-radicalization. Founded by two former members of Islamist extremist organizations, Maajid Usman Nawaz and Mohammed "Ed" Hussain, the Quilliam Foundation is a research and educational organization dedicated to providing policy makers, teachers, social workers, psychologists, police, and civil servants with the tools to recognize and counter violent extremism.[25] Established in 2003 and revised in 2011, the Prevent Strategy is a government initiative to counter radicalization. Its operational partner, the Channel Program, identifies individuals showing signs of disturbing behavior based upon strict criteria reviewed by a panel of experts and intervenes to counter radicalization. From April 2007 to December 2010, 1,120 people were referred to Channel. The majority of the referrals were 13–25 years old, and 90 percent were male. The vast majority (88%) were referred because of concerns about international terrorism, but 8 percent were referred because of concerns over "right-wing violent extremism." The rest were referred because of concerns about other kinds of extremism.[26] The program provides at-risk youth with support services such as anger management sessions, life skills work to help them deal with peer pressure and other stresses, mentoring, and social services as needed.[27]

Other countries have organizations and programs similar to those in the United Kingdom. The degree to which any of them actually works has been the subject of debate. One participant in the Prevent program was arrested for trying to bomb the London underground in September 2017.[28] However, no one knows how many of those who went through program might have engaged in violence had the intervention not occurred. Both the Quilliam Foundation and the Channel Program have been accused of being government tools for spying on Muslim communities. The Prevent strategy has also been accused of racial profiling.[29] These concerns highlight a problem faced by all counter-radicalization programs. Vulnerable populations distrust activities and organizations funded by the government.

Although the U.S. government recognizes the importance of countering terrorist ideology, it has not made much of an effort in this area. It supports other governments and nongovernmental organizations in their efforts to fight extremism, but it does not have comprehensive programs at home.[30] The federal government focuses almost entirely on Islamist extremism. Countering domestic extremism has been left almost entirely to not-for-profit organizations. In addition to monitoring hate groups, the Southern Poverty Law Center fights radicalization by developing and sharing educational materials.[31] The Anti-Defamation League also monitors hate groups, advocates for social justice, and produces education materials and resources to counter extremist ideology. However, a great deal more needs to be done in these areas.

MOVING FORWARD

A study of violent extremism would be incomplete without some concrete recommendations of how to counter the threat. Violent extremism will continue to be both a domestic and an international problem for the foreseeable future. The U.S. government will have to devote resources to countering it. Countering extremism requires a whole-of-government, whole-of-nation approach. Historically, the United States has relied heavily on the military to combat international terrorism and law enforcement to handle domestic extremism. This approach has allowed it to attack extremist organizations without countering the ideology or addressing the grievances that motivate them. While direct action against groups must continue, more effort must be devoted to addressing root causes of extremism. Somewhat different approaches to countering international and domestic extremism is necessary.

Countering Violent Islamist Extremism

Islamist extremism will continue to be the source of international terrorism for the foreseeable future. The Islamic State has been defeated, but the ISIS network survives. Other radical Islamist group will appear, and al-Qaeda may be reviving. Since 9/11, the United States has enjoyed considerable success combating such organizations. It has developed numerous strategic documents detailing ways to weaken terrorist organizations and degrade their networks. Through a combination of excellent intelligence gathering and direct action, the United States has eliminated a number of prominent terrorist leaders, including Osama bin Laden and several members of the ISIS hierarchy. U.S. Special Operations forces and American airpower have enabled the Iraqis to liberate territory from the Islamic State. Even though ISIS as a quasi-state has been vanquished, the struggle against the ISIS network and its extremist ideology must continue.

The United States needs to devote more effort and resources to countering the ideological threat. That effort requires funding research on radicalization, counter-radicalization, and deradicalization. It also requires replacing retributive with restorative justice for young people convicted of supporting terrorism who have not actually engaged in violence. A teenage boy or girl apprehended on the way to join a terrorist group needs rehabilitation and probation, not prison time. The Heartland Democracy approach used with the young Somali man from the Twin Cities should be applied more broadly. As the United States does not have a large number of marginalized Muslims at risk of radicalization, the cost of such programs should be fairly low.

Countering Domestic Extremism

Because far-right extremist groups pose a greater threat, more energy and resources need to be allocated to combating them. Until recently, the United States has been able to monitor and infiltrate far-right extremist groups. In the 1960s and 1970s, it crippled the KKK and dismantled the posse comitatus movement. Hate groups have reinvented themselves to appear more respectable and avoided open incitement of violence, making the job of law enforcement harder. As long as groups do not openly incite violence, they have broken no law. Because lone wolves perpetrate most of the attacks done in the name of their extremist ideology, far-right groups can easily disavow them and deny responsibility for their violent acts.

The first step in combating domestic extremism must be recognizing that it exists. Attacks upon people of color, Muslims, LGBQT individuals, and members of other marginalized groups on behalf of far-right ideologies are more than just hate crimes. Collectively, they amount to domestic terrorism and should be treated as such. Once that official recognition occurs, countering far-right extremism can be made a higher priority. The FBI should compile and publish a list of hate groups and monitor them more closely. A greater effort must be made to deny these groups online platforms. The time is long past for a serious discussion of the difference between free speech and hate speech. Paramilitary training by militias with anti-government ideologies might be outlawed. Enforcing such a ban would be difficult. A roundup of their members is just what these groups anticipate and welcome and should be avoided. Putting militias on the wrong side of the law would, however, give authorities the ability to move against them more easily. As with banning hate speech, such a move risks driving groups deeper underground and making them more dangerous.

Like organized crime, violent extremism cannot be eradicated. Like organized crime, however, it can be contained and reduced to the point where it has far less ability to hurt us. At present, people are being held captive by the fear of a grossly exaggerated foreign threat and being kept ignorant of a far more serious domestic one. Both the fear and the ignorance threaten our way of life more than any terrorist group every could. The best defense against any form of extremism is a pluralistic society that celebrates diversity. The United States is fast becoming such a society. The time has come to embrace rather than fear that demographic change.

Notes

INTRODUCTION

1. Jacob Poushter, *Majorities in Europe and North America Worried about Islamic Extremism* (Washington, DC: Pew Research Organization, Spring 2017), available at http://www.pewresearch.org/fact-tank/2017/05/24/majorities-in-europe-north -america-worried-about-islamic-extremism/, accessed February 13, 2018.

2. Ibid.

3. "How Serious a Threat Do You Think White Nationalism Poses to the United States?," August 2017, *Statista: the Statistical Portal*, available at https:// www.statista.com/statistics/738161/public-opinion-on-the-threat-of-white -nationalism-in-the-us/, accessed February 13, 2018.

4. *Countering Violent Extremism: Actions Needed to Define Strategy and Assess Progress of Federal Efforts* (Washington, DC: Government Accounting Office, 2017), p. 3.

5. Ibid., p. 3.

CHAPTER 1

1. Osama bin Laden, "World Islamic Front Statement," February 23, 1998, available in translation from the original Arabic at https://fas.org/irp/world/para /docs/980223-fatwa.htm, accessed November 6, 2017.

2. "What Is Violent Extremism," FBI website, available at https://www.fbi.gov /cve508/teen-website/what-is-violent-extremism, accessed December 13, 2018.

3. Bruce Hoffman, *Inside Terrorism* (New York: Columbia University Press, 3rd ed., 2017), pp. 73–76.

4. *Global Terrorism Index 2017: Measuring the Threat* (College Park, MD: Institute for Economics and Peace, 2017), p. 5.

5. *DOD Dictionary of Military and Associated Terms* (Washington, DC: DOD, 2017), p. 21.

6. Fr. John Sawicki, CSSp, PhD, "Why Terrorists Use Female and Child Suicide Bombers," *Health Progress*, July–August 2016, available at https://www.chausa.org/publications/health-progress/article/july-august-2016/why-terrorists-use-female-and-child-suicide-bombers, accessed November 13, 2017.

7. Ibid.

8. Hoffman, *Inside Terrorism*, p. 141.

9. *Inspire* (Fall 2010): 53–54, available at https://info.publicintelligence.net/InspireFall2010.pdf, accessed November 13, 2017.

10. Scott Keyes, "A Strange but True Tale of Voter Fraud and Bioterrorism," *Atlantic*, June 10, 2014, available at https://www.theatlantic.com/politics/archive/2014/06/a-strange-but-true-tale-of-voter-fraud-and-bioterrorism/372445/, accessed November 15, 2017.

11. Frank Leonard, "Are Suitcase Nukes a Genuine Concern," *New Atlas*, June 9, 2011, available at https://newatlas.com/suitcase-nukes-fact-or-fiction/18506/, accessed November 15, 2017.

12. "Nuclear Regulatory Commission (NRC) Fact Sheet on Dirty Bombs," available at http://www.mass.gov/eohhs/gov/departments/dph/programs/environmental-health/exposure-topics/radiation/radiological-emergency/fact-sheet-on-dirty-bombs.html, accessed December 2, 2017.

13. The idea of a grievance narrative has wide circulation among terrorism experts. For a particularly good discussion of the concept, see Ryan Hunter, M.A., and Daniel Heinke, "Radicalization of Islamist Terrorists in the Western World," September 1, 2011, available at https://leb.fbi.gov/articles/perspective/perspective-radicalization-of-islamist-terrorists-in-the-western-world, accessed December 20, 2018.

14. The phrase "propaganda of the deed" is usually attributed to Mikhail Bakunin, "Letters to a Frenchmen on the Present Crisis," 1870, available at https://www.marxists.org/reference/archive/bakunin/works/1870/letter-frenchman.htm, accessed December 13, 2018.

15. Monica Duffy Toft, "Networks Fighting Networks: Understanding Extremism and Radicalisation on a Smaller Scale," *Juncture*, 23, no. 1 (Summer 2016): 38.

16. Michael D. Silber and Arvin Bhatt, *Radicalization in the West: The Homegrown Threat* (New York: NYPD, 2007), p. 6

17. Faiza Patel, *Rethinking Radicalization* (New York: Brenan Center for Justice at the New York University of Law, 2011), p. 2.

18. Jytte Klausen, et al., "Toward a Behavioral Model of Homegrown Radicalization Trajectories," *Studies in Conflict and Terrorism*, 39 (2015): 39–67.

19. Adi Greif, "Double Alienation and Muslim Youth in Europe," USIP Brief, August 21, 2007, available at https://www.usip.org/publications/2007/08/double-alienation-and-muslim-youth-europe, accessed December 20, 2018.

20. Discussion of terrorist networks based on Mark Sageman, *Understanding Terrorist Networks* (Philadelphia, PA: University of Pennsylvania Press, 2004).

21. David Rapoport, "Four Waves of Modern Terrorism," in Audrey Cronin and James M. Ludes, eds., *Attacking Terrorism: Elements of Grand Strategy* (Washington, DC: Georgetown University Press, 2004), pp. 46–73.

22. "45 Years of Terrorism: Terrorist Attacks, 1970–2015, Concentration and Intensity," University of Maryland, Global Terrorism Database, available at https://www.start.umd.edu/gtd/images/START_GlobalTerrorismDatabase_TerroristAttacksConcentrationIntensityMap_45Years.png, accessed December 15, 2017.

23. *Global Terrorism Index 2017: Measuring and Understanding the Impact of Terrorism* (College Park, MD: Institute for Economics & Peace, 2017), p. 36.

24. Ibid., p. 35.

25. Ibid., p. 36.

26. Ibid., p. 36.

27. Miriam Valverde, "A Look at the Data on Domestic Terrorism and Who's behind It," *PolitiFact* (online), August 16, 2017, available at http://www.politifact.com/truth-o-meter/article/2017/aug/16/look-data-domestic-terrorism-and-whos-behind-it/, accessed December 15, 2017.

28. *Global Terrorism Index 2017*, p. 38.

29. "Deadly Statistics," available at http://www.lifeinsurancequotes.org/additional-resources/deadly-statistics/, accessed December 16, 2017.

30. Frank Holmes, "Global Cost of Terrorism Is at an All-Time High," *Business Insider* (online), March 28, 2016, available at http://www.businessinsider.com/global-cost-of-terrorism-at-all-time-high-2016-3, accessed December 16, 2017.

31. *Global Terrorism Index 2016* (College Park, MD: Institute for Economics and Peace, 2016), p. 62.

32. Alex Nowrashteh, "Terrorism Deaths by Ideology: Is Charlottesville an Anomaly?," CATO Institute, August 14, 2017, available at https://www.cato.org/blog/terrorism-deaths-ideology-charlottesville-anomaly, accessed December 14, 2018.

33. Jonathan Mahler and Julie Turkewitz, "Suspect in Dallas Attack Had Interest in Black Power Groups," *New York Times*, July 8, 2016, available at https://www.nytimes.com/2016/07/09/us/suspect-in-dallas-attack-had-interest-in-black-power-groups.html, accessed December 14, 2018.

CHAPTER 2

1. Osama bin Laden and Ayman al-Zawahiri, "Jihad against Jews and Crusaders," February 23, 1998, available at https://is.muni.cz/el/1423/jaro2010/MVZ203/OBL___AQ__Fatwa_1998.pdf, accessed March 28, 2018.

2. "Is Islamism a Threat? A Debate," *Middle East Quarterly* (online), 6, no. 4 (December 1999), available at https://www.meforum.org/articles/other/is-islamism-a-threat, accessed March 28, 2018.

3. Youssef H. Aboul-Enein, *Militant Islamist Ideology: Understanding the Threat* (Annapolis, MD: Naval Institute Press, 2010), p. 112.

4. "Religious Composition of Persian Gulf States," available at http://gulf2000.columbia.edu/images/maps/GulfReligionGeneral_lg.png, accessed March 30, 2018.

5. Hasan al-Banna, "Between Yesterday and Today," in *Complete Works of Hassan al-Bann, 1906–1949*, available at https://thequranblog.files.wordpress.com/2008/06/_7_-between-yesterday-today.pdf, accessed March 31, 2018.

6. Hasan al-Banna, "Al-Jihad," in ibid., available at https://thequranblog.files.wordpress.com/2008/06/_10_-al-jihad.pdf, accessed March 31, 2018.

7. Sayyid Qutb, *Milestones* (1964), English translation available at http://www .kalamullah.com/Books/MILESTONES.pdf, accessed March 31, 2018.

8. Rohan Gunaratna, *Inside Al-Qaeda: Global Network of Terror* (New York: Columbia University Press, 2002), p. 8.

9. Masami Nashino, "Muhammad Qutb's Islamist Thought: A Missing Link between Sayyid Qutb and al-Qaeda?," *NIDS Journal of Defense and Security*, 16 (December 2015): 137.

10. Yusef Abdoul-Enein, "The Late Sheikh Abdullah Azzam's Book—Part III," January 1, 2008, West Point Combatting Terrorism Center, available at https:// ctc.usma.edu/the-late-sheikh-abdullah-azzams-book-part-iii-radical-theories-on -defending-muslim-land-through/, accessed April 21, 2018.

11. Abdullah Azzam, *Join the Caravan* (ca. 1987), available at https://archive.org /stream/JoinTheCaravan/JoinTheCaravan_djvu.txt, accessed April 21, 2018.

12. Discussion of events that shaped bin Laden's worldview from Thomas R. Mockaitis, *Osama bin Laden* (Santa Barbara, CA: ABC-CLIO/Greenwood, 2010), pp. 18–20.

13. Jamal Kashoggi, cited in Peter Bergen, *The Osama bin Laden I Knew* (New York: Free Press, 2006), p. 41.

14. Steve Coll, *The Bin Ladens: An Arabian Family in the American Century* (New York: Penguin, 2008), pp. 301–303.

15. Bergen, *The Osama bin Laden I Knew*, pp. 27–28.

16. Quoted in Sharifa Zuhur, *A Hundred Osamas: Islamist Threats and the Future of Counterinsurgency* (Carlisle Barracks, PA: Strategic Studies Institute, 2005), p. 30.

17. Lawrence Wright, *The Looming Tower: Al-Qaeda and the Road to 9/11* (New York: Knopf, 2006), p. 104.

18. Ibid., p. 116.

19. Statement by Osama bin Laden, May 1998, in Raymond Ibrahim, ed. and trans., *The Al-Qaeda Reader* (New York: Broadway Books, 2007), p. 260.

20. Osama bin Laden, "Interview with Peter Arnett," *CNN*, March 1997, available at http://www.informationclearinghouse.info/article7204.htm, accessed April 28, 2018.

21. Abdullah Azzam, "Al-Qaeda al Sulbah," *Jihad*, 41 (April 1988), quoted in Bergen, *Osama bin Laden I Knew*, p. 74.

22. Hasan Abd-Rabbuh al Surayhi, quoted in ibid., p. 83.

23. Abu Mahmud quoted in Michael Scheuer, *Through Our Enemies Eyes: Osama bin Laden, Radical Islam, and the Future of America* (Washington, DC: Potomac Books, 2007), p. 110.

24. Bruce Riedel, *The Search for al-Qaeda: Its Leadership, Ideology, and Future* (Washington, DC: Brookings Institute Press, 2008), p. 47.

25. Coll, *The bin Ladens*, p. 46.

26. Reidel, *Search for al-Qaeda*, p. 47.

27. Murad Batal al-Shishani, "Understanding Strategic Change in al-Qaeda's Central Leadership after Bin Laden," *Terrorism Monitor*, 9, no. 23 (June 9, 2011), available at https://jamestown.org/program/understanding-strategic-change-in -al-qaedas-central-leadership-after-bin-laden/, accessed May 8, 2018.

28. *America at a Crossroads: The Men and Ideas behind Al-Qaeda*, PBS documentary, 2007, available at https://www.youtube.com/watch?v=9fRTBi1_YCo, accessed December 15, 2018.

29. Osama bin Laden, "Declaration of War against the Americans Occupying the Land of the Two Holy Places," first published in *Al Quds Al Arabi*, August 1996, available in translation at https://is.muni.cz/el/1423/jaro2010/MVZ448/OBL ___AQ__Fatwa_1996.pdf, accessed May 8, 2018.

30. Description of al-Qaeda organization from Jessica Stern, *Terror in the Name of God: Why Religious Militants Kill* (New York: Harper Collins, 2003), p. 250.

31. *9/11 Commission Report* (Washington, DC: Government Printing Office, 2004), p. 67.

32. Katherine Zimmerman, *The Al-Qaeda Network: A New Framework for Defining the Enemy* (Washington, DC: American Enterprise Institute, 2013), p. 14.

33. Ibid., p. 14.

34. Ibid., p. 39.

35. Victoria Barber, "The Evolution of al-Qaeda's Global Network," *Perspectives on Terrorism*, 9, no. 6 (December 2105): 1–35.

36. Ibid., p. 4.

37. Details on life of al-Zarqawi from Counterterrorism Project, "Abu Musab al-Zarqawi," n.d., available at https://www.counterextremism.com/extremists/abu -musab-al-zarqawi, accessed June 19, 2018.

38. Ibid.

39. Brian Fishman, "Revising the History of al-Qa'ida's Original Meeting with Abu Musab al-Zarqawi," *Sentinel*, 9, no. 10 (October 2016), available at https://ctc .usma.edu/revising-the-history-of-al-qaidas-original-meeting-with-abu-musab-al -zarqawi/, accessed June 19, 2018.

40. Mary Anne Weaver, "The Short, Violent Life of Abu Musab al-Zarqawi," *Atlantic* (July/August 2006), available at https://www.theatlantic.com/magazine /archive/2006/07/the-short-violent-life-of-abu-musab-al-zarqawi/304983/, accessed June 20, 2018.

41. Ibid.

42. "Al-Qaeda in the Arabian Peninsula (AQAP)," *Council on Foreign Relations* (June 2015), available at https://www.cfr.org/backgrounder/al-qaeda-arabian -peninsula-aqap, accessed June 21, 2018.

43. Ibid.

44. "Al-Qaeda in Yemen," Stanford University, Mapping Militant Organizations Project (July 2015), available at http://web.stanford.edu/group/mappingmilitants /cgi-bin/groups/view/23, accessed June 21, 2018.

45. Quotes and details from "Underwear Bomber Abdulmutallab Sentenced to Life," *BBC online* (February 16, 2012), available at https://www.bbc.com/news /world-us-canada-17065130, accessed June 22, 2018.

46. "Cargo Plane Bomb Found in Britain Was Primed to Blow Up over U.S.," *The Guardian* (November 10, 2010), available at https://www.theguardian.com/world /2010/nov/10/cargo-plane-bomb-us-alqaida, accessed June 22, 2018.

47. "The Ultimate Mowing Machine," *Inspire*, no. 2 (October 2010): 53, available at https://azelin.files.wordpress.com/2010/10/inspire-magazine-2.pdf, accessed June 22, 2018.

48. Catherine E. Shoichet and Josh Levs, "Al-Qaeda Branch Reveals Charlie Hebdo Attack Was Years in the Making" (January 21, 2015), available at https:// www.cnn.com/2015/01/14/europe/charlie-hebdo-france-attacks/index.html, accessed June 22, 2018.

49. Oscar Gakuo Mwangi, "Stat Collapse, al-Shabab, Islamism, and Legitimacy in Somalia," *Politics, Religion and Ideology*, 13, no. 4 (December 2012): 520.

50. Ibid., p. 518.

51. Ibid., p. 519.

52. Details on al-Shabab terrorist attacks from "Shabaab," Mapping Terrorist Organizations data base, Stanford University, available at http://web.stanford .edu/group/mappingmilitants/cgi-bin/groups/view/61?highlight=somalia #attacks, accessed December 15, 2018.

53. For details on planning the operation, see *Report of the 9/11 Commission*, 148–173.

54. Ibid., p. 169.

55. "How Much Did the 9/11 Attacks Cost?," Institute for the Analysis of Global Security, available at http://www.iags.org/costof911.html, accessed July 4, 2018.

56. House of Commons (UK), *Report of the Official Account of the London— Bombings on 7th July 2005* (HC 1087) (London: Her Majesty's Stationary Office, 2006), p. 20, available at https://assets.publishing.service.gov.uk/govern ment/uploads/system/uploads/attachment_data/file/228837/1087.pdf, accessed July 5, 2018.

57. Ibid., p. 20.

58. Jennifer Cole, "Operation Crevice Trial Ends," *Royal United Services Institute* (May 2, 2007), available at https://rusi.org/commentary/operation-crevice-trial -ends, accessed July 5, 2018.

59. Ibid.

60. Fernando Reinares, "Jihadist Radicalization and the 2004 Madrid Bomb-ing Network," *Sentinel*, 2, no. 11 (November 2009), available at https://ctc.usma .edu/jihadist-radicalization-and-the-2004-madrid-bombing-network/, accessed July 19, 2018.

61. Javier Jordan, et al., "Strengths and Weaknesses of Grassroot Jihadist Net-works: The Madrid Bombings," *Studies in Conflict & Terrorism*, 31 (2008): 18.

62. Phil Williams, "In Cold Blood: The Madrid Bombings," *Perspectives on Terror-ism*, 2, no. 9 (2008): 19–24.

63. Ibid.

64. Ibid.

65. Joseph Felter and Brian Fishman, "Al-Qaeda's Foreign Fighters in Iraq: A First Look at the Sinjar Records," *Harmony Project* (West Point: Counterterrorism Cen-ter, 2007), available at https://www.files.ethz.ch/isn/45910/CTCForeignFighter .19.Dec07.pdf, accessed July 21, 2018.

66. *9/11 Commission Report*, available at https://9-11commission.gov/report /911Report_Exec.htm, accessed July 21, 2018.

67. Michael Buchanan, "London Bombs Cost Just Hundreds," *BBC*, January 3, 2006, available at http://news.bbc.co.uk/2/hi/uk_news/4576346.stm, accessed July 21, 2018.

68. Discussion of funding from *9/11 Commission Report*, pp. 169–172.

69. Thomas R. Mockaitis, "The Abbottabad Files: An Enduring Resource," *Georgetown Journal of International Affairs* (online), February 7, 2018, available at https://www.georgetownjournalofinternationalaffairs.org/online-edition/2018 /2/6/the-abbottabad-files-enduring-impact, accessed August 8, 2018.

CHAPTER 3

1. Aida Arosoaie, "Doctrinal Differences between ISIS and Al Qaeda: An Account of Ideologues," *Counter Terrorist Trends and Analyses*, 7, no. 7 (August 2015): 31–37.

2. Fawaz A. Gerges, *A History of ISIS* (Princeton, NJ: Princeton University Press, 2016), p. 100.

3. Ibid., p. 101.

4. "The Islamic State of Iraq and the Iraq War," in Patrick B. Johnston, et al., *Foundations of the Islamic State: Management, Money, and Terror in Iraq, 2005–2010* (Santa Monica, CA: Rand, 2016), p. 17.

5. Ibid., p. 20.

6. Ibid., p. 23.

7. Ibid., p. 47.

8. Gerges, *A History of ISIS*, pp. 119–120.

9. Patrick Garrity, "Paris Attacks: What Does 'Daesh' Mean and Why Does ISIS Hate It?," *NBC News*, available at https://www.nbcnews.com/storyline /isis-terror/paris-attacks-what-does-daesh-mean-why-does-isis-hate-n463551, accessed December 17, 2018.

10. Ibid.

11. Ibid., p. 133.

12. Details of al-Baghdadi's life from ibid., pp. 129–131.

13. Laith Alkhouri and Alex Kassirer, "Governing the Caliphate: The Islamic State Picture," *Sentinel*, 8, no. 8 (August 2015), p. 17.

14. Details on governance from ibid., pp. 17–20.

15. *The Islamic State*, VICE News Documentary, August 14, 2014, available at https://www.youtube.com/watch?v=AUjHb4C7b94&has_verified=1&bpctr =1542401918, accessed November 2018.

16. Alkhouri and Kassirer, "Governing the Caliphate," p. 20.

17. Details of administration in Mosul from Rukmini Callimachi, "The ISIS Files," *New York Times*, April 4, 2018, available at https://www.nytimes.com /interactive/2018/04/04/world/middleeast/isis-documents-mosul-iraq.html, accessed November 17, 2018.

18. Ibid.

19. Details on morality crimes from Thanassis Cambanis and Rebecca Collard, "How ISIS Runs a City," *Time*, February 26, 2015, available at http://time.com /3720063/isis-government-raqqa-mosul/, accessed November 17, 2018.

20. Callimachi, "The ISIS Files."

21. Thomas P. Thornton, "Terror as a Weapon of Political Agitation," in Harry Eckstein, ed., *Internal War: Problems and Approaches* (Westport, CT: Greenwood, 1964), p. 72.

22. Brian Dodwell, Daniel Milton, and Don Rassler, *The Caliphate's Global Workforce: An Inside Look at the Islamic State's Foreign Fighter Paper Trail* (West Point, NY: Center for Combatting Terrorism Center, 2016), pp. 7–8.

23. "Beijing Policies in Xinjiang Driving Chinese Muslims to Join Ranks of Islamic State, Says US Think Tank," *South China Morning Post*, July 20, 2018, available at https://www.scmp.com/news/china/policies-politics/article/1992418/beijing -policies-xinjiang-driving-chinese-muslims-join, accessed February 20, 2019.

24. Dodwell, et al., *The Caliphate's Global Workforce*, p. 11.

25. Age date from ibid., pp. 12–13.

26. Ibid., p. 13.

27. Ibid., p. 15.

28. Educational data from ibid., p. 16.

29. Ibid., p. 16.

30. Ibid., p. 18.

31. Employment data from ibid., p. 21.

32. Ibid. p. 22.

33. Data from Sinjar and ISIS records from ibid., p. 29.

34. Ibid., p. 29.

35. Ibid., p. 27.

36. Brian Jenkins, "Foreword" to Alexander Meleagrou-Hitchens, Seamus Hughes, Bennett Clifford, *Travelers: American Jihadis in Syria and Iraq* (George Washington University: Program on Extremism, 2018), p. x.

37. Robert Pape, et al., *The American Face of ISIS: Analysis of ISIS-related Terrorism in the US March 2014–August 2016* (Chicago, IL: University of Chicago Center for Counterterrorism Policy, 2017).

38. Ibid., p. 5.

39. Findings of the report from Ibid., pp. 5, 11.

40. Ibid., p. 17.

41. Ibid., p. 12.

42. Age and gender figures from Meleagrou-Hitchens, et al., *Travelers*, p. 16.

43. Ibid, pp. 39–40.

44. Florence Gaub and Julia Lisiecka, "Women in Daesh: Jihadist 'Cheerleaders,' Active Operatives?," *European Union for Security Studies* (October 2016), available at https://www.iss.europa.eu/sites/default/files/EUISSFiles/Brief_27_Women_in_Daesh.pdf, accessed November 19, 2018.

45. Amanda N. Spencer, "The Hidden Face of Terrorism: An Analysis of the Women in Islamic State," *Journal of Strategic Security*, 9, no. 3, *Special Issue: Emerging Threats* (Fall 2016), p. 90.

46. Details on role of women in ISIS from ibid., p. 2.

47. Katrin Bennhold, "Jihad and Girl Power: How ISIS Lured 3 London Girls," *New York Times*, August 7, 2015, available at https://www.nytimes.com/2015/08/18/world/europe/jihad-and-girl-power-how-isis-lured-3-london-teenagers.html, accessed November 19, 2018.

48. Ibid., p. 79.

49. Miriam Fernandez, et al., "Understanding the Roots of Radicalisation on Twitter," in *WebSci 18*: 10th ACM Conference on Web Science, 27–30 May 2018, Amsterdam, Netherlands, ACM (Association for Computing Machinery), available at http://dx.doi.org/doi:10.1145/3201064.3201082, accessed November 21, 2018. The article contains an excellent review of the literature.

50. Ines von Behr, et al., *Radicalisation in the Digital Era: The Use of the Internet in 15 Cases of Terrorism and Extremism* (Cambridge, UK: Rand Europe, 2013), p. xii.

51. Conclusions from ibid., p. 24. This study took place before the rise of ISIS, which has a much more sophisticated social media strategy. Nonetheless, later studies have not conclusively challenged its results.

52. Azeem Ibrahim, "ISIS in Libya: A Threat or a Deadend?," *Strategic Studies Institute*, September 2018, available at https://ssi.armywarcollege.edu/index.cfm /articles/ISIS-In-Libya/2018/09/26#end10, accessed November 22, 2018.

53. Charlie Winter, *"Libya: The Strategic Gateway for the Islamic State," Translation and Analysis of IS Recruitment Propaganda for Libya* (London: Quillium Foundation, 2015), p. 6, available at https://www.ibs-ops.com/fileadmin/files/downloads /libya-the-strategic-gateway-for-the-is.pdf, accessed November 22, 2018.

54. Gregory Waters and Robert Postings, *Spiders of the Caliphate: Mapping the Islamic State's Global Support Network on Facebook* (New York: Counter Extremism Project, 2018), p. 9.

55. Richard Barrett, "The Islamic State Goes Global," *Sentinel*, 8, no. 11 (November/December 2015), p. 2.

56. Rukmini Callimachi, "How a Secretive Branch of ISIS Built a Global Network of Killers," *New York Times*, August 3, 2016, available at https://www.nytimes.com /2016/08/04/world/middleeast/isis-german-recruit-interview.html, accessed November 27, 2018.

57. Ibid.

58. Ibid.

59. Ibid.

60. Ibid.

61. Timeline and details of Paris attack from "2015 Paris Attacks: Fast Facts," *CNN*, available at https://www.cnn.com/2015/12/08/europe/2015-paris-terror -attacks-fast-facts/index.html, accessed November 24, 2018.

62. Jean Charles Brisard and Kevin Jackson, "The Islamic State's External Operations and the French-Belgian Nexus," *Sentinel*, 9, no. 11 (November/December 2016): 13.

63. Details on the cell members from Paul Cruickshank, "The Inside Story of the Paris and Brussels Attacks," *CNN*, October 30, 2017, available at https://www .cnn.com/2016/03/30/europe/inside-paris-brussels-terror-attacks/index.html, accessed November 27, 2018.

64. "Belgium: Extremism and Counter-Extremism," Countering Extremism Project, 2018, available at https://www.counterextremism.com/sites/default /files/country_pdf/BE-11272018.pdf, accessed November 28, 2018.

65. Pieter van Ostaeyen, "Belgian Radical Networks and the Road to the Brussels Attacks," *CTC Sentinel*, 9, no. 6 (June 2016): 9.

66. Ibid., p. 7.

67. Ibid., p. 7.

68. Details on Sinai Wilayat terrorism from "Egypt: Extremism and Counterextremism," Counterextremism Project, 2018, available at https://www .counterextremism.com/countries/egypt, accessed November 29, 2018.

69. Details on attacks against Christians in Egypt from ibid.

70. "Manchester Arena Attack: Bomb 'Injured More Than 800,'" available at https://www.bbc.com/news/uk-england-manchester-44129386, accessed December 17, 2018.

71. Information on attack and background of perpetrator from Intelligence and Security Committee of Parliament, *The 2017 Attacks: What Needs to Change?* (London: HMSO, 2018).

72. Ekin Karasin, "ISIS: 'We Killed Your Children.' Terror Group Claim Responsibility for Manchester Bombing 'In the Midst of a Gathering of the Crusaders,'" *Daily Mail* (online), May 23, 2017, available at https://www.dailymail.co.uk/news/article-4534612/ISIS-claim-responsibility-Manchester-bombing.html, accessed November 29, 2018.

73. *The 2017 Attacks*, p. 10.

74. Fernando Reinares and Carola García-Calvo, "'Spaniards, You Are Going to Suffer': The Inside Story of the August 2017 Attacks in Barcelona and Cambrils," *CTC Sentinel*, 11, no. 1 (January 2018): 4.

75. Details on backgrounds of cell members from ibid, pp. 5–6.

76. Ibid., p. 8.

77. Quoted in ibid., p. 8.

78. Ibid., p. 8.

79. Tim Lister, et al., "ISIS Goes Global: 143 Attacks in 29 Countries Have Killed 2,043," *CNN*, February 12, 2018, available at https://www.cnn.com/2015/12/17/world/mapping-isis-attacks-around-the-world/index.html, accessed November 29, 2018.

80. Map of ISIS attacks in ibid.

81. "After the Caliphate: Has ISIS Been Defeated," *BBC News*, February 7, 2019, available at https://www.bbc.com/news/world-middle-east-45547595, February 21, 2019.

82. Mia Bloom and Chelsea Daymon, "Assessing the Future Threat: ISIS's Virtual Caliphate," *Orbis*, 62, no. 3 (Summer 2018): 376.

CHAPTER 4

1. "What Are Known Violent Extremist Groups," *FBI*, available at https://www.fbi.gov/cve508/teen-website/what-are-known-violent-extremist-groups, accessed December 18, 2018.

2. "Frequently Asked Questions about Hate Groups," available at https://www.splcenter.org/20171004/frequently-asked-questions-about-hate-groups, accessed December 18, 2018.

3. "Hate Group," Anti-Defamation League, available at https://www.adl.org/resources/glossary-terms/hate-group, accessed December 18, 2018.

4. Charles Kurzman and David Schanzer, *Law Enforcement Assessment of the Violent Extremism Threat* (Durham, NC: Duke University Triangle Center on Terrorism and Homeland Security, 2015), p. 3.

5. Ant-Defamation League, *A Dark and Constant Rage: 25 Years of Right-Wing Terrorism in the United States* (Washington, DC: ADL, 2017), p. 3.

6. Antidefamation League, *ADL Report: White Supremacist Murders More Than Doubled in 2017* (New York: ADL, 2018), available at https://www.adl.org/news/press-releases/adl-report-white-supremacist-murders-more-than-doubled-in-2017, accessed May 13, 2018.

7. Ibid.

8. Ibid.

9. Kathleen Belew, *Bring the War Home: The White Power Movement and Paramilitary America* (Cambridge, MA: Harvard University Press, 2018) discusses this connection in depth.

10. Anti-Defamation League, *State of the Ku Klux Klan in the United States* (New York: ADL, 2016), p. 1, available at https://www.adl.org/sites/default/files /documents/assets/pdf/combating-hate/tattered-robes-state-of-kkk-2016.pdf, accessed August 14, 2018.

11. Rick Najera, "Make America Great Again Is a Cover for Make America White Again," *Huffington Post*, August 29, 2016, available at https://www.huffingtonpost .com/rick-najera/make-america-great-again-_1_b_8056888.html, accessed February 21, 2019.

12. "Jason Kessler on His 'Unite the Right Rally' Move to DC," *NPR*, *Morning Edition*, April 10, 2018, available at https://www.npr.org/2018/08/10/637390 626/a-year-after-charlottesville-unite-the-right-rally-will-be-held-in-d-c, accessed August 13, 2018.

13. Southern Poverty Law Center, "Stormfront," available at https://www.splcenter .org/fighting-hate/extremist-files/group/stormfront, accessed August 13, 2018.

14. Stormfront website, available at https://www.stormfront.org/forum/, accessed August 15, 2018.

15. Dr. Ford, "An Introduction to Stormfront and the Pro-White Movement. Part I: What We Want and Why," available at https://www.stormfront.org/forum /t968576/, accessed August 15, 2018. It is not clear whether or not "Dr. Ford" is a screen name.

16. Ibid.

17. Ibid.

18. Don Black, "Guidelines for Posting," available at https://www.stormfront .org/forum/t4359/, accessed August 15, 2018.

19. Stormfront blog, available at https://www.stormfront.org/forum/t1254526/, accessed August 15, 2018.

20. Heidi Beirich, *White Homicide Worldwide: Stormfront, the Leading White Suprem- acist Web Forum Has Another Distinction—Murder Capital of the Internet* (Montgom- ery, AL: Southern Poverty Law Center, 2014), available at file:///C:/Documents/ Tom/Terrorism%20Book/Right/white-homicide-worldwide.pdf, accessed August 15, 2018.

21. Ibid., pp. 4–5.

22. Ibid., p. 5

23. "The AFP Mission Statement," available at http://theamericanfreedomparty .us/mission-statement/, accessed August 16, 2018.

24. Robert Litoff, "Jews and Their Effect on Russian American Relations," April 19, 2015, available at http://theamericanfreedomparty.us/jews-and-their-effect-on -russian-american-relations/, accessed August 16, 2018. Details of AFP platform from "Platform," available at http://theamericanfreedomparty.us/platform/, accessed August 16, 2018.

25. ADL, "American Third Position: Academic Racists Take the Reign from the Young," available at https://www.adl.org/news/article/american-third-position -academic-racists-take-the-reins-from-young, accessed February 26, 2019.

26. "Death of CCC Founder a Symbolic End of Segregationist Era," *Intelligence Report*, SPLC (Summer 2015), available at https://www.splcenter.org/fighting -hate/intelligence-report/2015/death-ccc-founder-symbolic-end-segregationist -era, accessed August 22, 2018.

27. All quotes of CCC, "Statement of Principles," available at http://conservative -headlines.org/statement-of-principles/, accessed August 23, 2018.

28. News items and bumper sticker, available at http://conservative-headlines
.org/, accessed December 18, 2018.

29. David A. Graham, "The White-Supremacist Group That Inspired a Racist Manifesto. How Did the Council of Conservative Citizens Become America's
Biggest White-Nationalist Organization, and Why Do Politicians Keep Dealing
With It?," *The Atlantic*, June 22, 2015, available at https://www.theatlantic.com
/politics/archive/2015/06/council-of-conservative-citizens-dylann-roof/396467/,
accessed August 23, 2018. Huckabee addressed the group by video.

30. Ibid, accessed August 23, 2018.

31. "About Us," Identity Evropa, available at https://www.identityevropa.com
/about-us, accessed September 20, 2018.

32. Ibid.

33. "Identity Evropa," Southern Poverty Law Center, available at https://www
.splcenter.org/fighting-hate/extremist-files/group/identity-evropa, accessed
September 20, 2018.

34. "Action Report," Identity Evropa, available at https://www.identityevropa
.com/action-report, September 20, 2018.

35. Alfred W. Clark, "'Cuckservative,' a Definition," July 17, 2015, available at
https://www.radixjournal.com/2015/07/2015-7-16-cuckservative-a-definition/,
accessed August 25, 2018.

36. See the AfriForum website, https://www.afriforum.co.za/about/about
-afriforum/, accessed August 26, 2018.

37. President Trump's tweet quoted in "South Africa Hits Back at Trump over
Land Seizure Tweet," *CBS online*, August 23, 2018, available at https://www
.cbsnews.com/news/south-africa-hits-back-at-trump-over-land-seizure-tweet/,
accessed August 26, 2018.

38. NPR, All Things Considered, "Trump Brings Attention to Polarizing South
Africa Land Reform Issue," August 25, 2018, available at https://www.npr.org
/2018/08/25/641927183/trump-brings-attention-to-polarizing-south-africa-land
-reform-issue, accessed August 26, 2018.

39. The site reposted a tweet about the alleged swearing in on December 4, 2018,
available at https://www.facebook.com/AltRight/, accessed December 18, 2018.

40. "Was Ilhan Omar Sworn in with Her Hand on the Quran?," n.d., available
at https://www.snopes.com/fact-check/ilhan-omar-sworn-quran/, accessed
December 18, 2018.

41. December 4, 2018, post, available at https://www.facebook.com/AltRight/,
accessed December 18, 2018.

42. Emmanuel Spraguer, "Antiracism Is Immoral," available at http://
alternativeright.com/, accessed December 19, 2018.

43. "National Socialist Movement," Southern Poverty Law Center, available at
https://www.splcenter.org/fighting-hate/extremist-files/group/national-socialist
-movement, September 11, 2018.

44. "25 Points of National Socialism," National Socialist Movement Website,
available at http://www.nsm88.org/25points/25pointsengl.html, accessed February 21, 2019.

45. Ibid., accessed September 11, 2018.

46. "Vanguard America Platform," available at http://vanguardamerica.online
/platform/, September 13, 2018.

47. ACT for America, available at https://www.actforamerica.org/, accessed September 24, 2018.

48. SPLC, "ACT for America," available at https://www.splcenter.org/fighting -hate/extremist-files/group/act-america, accessed February 26, 2019.

49. "Meet Our Founder," ACT for America, available at https://www .actforamerica.org/aboutbrigitte, accessed September 21, 2018.

50. "Mission," ACT for America, available at https://www.actforamerica.org /Mission, accessed September 21, 2018.

51. Quoted in Peter Beinart, "America's Most Prominent Anti-Muslim Activist Is Welcome at the White House," *The Atlantic* online, March 21, 2017, available at https://www.theatlantic.com/politics/archive/2017/03/americas-most-anti -muslim-activist-is-welcome-at-the-white-house/520323/, accessed September 21, 2018.

52. Quoted in Laurie Goodstein, "Drawing Crowds with Anti-Islam Message," *New York Times*, March 7, 2011, p. A1, available at https://archive.nytimes.com /www.nytimes.com/2011/03/08/us/08gabriel.html, accessed September 21, 2018.

53. ACT for America Facebook page, available at https://www.facebook.com /actforamerica/, accessed September 24, 2018.

54. ACT for Brandon Mississippi, available at https://www.facebook.com /ActForAmericaBrandonMs/, accessed September 24, 2018.

55. Soldiers of Odin USA official Facebook page, available at https://www .facebook.com/pg/soldiersofodinusaofficial/about/?ref=page_internal, accessed September 24, 2018.

56. Ibid., accessed September 24, 2018.

57. "About," Counter Jihad Organization Facebook page, available at https:// www.facebook.com/pg/CounterJihadCoalition/about/?ref=page_internal, accessed October 9, 2018.

58. Countering Jihad website, available at https://counterjihadcoalition.org/, accessed October 9, 2018.

59. "Islam in a Nutshell: Violent or Peaceful?," available at https:// counterjihadcoalition.org/wp-content/uploads/2015/04/Islam-In-A-Nutshell _r2.pdf, accessed October 9, 2018.

60. "ISIS Is Islam," available at https://counterjihadcoalition.org/wp-content /uploads/2015/04/Islam-in-a-Nutshell-ISIS-is-Islam.pdf, accessed October 9, 2018.

61. "About" AFDI, available at http://afdi.us/about/, accessed October 10, 2018.

62. Ibid., accessed October 10, 2018.

63. Ibid., accessed October 10, 2018.

64. "Anti-Muslim Activist Pamela Geller Promotes Anti-Refugee Rhetoric," available at https://www.adl.org/blog/anti-muslim-activist-pamela-geller-promo tes-anti-refugee-rhetoric, accessed October 10, 2018; Gellers website, https:// gellerreport.com/?s=black+lives, contains numerous articles attacking the Black Lives Matter movement, accessed February 27, 2019.

65. Ibid., accessed October 10, 2018.

66. Jihad Watch, "Why Jihad Watch," available at https://www.jihadwatch.org /why-jihad-watch, accessed February 27, 2019.

67. Southern Poverty Law Center, "Christian Identity," available at https://www.splcenter.org/fighting-hate/extremist-files/ideology/christian-identity, accessed February 21, 2019.

68. "Kingdom Identity Ministries," available at https://www.splcenter.org/fighting-hate/extremist-files/group/kingdom-identity-ministries, accessed September 17, 2018.

69. Kingdom Identity Ministries, "Doctrinal Statement of Beliefs," available at http://www.kingidentity.com/doctrine.htm, accessed September 17, 2018.

70. "Kingdom Identity Ministries," available at https://www.splcenter.org/fighting-hate/extremist-files/group/kingdom-identity-ministries, accessed September 17, 2018.

71. Levitas, *The Terrorist Next Door*, discusses the evolution of the evolution of the militia movement.

72. For a discussion of the origin of the militia movement, see Darren Malloy, "Conversing with the Dead: The Militia Movement and American History," *Journal of American Studies*, 38, no. 3 (December 2004): 439–456.

73. Spencer Sunshine, "Profiles on the Right: Three Percenters," January 5, 2015, available at https://web.archive.org/web/20171105005930/http://www.politicalresearch.org/2016/01/05/profiles-on-the-right-three-percenters/, accessed February 27, 2019.

74. *The Three Percenters—Original—National Bylaws: A Guide to Being a Three Percenter*, available at https://docs.wixstatic.com/ugd/6ecfe6_40d0b0f5b-b144a87ab351f8d93e2bee0.pdf, accessed October 6, 2018.

75. Ibid., pp. 31–32.

76. "The Three Percenters—Original" Facebook page, available at https://www.facebook.com/pg/ThreePercenters/posts/?ref=page_internal, accessed October 8, 2018.

77. "About Oath Keepers," available at https://oathkeepers.org/about/, accessed October 8, 2018.

78. "Help Us Launch the Oath Keepers Spartan Group Training Program," available at https://oathkeepers.org/2018/08/help-us-launch-the-oath-keepers-spartan-training-group-program/, October 8, 2018.

79. "Black Lives Matter Strikes Again," August 14, 2016, available at https://www.facebook.com/pg/OKNational/posts/?ref=page_internal, accessed October 8, 2018.

80. FBI Counterterrorism Analysis Section, "Sovereign Citizens: A Growing Threat to Law Enforcement," September 1, 2001, available at https://leb.fbi.gov/articles/featured-articles/sovereign-citizens-a-growing-domestic-threat-to-law-enforcement; Southern Poverty Law Center, "Sovereign Citizens," available at https://www.splcenter.org/fighting-hate/extremist-files/ideology/sovereign-citizens-movement, accessed October 9, 2018.

81. "Our Mission," available at http://www.fightwhitegenocide.com/mission/, accessed September 17, 2018.

82. "New Nation News," available at http://www.newnation.org/, accessed September 17, 2018.

83. Mission Statement, "The Occidental Observer," available at https://www.theoccidentalobserver.net/mission/, accessed September 17, 2018.

84. "'Racism Is a Crime, Not an Opinion': Jewish Goyophobia and the War on White," available at https://www.theoccidentalobserver.net/2018/09/11/racism-is-a-crime-not-an-opinion-jewish-goyophobia-and-the-war-on-white/, accessed September 17, 2018.

85. Details on Reddit and its users from Keegan Hanks, "The Most Violent Racist Internet Content Isn't on Stormfront or VNN Anymore," available at https://www.splcenter.org/hatewatch/2015/03/11/most-violently-racist-internet-content-isnt-stormfront-or-vnn-anymore, accessed September 17, 2018.

86. Gavin McInnes, "About Us," available at http://proudboysusa.com/aboutus/, accessed December 21, 2018.

87. George Hawley, "The Demography of the Alt-Right," *Institute for Family Studies*, August 9, 2018, available at https://ifstudies.org/blog/the-demography-of-the-alt-right, accessed October 10, 2018.

88. Ibid.

89. Ibid.

90. Ibid.

91. Thomas Chadwick, quoted in Ruth Serven Smith and Allison Wrabel, "'Serial Rioters' Charged in Rally Violence," *The Daily Progress*, October 2, 2018, available at https://www.dailyprogress.com/news/local/serial-rioters-charged-in-rally-violence/article_14d0ec88-c659-11e8-a61d-57feee131da1.html, accessed October 15, 2018.

92. Quoted in Paul Dugan, "Four Alleged Members of Hate Group Charged in 2017 'Unite the Right' Rally in Charlottesville," *Washington Post* (online), October 2, 2018, available at https://www.washingtonpost.com/local/public-safety/federal-officials-to-announce-additional-charges-in-2017-unite-the-right-rally-in-charlottesville/2018/10/02/60881262-c651-11e8-9b1c-a90f1daae309_story.html, accessed October 15, 2018.

93. Details of the plot and quotes from Ted Genoways, "The Only Good Muslim Is a Dead Muslim," *New Republic* (June 2017): 31–41.

94. Details of these hate crimes from "Ten Sentenced in Hate Crime Case," FBI News, June 16, 2015, available at https://www.fbi.gov/news/stories/ten-sentenced-in-hate-crime-case, accessed October 16, 2018.

95. Oath Keepers, "National Call to Action to Assist in Hurricane Florence Disaster Relief," September 11, 2018, available at https://oathkeepers.org/2018/09/national-call-to-action-to-assist-in-hurricane-florence-disaster-relief/, accessed February 27, 2019.

CHAPTER 5

1. Ben Zimmer, "The Phrase 'Lone Wolf' Goes Back Centuries," *Wall Street Journal* (online), December 19, 2014, available at https://www.wsj.com/articles/the-phrase-lone-wolf-goes-back-centuries-1419013651, accessed May 9, 2018.

2. *Dialect Notes*, V, Parts I–X (1919–1927) (New Haven, CT: Tuttle, Morehouse & Taylor, 1927), p. 454, available at https://books.google.com/books?id=lxwOAAAAIAAJ&pg=PA454#v=onepage&q=lone%20wolf&f=false, accessed May 9, 2018.

3. "Lone Wolf Attacks are Becoming More Common—And More Deadly," *Frontline,* July 14, 2016, available at https://www.pbs.org/wgbh/frontline/article/lone-wolf-attacks-are-becoming-more-common-and-more-deadly/, accessed October 20, 2018.

4. Ibid.

5. Jeffrey D. Simon, *Lone Wolf Terrorism: Understanding the Growing Threat* (New York: Prometheus Books, 2013), p. 47.

6. Details on Kurbegovic from Simon, *Lone Wolf Terrorism*, pp. 401–409.

7. Ibid.

8. Ibid.

9. Theodore Kaczynski, "Industrial Society and Its Future," 1995, available at http://editions-hache.com/essais/pdf/kaczynski2.pdf, accessed October 24, 2018.

10. *LVMPD Criminal Investigative Report of the October 1, 2017 Mass Casualty Shooting*, August 3, 2018, p. 126, available at https://www.lvmpd.com/en-us/Documents/1-October-FIT-Criminal-Investigative-Report-FINAL_080318.pdf, accessed October 29, 2018. Details on attack from ibid., pp. 125–126.

11. Matt Lysiak, "Why Adam Lanza Killed Those 20 Children," *Newsweek Global*, 162, no. 4 (January 24, 2014): 77–84.

12. Lisa Marie Segarra, "What to Know about Republic of Florida, the White Supremacist Militia That Nikolas Cruz Attended," *Time.com*, February 16, 2018, available at http://time.com/5161203/republic-of-florida-nikolas-cruz-white-supremacist-militia/, accessed November 23, 2018.

13. "Homegrown Violent Extremism," February 15, 2013, available at https://www.fbi.gov/audio-repository/news-podcasts-thisweek-homegrown-violent-extremism.mp3/view, accessed December 20, 2018.

14. Statement by Abū Muhammad al-'Adnānī ash-Shāmī, September 22, 2014, available at https://scholarship.tricolib.brynmawr.edu/bitstream/handle/10066/16495/ADN20140922.pdf, accessed November 23, 2018.

15. Details on Hasan's radicalization from 2000 to 2009 from "Nidal Hasan," Counter Extremism Project, available at https://www.counterextremism.com/extremists/nidal-hasan, accessed November 2, 2018.

16. Ibid.

17. Details on Tamerlan Tsarnaev from House of Representatives Committee on Homeland Security, *The Road to Boston: Counterterrorism Challenges and Lessons from the Marathon Bombings*, March 2014, pp. 9–15, available at https://homeland.house.gov/files/documents/Boston-Bombings-Report.pdf, accessed November 3, 2018.

18. Ibid., p. 10.

19. Ibid., p. 37.

20. "Search of Tsarnaevs' Phones, Computers Finds No Indication of Accomplice, Source Says," *NBC News* (online), April 23, 2013, available at http://usnews.nbcnews.com/_news/2013/04/23/17877288-search-of-tsarnaevs-phones-computers-finds-no-indication-of-accomplice-source-says?lite, accessed November 4, 2018.

21. Details on life of Muhammad Youssef Abdulazeez from "Muhammad Youssef Abdulazeez," Counter Extremism Project, available at https://www.counterextremism.com/extremists/muhammad-youssef-abdulazeez, accessed November 4, 2018.

22. Quote and details on radicalization from ibid.

23. Matt Hamilton, "San Bernardino Shooting Suspect Endured Turbulent Home Life, According to Court Documents," *Los Angeles Times* (online), December 3, 2015, available at http://www.latimes.com/local/lanow/la-me-san-bernardino -shooter-endured-turbulent-home-life-according-to-court-documents-20151203 -story.html, accessed November 4, 2018.

24. James Comey, quoted in Al Baker and Mark Santora, "San Bernardino Attackers Discussed Jihad in Private Messages, F.B.I. Says," *New York Times*, December 16, 2015, available at https://www.nytimes.com/2015/12/17/us /san-bernardino-attackers-discussed-jihad-in-private-messages-fbi-says.html, accessed November 4, 2018.

25. "Jihadi Bride Led the Way at Party Massacre," *Daily Mail*, December 6, 2015, available at https://www.dailymail.co.uk/news/article-3348102/I-think -married-terrorist-Tashfeen-Malik-shot-Syed-Farook-hesitated-attack-killed-14 -FBI-investigate-radicalized-husband.html, accessed November 4, 2018.

26. Mark Berman, "One Year after the San Bernardino Attack, Police Offer a Possible Motive as Questions Still Linger," *Washington Post*, December 2, 2016, available at https://www.washingtonpost.com/news/post-nation/wp/2016/12/02 /one-year-after-san-bernardino-police-offer-a-possible-motive-as-questions-still -linger/, accessed November 4, 2018.

27. "Jihadi Bride."

28. Quoted in Alan Blinder, et al., "Omar Mateen Posted to Facebook Amid Orlando Attack, Lawmaker Says," *New York Times*, June 16, 2016, available at https://www.nytimes.com/2016/06/17/us/orlando-shooting.html, accessed November 5, 2018.

29. Dan Barry, et al., "'Always Agitated. Always Mad': Omar Mateen, According to Those Who Knew Him," *New York Times*, June 18, 2016, available at https:// www.nytimes.com/2016/06/19/us/omar-mateen-gunman-orlando-shooting .html, accessed November 5, 2018.

30. Alan Binder, et al., "Omar Mateen: From Early Promise to F.B.I. Surveillance," *New York Times*, June 12, 2016, available at https://www.nytimes.com/2016/06 /13/us/omar-mateen-early-signs-of-promise-then-abuse-and-suspected-terrorist -ties.html, accessed November 5, 2018.

31. Barry, "Always Agitated."

32. Jane Coaston, "New Evidence Shows the Pulse Nightclub Shooting Wasn't about Anti-LGBTQ Hate," *Vox*, available at https://www.vox.com/policy-and -politics/2018/4/5/17202026/pulse-shooting-lgbtq-trump-terror-hate, accessed November 5, 2018.

33. "Sayfullo Habibullaevic Saipov," Counter Extremism Project, available at https://www.counterextremism.com/extremists/sayfullo-habibullaevic-saipov, accessed November 5, 2018.

34. Charge sheet for Sayfullo Habibullaevic Saipov, November 1, 2017, available at https://www.justice.gov/usao-sdny/press-release/file/1008081/download, accessed November 5, 2018.

35. Andrew Macdonald [William Pearce], *The Turner Diaries* (1978), available at https://www.e-reading.club/bookreader.php/133469/The_Turner_Diaries.pdf, accessed November 7, 2018.

36. Louis Beam, "Leaderless Resistance," 1983, available at http://www
.louisbeam.com/leaderless.htm, accessed November 7, 2018.

37. Chris Swecker, "Eric Rudolph," FBI history page, available at https://www
.fbi.gov/history/famous-cases/eric-rudolph, accessed November 8, 2018.

38. "Rudolph's Mother: Son Not a Monster," *CNN*, August 22, 2005, available
at https://web.archive.org/web/20140715230302/http://www.cnn.com/2005
/LAW/08/22/rudolph.mother/index.html?_s=PM%3ALAW, accessed November 8, 2018.

39. Eric Rudolph, "Racism," Army of God, available at http://armyofgod.com
/EricRudolphRacism.html, accessed November 8, 2018. The "Army of God" website contains a collection of Rudolph's writings.

40. "The Turner Diaries," Anti-Defamation League, https://www.adl.org
/education/resources/backgrounders/turner-diaries, November 8, 2018.

41. "McVeigh's Apr. 26 Letter to Fox News," April 26, 2001, available https://
www.foxnews.com/story/mcveighs-apr-26-letter-to-fox-news, accessed November 8, 2018.

42. "Key Points from the Norway Shooting Suspect's Purported Manifesto,"
CNN, July 24, 2011, available at http://www.cnn.com/2011/WORLD/europe
/07/24/norway.manifesto.highlights/index.html, accessed November 12, 2018.
An English translation of the manifesto is available at http://www.deism.com
/images/breivik-manifesto-2011.pdf, accessed November 12, 2018.

43. "Norway's Mass Killer Breivik Declared Sane," *BBC online*, April 10, 2012,
available at https://www.bbc.com/news/world-europe-17663958, accessed
November 12, 2018.

44. "Norway Killer: Anders Behring Breivik Was a 'Mummy's Boy,'" *Daily Telegraph*, July 25, 2011, available at https://www.telegraph.co.uk/news/worldnews
/europe/norway/8659746/Norway-killer-Anders-Behring-Breivik-was-a-mummys
-boy.html, accessed November 12, 2018.

45. Ibid.

46. "Key Points from the Norway Shooting Suspect's Purported Manifesto."

47. Roof's word according to a survivor of the massacre, quoted in Susan San-
chez and Ed Payne, "Charleston Church Shooting: Who Is Dylan Roof?," December 16, 2016, *CNN online*, available at https://www.cnn.com/2015/06/19/us
/charleston-church-shooting-suspect/index.html, accessed November 11, 2018.

48. Dylan Roof, "Manifesto," available at https://www.nytimes.com
/interactive/2016/12/13/universal/document-Dylann-Roof-manifesto.html,
accessed November 11, 2018.

49. Ibid.

50. Ibid.

51. Details on Dylan Roof's background from Frances Robles and Nikita Stewart, "Dylan Roof's Past Reveals Trouble at Home and at School," *New York Times*,
June 16, 2015, available at https://www.nytimes.com/2015/07/17/us/charleston
-shooting-dylann-roof-troubled-past.html, accessed November 12, 2018.

52. Jennifer Levitz and John Kamp, "Charleston Shooting Suspect Became
a Loner in Recent Years," *Wall Street Journal*, June 18, 2015, available at https://
www.wsj.com/articles/charleston-church-shooting-suspect-dylann-roof-became
-a-loner-in-recent-years-1434644808, accessed November 12, 2018.

53. Ibid.; Robles and Stewart, "Dylan Roof's Past Reveals Trouble at Home and
at School."

54. Melissa Gomez, "Charlottesville Car Attack Suspect Pleads Not Guilty to Federal Hate Crimes," *New York Times*, July 5, 2018, available at https://www.nytimes.com/2018/07/05/us/charlottesville-plea-hate-crimes.html, accessed November 12, 2018.

55. "Charlottesville: Who Is Suspect James Alex Fields, Jr.?," *BBC News online*, August 14, 2017, available at https://www.bbc.com/news/world-us-canada-40923489, accessed November 12, 2018.

56. James Pilcher, "Charlottesville Suspect's Beliefs Were 'Along the Party Lines of the Neo-Nazi Movement,' Ex-Teacher Says," *Cincinnati Enquirer*, August 13, 2017, available at https://www.cincinnati.com/story/news/local/northern-ky/2017/08/13/charlottesville-suspects-beliefs-were-along-party-lines-neo-nazi-movement-ex-teacher-says/563139001/, accessed November 12, 2018.

57. "Charlottesville: Who is Suspect James Alex Fields, Jr.?"

58. Vanguard America Tweet, August 12, 2017, quoted in its entirety in "Charlottesville Driver Who Killed One Rallied with Alt-Right Vanguard America Group," Southern Poverty Law Center, available at https://www.splcenter.org/hatewatch/2017/08/12/alleged-charlottesville-driver-who-killed-one-rallied-alt-right-vanguard-america-group, accessed November 12, 2018.

59. Brenton Tarrant, *The Great Replacement: Towards a New Society*, available at https://milnenews.com/2019/03/15/christchurch-mosque-shooter-brenton-tarrants-full-manifesto/, accessed March 28, 2019.

60. Details on life of Brenton Tarrant from David D. Kirkpatrick, "Massacre Suspect Traveled the World but Lived on the Internet," *New York Times*, May 15, 2019, available at https://www.nytimes.com/2019/03/15/world/asia/new-zealand-shooting-brenton-tarrant.html, accessed March 28, 2019.

CHAPTER 6

1. *DOD Dictionary of Military and Related Terms* (Washington, DC: Government Printing Office, 2018), p. 252.

2. "Saddam's Chemical Weapons Campaign: Halabja, March 16, 1988," U.S. Department of State, Bureau of Public Affairs, March 14, 2003, available at https://2001-2009.state.gov/r/pa/ei/rls/18714.htm, accessed December 9, 2018.

3. Information on the Syrian weapons program and attacks from Robert J. Bunker, "Strategic Insights: The Assad Regime and Chemical Weapons," Strategic Studies Institute, May 18, 2018, available at http://strategicstudiesinstitute.army.mil/index.cfm/articles/Assad-Regime-Chemical-Weapons/2018/05/18, accessed December 9, 2018.

4. For a detailed discussion of the Tokyo subway attack, see "The Sarin Gas Attack in Japan and the Related Forensic Investigation," Organization for the Prohibition of Chemical Weapons, June 1, 2001, available at https://www.opcw.org/media-centre/news/2001/06/sarin-gas-attack-japan-and-related-forensic-investigation, accessed December 10, 2018.

5. Alan Taylor, "Bhopal: The World's Worst Industrial Disaster, 30 Years Later," *The Atlantic*, December 2, 2014, available at https://www.theatlantic.com/photo/2014/12/bhopal-the-worlds-worst-industrial-disaster-30-years-later/100864/, accessed December 10, 2018.

6. Robert Kessler, "Outbreak: The Pandemic Strikes," EcoHealth Alliance, 2018, available at https://www.ecohealthalliance.org/2018/05/outbreak-pandemic-stri kes, accessed December 10, 2018.

7. Joby Warrick, "FBI Investigation of 2001 Anthrax Attacks Concluded; U.S. Releases Details," *Washington Post*, February 20, 2010, available at http://www .washingtonpost.com/wp-dyn/content/article/2010/02/19/AR2010021902369 .html, accessed December 10, 2018.

8. "Smallpox," Centers for Disease Control, available at https://www.cdc.gov /smallpox/vaccine-basics/index.html, accessed December 10, 2018.

9. Chris L. Barrett, Stephen G. Eubank, and James P. Smith, "If Smallpox Strikes Portland. . . .," *Scientific American* (March 2005): 54–61.

10. Details on the attack and perpetrators from Scot Keyes, "A Strange but True Tale of Voter Fraud and Bioterrorism," *The Atlantic*, June 10, 2014, available at https://www.theatlantic.com/politics/archive/2014/06/a-strange-but-true-tale -of-voter-fraud-and-bioterrorism/372445/, accessed December 10, 2018.

11. Amy E. Smithson, "Grounding the Threat in Reality," in Amy E. Smithson and Leslies-Anne Levy, *Ataxia: The Chemical and Biological Terrorism Threat and the US Response* (Washington, DC: Henry L. Stimson Center, 2000), pp. 34–35.

12. "'Suitcase Nukes': A Reassessment," Middlebury Institute of International Security, September 23, 2002, available at https://www.nonproliferation.org /suitcase-nukes-a-reassessment/, accessed December 11, 2018; Katherine Shrader and Associated Press, "Suitcase Nukes Closer to Fiction Than Reality," November 10, 2007, available at https://usatoday30.usatoday.com/tech/science/2007-11-10 -suitcasenukes_N.htm, accessed December 11, 2018.

13. Details on the challenges of building an improvised nuclear device and its unlikely occurrence from Carson Mark, et al., *Can Terrorists Build Nuclear Weapons?* (Washington, DC: Nuclear Control Institute, n.d.), available at https://www.nci.org /k-m/makeab.htm, accessed December 11, 2018.

14. Details on dirty bombs from COL Asaf Durakovic, MC USA(R), "Medical Effects of Tranuranic 'Dirty Bomb,'" *Military Medicine*, 82 (March/April 2017): e1591–e1595; Mihai Velicof and Simona Miclăuừ, "An Analysis of Radiological Dispersal Devices in Terms of Nuclear Hazard," Land Forces Academy of Romania, *Technical Sciences*, 58, no. 2 (June 2010): 267–276; James M. Acton, M. Brooke Rogers and Peter D. Zimmermann, "Beyond the Dirty Bomb: Rethinking Radiological Terror," *Survival*, 49, no. 3 (Autumn 2007): 151–168.

15. Acton, et al., "Beyond the Dirty Bomb," p. 156.

16. Nicole Perlroth, "Chinese and Iranian Hackers Renew Their Attacks on U.S. Companies," *New York Times*, February 18, 2019, available at https://www .nytimes.com/2019/02/18/technology/hackers-chinese-iran-usa.html, accessed February 24, 2019.

17. Josh Fruhlinger, "What Is Stuxnet, Who Created It and How Does It Work?," CSO, August 22, 2017, available at https://www.csoonline.com/article/3218104 /malware/what-is-stuxnet-who-created-it-and-how-does-it-work.html, accessed December 12, 2018.

18. Details on the Estonian cyberattack from Damien McGuinness, "How a Cyber Attack Transformed Estonia," *BBC*, April 27, 2017, available at https:// www.bbc.com/news/39655415, accessed December 12, 2018.

19. Sarah P. White, "Understanding Cyber Warfare: Lessons from Russia-Georgia War," *Modern War Institute*, March 20, 2018, available at https://mwi.usma.edu/understanding-cyberwarfare-lessons-russia-georgia-war/, accessed February 24, 2019.

20. Andy Greenberg, "Next-Gen Air Traffic Control Vulnerable to Hackers Spoofing Planes out of Thin Air," *Forbes*, July 25, 2012, available at https://www.forbes.com/sites/andygreenberg/2012/07/25/next-gen-air-traffic-control-vulnerable-to-hackers-spoofing-planes-out-of-thin-air/#34ef4af45927, accessed December 12, 2018.

21. Details on power grid intrusions from Robert M. Lee and Sergio Caltagirone, "Hackers Got into America's Power Grid. But Don't Freak Out," *Fortune*, September 11, 2017, available at http://fortune.com/2017/09/11/dragonfly-2-0-symantec-hackers-power-grid/, accessed December 12, 2018.

22. "Engineers Who Hacked into L.A. Traffic Signal Computer, Jamming Streets, Sentenced," *LA Times Blog*, December 1, 2009, available at https://latimesblogs.latimes.com/lanow/2009/12/engineers-who-hacked-in-la-traffic-signal-computers-jamming-traffic-sentenced.html, accessed December 12, 2018.

23. Details on traffic signal interference from Faiz Saddiqui, "Can Hackers Take over Traffic Lights?," *Washington Post*, August 8, 2015, available at https://www.washingtonpost.com/local/could-a-hacker-gain-control-of-dcs-traffic-system/2015/08/08/7cb7cf94-201a-11e5-bf41-c23f5d3face1_story.html, accessed December 12, 2018.

24. Ibid.

25. State of New Jersey Office of Homeland Security and Preparedness, "ISIS: Escalating Threats Against US Military Personnel," March 22, 2015, available at https://www.njhomelandsecurity.gov/analysis/isis-threats-to-military, accessed December 12, 2018.

26. Christopher Cox, "Cyber Capabilities and Intent of Terrorist Forces," *Information Security Journal: A Global Perspective*, 24 (2015): 35–36.

27. Australian Cyber Security Centre, *2016 Threat Report*, pp. 8–9, available at https://www.internationalaffairs.org.au/australianoutlook/is-cyberterrorism-a-threat/, accessed December 12, 2018.

CONCLUSIONS AND RESPONSES

1. Tim Lister, et al., "ISIS Goes Global: 143 Attacks in 29 Countries," *CNN*, February 12, 2018, available at https://www.cnn.com/2015/12/17/world/mapping-isis-attacks-around-the-world/index.html, accessed February 25, 2019. This figure does not include those killed in Syrian Civil war or the fighting in Iraq. The period covered includes the most extensive wave of ISIS attacks outside the Middle East.

2. "United States Crime Rates, 1960–2017," available at http://www.disastercenter.com/crime/uscrime.htm, accessed November 30, 2018.

3. "Overdose Death Rates," National Institute of Drug Abuse, available at https://www.drugabuse.gov/related-topics/trends-statistics/overdose-death-rates, accessed November 30, 2018; "2017 Estimates Show Vehicle Fatalities Topped

40,000 for Second Straight Year," National Safety Council, available at https://www
.nsc.org/road-safety/safety-topics/fatality-estimates, accessed November 30, 2018.

4. Chip Grabow and Lisa Row, "The U.S. Has Had 57 Times as Many School
Shootings as the Other Major Industrialized Nations Combined," *CNN*, May 21,
2018, available at https://www.cnn.com/2018/05/21/us/school-shooting-us
-versus-world-trnd/index.html, accessed November 30, 2018.

5. David Mosher and Sky Gould, "The Odds That a Gun Will Kill the Average American May Surprise You," *Business Insider*, October 29, 2018, available at
https://www.businessinsider.com/us-gun-death-murder-risk-statistics-2018-3/,
accessed December 1, 2018.

6. Stephen Leadhy, "Hidden Costs of Climate Change Running Hundreds of
Billions a Year," *National Geographic*, September 27, 2017.

7. Melissa Denchak, "Are the Effects of Global Warming Really That Bad?,"
available at https://www.nrdc.org/stories/are-effects-global-warming-really
-bad, accessed December 1, 2018.

8. Donald Trump quoted in Jenna Johnson and Abigail Hauslohner, "'I Think
Islam Hates Us': A Timeline of Trump's Comments about Islam and Muslims,"
Washington Post, May 20, 2017, https://www.washingtonpost.com/news
/post-politics/wp/2017/05/20/i-think-islam-hates-us-a-timeline-of-trumps
-comments-about-islam-and-muslims/, December 1, 2018.

9. Miriam Valverde, "A Look at the Data on Domestic Terrorism and Who's
Behind It," *Politifact*, August 16, 2017, available at https://www.politifact.com
/truth-o-meter/article/2017/aug/16/look-data-domestic-terrorism-and-whos
-behind-it/, accessed December 1, 2018. The article note puts the numbers at 106
killed by far-right extremists, and 119 by radical Islamists. However, several violent incidents, including the October 2018 attack on the Tree of Life Synagogue in
Pittsburgh, Pennsylvania, brings the total to 121.

10. Maya Berry and Kai Wiggins, "FBI Stats on Hate Crimes Are Scary. So Is
What's Missing," *CNN*, November 14, 2018, available at https://www.cnn.com
/2018/11/14/opinions/fbi-hate-crimes-data-whats-missing-berry-wiggins
/index.html, accessed December 1, 2018.

11. "2017 Hate Crime Statistics," FBI, available at https://ucr.fbi.gov/hate
-crime/2017/tables/table-1.xls, accessed December 1, 2018.

12. "The Year in Hate: Trump Buoyed White Supremacists in 2017, Sparking
Backlash among Black Nationalist Groups," Southern Poverty Law Center, February 21, 2018, available at https://www.splcenter.org/news/2018/02/21/year
-hate-trump-buoyed-white-supremacists-2017-sparking-backlash-among-black
-nationalist, accessed December 1, 2018. Black nationalists espouse racists' rhetoric
but are fewer in number and far less violent than their white counterparts. In 2016,
7 police officers were murdered in two incidents, but it is not clear whether the perpetrators were motivated by black nationalist ideology or simply rage over police
shootings of African Americans.

13. *Washington Post-ABC News* Poll August 16–20, 2017, available at http://apps
.washingtonpost.com/g/page/politics/washington-post-abc-news-poll-aug-16
-20-2017/2235/, accessed December 2, 2018.

14. May Oppenheim, "22 Million Americans Support Neo-Nazis, New Poll Indicates," *Independent*, August 22, 2017, available at https://www.independent.co.uk

/news/world/americas/us-neo-nazi-support-american-public-charlottesville-white-supremacists-kkk-far-right-poll-a7907091.html, accessed December 2, 2018.

15. Christal Hayes, "ISIS in Our Own Backyard: Group's U.S. Followers Are Diverse, in Places Large and Small," *USA Today*, January 4, 2018, available at https://www.usatoday.com/story/news/2018/01/04/fight-against-isis-teenager-playing-basketball-fbi-agent-and-couple-their-honeymoon-heres-how-isis-s/953954001/, accessed February 25, 2019.

16. "The Year in Hate."

17. Information on speakers and groups from "The People, Groups and Symbols of Charlottesville," Southern Poverty Law Center, available at https://www.splcenter.org/news/2017/08/15/people-groups-and-symbols-charlottesville, accessed December 3, 2018.

18. "Living Islam," available at http://www.livingislam.org/index.html, accessed December 3, 2018.

19. Rabbi Michael White and Rabbi Jerome Davidson, "Hate Speech Has No Place in a Synagogue," *ADL*, April 9, 2013, http://jewishweek.timesofisrael.com/hate-speech-has-no-place-in-a-synagogue/, accessed February 25, 2019.

20. "At What Age Is the Brain Fully Developed?," *Mental Health Daily*, n.d., available at https://mentalhealthdaily.com/2015/02/18/at-what-age-is-the-brain-fully-developed/, accessed December 20, 2018.

21. Dina Temple-Raston, "Jihadi Rehab May Be an Alternative to Prison for Young ISIS Recruits," NPR, November 28, 2017, available at https://www.npr.org/2017/11/28/566877270/jihadi-rehab-may-be-an-alternative-to-prison-for-young-isis-recruits, accessed December 6, 2018.

22. Steve Karnowski, "Minnesota Terror Sentences Expected to Set National Pattern," *TwinCities.com*, November 19, 2016, available at https://www.twincities.com/2016/11/19/minnesota-terror-sentences-expected-to-set-national-pattern/, accessed December 6, 2018.

23. John Horgan, "Deradicalization or Disengagement? A Process in Need of Clarity and a Counterterrorism Initiative in Need of Evaluation," *Perspectives on Terrorism*, 2, no. 4 (2008), available at http://www.terrorismanalysts.com/pt/index.php/pot/article/view/32/html, accessed December 6, 2018.

24. Details on the group and its accomplishments available at https://www.lifeafterhate.org/about-us-1/, accessed December 6, 2018.

25. Quilliam Foundation, available at https://www.quilliaminternational.com/, accessed December 7, 2018. Ed Hussain, *The Islamist: Why I Joined Radical Islam in Britain, What I Saw Inside and Why I Left* (New York: Penguin, 2007) describes how the author became radicalized and deradicalized.

26. *Prevent Strategy*, House of Commons Command Paper, Cm 8092 (London: HMSO, 2011), p. 59.

27. *Channel Duty Guidance: Protecting Vulnerable People from Being Drawn into Terrorism* (London: Her Majesty's Stationary Office, 2015), p. 17.

28. Patrick Poole, "London Tube Bomber Was Part of 'Deradicalization' Program," *PJ Media*, September 20, 2017, available at https://pjmedia.com/homeland-security/2017/09/20/london-tube-bomber-part-deradicalization-program/amp/, accessed December 7, 2018.

29. Dominic Casiani, "Analysis: The Prevent Strategy and Its Problems," *BBC News*, August 26, 2014, available at https://www.bbc.com/news/uk-28939555, accessed December 8, 2018.

30. "Programs and Initiatives," U.S. Department of State, available at https://www.state.gov/j/ct/programs/index.htm#CVE, accessed December 8, 2018.

31. See, for example, SPLC's "Teaching Tolerance Program," available at https://www.splcenter.org/teaching-tolerance, accessed December 8, 2018.

Select Bibliography

PRIMARY SOURCES

Official Documents

Australian Cyber Security Centre. *2016 Threat Report*. Australian Institute of International Affairs. https://www.internationalaffairs.org.au/australianoutlook/is-cyberterrorism-a-threat/ (accessed December 12, 2018).

Channel Duty Guidance: Protecting Vulnerable People from Being Drawn into Terrorism. London: Her Majesty's Stationary Office, 2015.

Charge sheet for Sayfullo Habibullaevic Saipov (November 1, 2017). https://www.justice.gov/usao-sdny/press-release/file/1008081/download (accessed November 5, 2018).

Countering Violent Extremism: Actions Needed to Define Strategy and Assess Progress of Federal Efforts. Washington, DC: Government Accounting Office, 2017.

DOD Dictionary of Military and Related Terms. Washington, DC: Government Printing Office, 2018.

FBI Counterterrorism Analysis Section. "Sovereign Citizens: A Growing Threat to Law Enforcement" (September 1, 2001). https://leb.fbi.gov/articles/featured-articles/sovereign-citizens-a-growing-domestic-threat-to-law-enforcement (accessed October 9, 2018).

House of Commons (UK). *Report of the Official Account of the London Bombings on 7th July 2005* (HC 1087). London: Her Majesty's Stationary Office, 2006.

House of Representatives Committee on Homeland Security. *The Road to Boston: Counterterrorism Challenges and Lessons from the Marathon Bombings*, March 2014. https://homeland.house.gov/files/documents/Boston-Bombings-Report.pdf (accessed November 3, 2018).

LVMPD Criminal Investigative Report of the October 1, 2017 Mass Casualty Shooting (August 3, 2018). https://www.lvmpd.com/en-us/Documents/1-October

-FIT-Criminal-Investigative-Report-FINAL_080318.pdf (accessed October 29, 2018).

9/11 Commission Report. Washington, DC: Government Printing Office, 2004.

"Nuclear Regulatory Commission (NRC) Fact Sheet on Dirty Bombs." Mass.gov. http://www.mass.gov/eohhs/gov/departments/dph/programs/environ mental-health/exposure-topics/radiation/radiological-emergency/fact -sheet-on-dirty-bombs.html (accessed December 2, 2017).

Prevent Strategy. House of Commons Command Paper, Cm 8092. London: HMSO, 2011.

"Programs and Initiatives." U.S. Department of State. https://www.state.gov/j/ct /programs/index.htm#CVE (accessed December 8, 2018).

"Saddam's Chemical Weapons Campaign: Halabja, March 16, 1988." U.S. Depart- ment of State, Bureau of Public Affairs (March 14, 2003). https://2001-2009 .state.gov/r/pa/ei/rls/18714.htm (accessed December 9, 2018).

Silber, Michael D., and Arvin Bhatt. *Radicalization in the West: The Homegrown Threat*. New York: NYPD, 2007.

"Smallpox." Centers for Disease Control. https://www.cdc.gov/smallpox /vaccine-basics/index.html (December 10, 2018).

State of New Jersey Office of Homeland Security and Preparedness. "ISIS: Esca- lating Threats against US Military Personnel" (March 22, 2015). https:// www.njhomelandsecurity.gov/analysis/isis-threats-to-military (accessed December 12, 2018).

Swecker, Chris. "Eric Rudolph." FBI history page. https://www.fbi.gov/history /famous-cases/eric-rudolph (accessed November 8, 2018).

The 2017 Attacks: What Needs to Change? London: HMSO, 2018.

"2017 Hate Crime Statistics." FBI. https://ucr.fbi.gov/hate-crime/2017/tables /table-1.xls (accessed December 1, 2018).

"What Are Known Violent Extremist Groups." https://www.fbi.gov/cve508/teen -website/what-are-known-violent-extremist-groups (accessed December 18, 2018).

Extremist Material

"About." American Freedom Defense Initiative. http://afdi.us/about/ (accessed October 10, 2018).

"About Oath Keepers." Oath Keepers. https://oathkeepers.org/about/ (accessed October 8, 2018).

"About Us." Identity Evropa. https://www.identityevropa.com/about-us (accessed September 20, 2018).

"The AFP Mission Statement." http://theamericanfreedomparty.us/mission -statement/ (accessed August 16, 2018).

al-Banna, Hasan. "Between Yesterday and Today." *Complete Works of Hassan al- Banna, 1906–1949*. https://thequranblog.files.wordpress.com/2008/06/_7 _-between-yesterday-today.pdf (accessed March 31, 2018).

Azzam, Abdullah. *Join the Caravan* (c.a. 1987). https://archive.org/stream /JoinTheCaravan/JoinTheCaravan_djvu.txt (accessed April 21, 2018).

Bakunin, Mikhail. "Letters to a Frenchmen on the Present Crisis" (1870). https://www.marxists.org/reference/archive/bakunin/works/1870/letter-frenchman.htm (accessed December 13, 2018).

Beam, Louis. "Leaderless Resistance" (1983). http://www.louisbeam.com/leaderless.htm (accessed November 7, 2018).

bin Laden, Osama. "Declaration of War against the Americans Occupying the Land of the Two Holy Places." First published in Al Quds Al Arabi (August 1996). https://is.muni.cz/el/1423/jaro2010/MVZ448/OBL___AQ__Fatwa_1996.pdf (accessed May 8, 2018).

bin Laden, Osama. "Interview with Peter Arnett." CNN (March 1997). http://www.informationclearinghouse.info/article7204.htm (accessed April 28, 2018).

bin Laden, Osama. "World Islamic Front Statement" (February 23, 1998). https://fas.org/irp/world/para/docs/980223-fatwa.htm (accessed November 6, 2017).

bin Laden, Osama, and Ayman al-Zawahiri. "Jihad against Jews and Crusaders" (February 23, 1998). https://is.muni.cz/el/1423/jaro2010/MVZ203/OBL___AQ__Fatwa_1998.pdf (accessed March 28, 2018).

Breivik, Anders. "Manifesto." An English Translation of the manifesto is available at http://www.deism.com/images/breivik-manifesto-2011.pdf (accessed November 12, 2018).

Clark, Alfred W. "'Cuckservative,' a Definition" (July 17, 2015). https://www.radixjournal.com/2015/07/2015-7-16-cuckservative-a-definition/ (accessed August 25, 2018).

Ford, Dr. "An Introduction to Stormfront and the Pro-White Movement. Part I: What We Want and Why." https://www.stormfront.org/forum/t968576/ (accessed August 15, 2018).

Ibrahim, Raymond, ed. and trans. The Al-Qaeda Reader. New York: Broadway Books, 2007.

Ibrahim, Yahya. "The Ultimate Mowing Machine." Inspire (Fall 2010): 53–54. https://info.publicintelligence.net/InspireFall2010.pdf (accessed November 13, 2017).

"ISIS Is Islam." https://counterjihadcoalition.org/wp-content/uploads/2015/04/Islam-in-a-Nutshell-ISIS-is-Islam.pdf (accessed October 9, 2018).

Kaczynski, Theodore. "Industrial Society and Its Future" (1995). http://editions-hache.com/essais/pdf/kaczynski2.pdf (accessed October 24, 2018).

Kingdom Identity Ministries. "Doctrinal Statement of Beliefs." http://www.kingidentity.com/doctrine.htm (accessed September 17, 2018).

Litoff, Robert. "Jews and Their Effect on Russian American Relations" (April 19, 2015). http://theamericanfreedomparty.us/jews-and-their-effect-on-russian-american-relations/ (accessed August 16, 2018).

Macdonald, Andrew [William Pearce]. The Turner Diaries. Hillsboro, WV: National Vanguard Books, 1978. https://www.e-reading.club/bookreader.php/133469/The_Turner_Diaries.pdf (accessed November 7, 2018).

McVeigh, Timothy. "McVeigh's Apr. 26 Letter to Fox News" (April 26, 2001). https://www.foxnews.com/story/mcveighs-apr-26-letter-to-fox-news (accessed November 8, 2018).

"Mission." ACT for America. https://www.actforamerica.org/Mission. September 21, 2018.

"Mission Statement." The Occidental Observer. https://www.theoccidentalobser
    ver.net/mission/ (accessed September 17, 2018).
"Our Mission." Fight White Genocide. http://www.fightwhitegenocide.com
    /mission/ (accessed September 17, 2018).
Qutb, Sayyid. *Milestones* (1964). http://www.kalamullah.com/Books/MILE
    STONES.pdf (accessed March 31, 2018).
Roof, Dylan. "Manifesto." https://www.nytimes.com/interactive/2016/12/13
    /universal/document-Dylann-Roof-manifesto.html (accessed November
    11, 2018).
Rudolph, Eric. "Racism." http://armyofgod.com/EricRudolphRacism.html/
    (accessed November 8, 2018).
Spraguer, Emmanuel. "Antiracism Is Immoral." http://alternativeright.com/
    (accessed December 19, 2018).
Statement by Isis leaders Abū Muhammad al-'Adnānī ash-Shāmī (September
    22, 2014). https://scholarship.tricolib.brynmawr.edu/bitstream/handle
    /10066/16495/ADN20140922.pdf (accessed November 23, 2018).
"Statement of Principles." http://conservative-headlines.org/statement-of
    -principles/ (accessed August 23, 2018).
Tarrant, Brenton. *The Great Replacement: Towards a New Society*. https://milnenews
    .com/2019/03/15/christchurch-mosque-shooter-brenton-tarrants-full
    -manifesto/ (accessed March 28, 2019).
The Three Percenters—Original—National Bylaws: A Guide to Being a Three Percenter.
    https://docs.wixstatic.com/ugd/6ecfe6_40d0b0f5bb144a87ab351f8d93e-
    2bee0.pdf (accessed October 6, 2018).
"25 Points of National Socialism." http://www.nsm88.org/25points/25pointsengl
    .html (accessed September 11, 2018).
"The Ultimate Mowing Machine." *Inspire*, no. 2 (October 2010). https://azelin.files
    .wordpress.com/2010/10/inspire-magazine-2.pdf (accessed June 22, 2018).
"Vanguard America Platform." http://vanguardamerica.online/platform/ (accessed
    September 13, 2018).

SECONDARY SOURCES

Books

Aboul-Enein, Youssef H. *Militant Islamist Ideology: Understanding the Threat*. Annap-
    olis, MD: Naval Institute Press, 2010.
Beirich, Heidi. *White Homicide Worldwide: Stormfront, the Leading White Supremacist
    Web Forum Has Another Distinction—Murder Capital of the Internet*. Mont-
    gomery, AL: Southern Poverty Law Center, 2014.
Belew, Kathleen. *Bring the War Home: The White Power Movement and Paramilitary
    America*. Cambridge, MA: Harvard University Press, 2018.
Bergen, Peter. *The Osama bin Laden I Knew*. New York: Free Press, 2006.
Coll, Steve. *The Bin Ladens: An Arabian Family in the American Century*. New York:
    Penguin, 2008.
Dodwell, Brian, Daniel Milton, and Don Rassler. *The Caliphate's Global Workforce:
    An Inside Look at the Islamic State's Foreign Fighter Paper Trail*. West Point, NY:
    Center for Combatting Terrorism Center, 2016.

Gerges, Fawaz A. *A History of ISIS*. Princeton, NJ: Princeton University Press, 2016.

Global Terrorism Index, 2016. College Park, MD: Institute for Economics and Peace, 2016.

Global Terrorism Index, 2017: Measuring and Understanding the Impact of Terrorism. College Park, MD: Institute for Economics & Peace, 2017.

Gunaratna, Rohan. *Inside Al-Qaeda: Global Network of Terror*. New York: Columbia University Press, 2002.

Hoffman, Bruce. *Inside Terrorism*, 3rd ed. New York: Columbia University Press, 2017.

Hussain, Ed. *The Islamist: Why I Joined Radical Islam in Britain, What I Saw Inside and Why I Left*. New York: Penguin, 2007.

Kurzman, Charles, and David Schanzer. *Law Enforcement Assessment of the Violent Extremism Threat*. Durham, NC: Duke University Triangle Center on Terrorism and Homeland Security, 2015.

Levitas, Daniel. *The Terrorist Next Door: The Militia Movement and the Radical Right*. New York: St. Martin, 2004.

Meleagrou-Hitchens, Alexander, Seamus Hughes, and Bennett Clifford. *Travelers: American Jihadis in Syria and Iraq*. Washington, DC: George Washington University: Program on Extremism, 2018.

Mockaitis, Thomas R. *The New Terrorism: Myths and Reality*. Westport, CT: Praeger, 2007.

Mockaitis, Thomas R. *Osama bin Laden*. Santa Barbara, CA: ABC-CLIO/Greenwood, 2010.

Pape, Robert, et al. *The American Face of ISIS: Analysis of ISIS-Related Terrorism in the US March 2014–August 2016*. Chicago, IL: University of Chicago Center for Counterterrorism Policy, 2017.

Patel, Faiza. *Rethinking Radicalization*. New York: Brenan Center for Justice at the New York University of Law, 2011.

Riedel, Bruce. *The Search for al-Qaeda: Its Leadership, Ideology, and Future*. Washington, DC: Brookings Institute Press, 2008.

Sageman, Mark. *Understanding Terrorist Networks*. Philadelphia, PA: University of Pennsylvania Press, 2004.

Scheuer, Michael. *Through Our Enemies' Eyes: Osama bin Laden, Radical Islam, and the Future of America*. Washington, DC: Potomac Books, 2007.

Simon, Jeffrey D. *Lone Wolf Terrorism: Understanding the Growing Threat*. New York: Prometheus Books, 2013.

Stern, Jessica. *Terror in the Name of God: Why Religious Militants Kill*. New York: Harper Collins, 2003.

von Behr, Ines, et al. *Radicalisation in the Digital Era: The Use of the Internet in 15 Cases of Terrorism and Extremism*. Cambridge, UK: Rand Europe, 2013.

Winter, Charlie. *"Libya: The Strategic Gateway for the Islamic State," Translation and Analysis of IS Recruitment Propaganda for Libya*. London: Quilliam Foundation, 2015. https://www.ibs-ops.com/fileadmin/files/downloads/libya-the-strategic-gateway-for-the-is.pdf (accessed November 22, 2018).

Wright, Lawrence. *The Looming Tower: Al-Qaeda and the Road to 9/11*. New York: Knopf, 2006.

Zimmerman, Katherine. *The Al-Qaeda Network: A New Framework for Defining the Enemy*. Washington, DC: American Enterprise Institute, 2013.

Zuhur, Sharifa. *A Hundred Osamas: Islamist Threats and the Future of Counterinsurgency.* Carlisle Barracks, PA: Strategic Studies Institute, 2005.

Articles

Abdoul-Enein, Yusef. "The Late Sheikh Abdullah Azzam's Book- Part III" (January 1, 2008). West Point Combatting Terrorism Center. https://ctc.usma.edu/the-late-sheikh-abdullah-azzams-book-part-iii-radical-theories-on-defending-muslim-land-through/ (accessed April 21, 2018).

Acton, James M., M. Brooke Rogers, and Peter D. Zimmermann. "Beyond the Dirty Bomb: Re-thinking Radiological Terror." *Survival*, 49, no. 3 (Autumn 2007): 151–168.

Alkhouri, Laith, and Alex Kassirer. "Governing the Caliphate: The Islamic State Picture." *Sentinel*, 8, no. 8 (August 2015): 17–20.

"Al-Qaeda in the Arabian Peninsula (AQAP)." *Council on Foreign Relations* (June 2015). https://www.cfr.org/backgrounder/al-qaeda-arabian-peninsula-aqap (accessed June 21, 2018).

Arosoaie, Aida. "Doctrinal Differences between ISIS and Al Qaeda: An Account of Ideologues." *Counter Terrorist Trends and Analyses*, 7, no. 7 (August 2015): 31–37.

Baker, Al, and Mark Santora. "San Bernardino Attackers Discussed Jihad in Private Messages, F.B.I. Says," *New York Times*, December 16, 2015. https://www.nytimes.com/2015/12/17/us/san-bernardino-attackers-discussed-jihad-in-private-messages-fbi-says.html (accessed November 4, 2018).

Barber, Victoria. "The Evolution of al-Qaeda's Global Network." *Perspectives on Terrorism*, 9, no. 6 (December 2015): 1–35.

Barrett, Chris L., Stephen G. Eubank, and James P. Smith. "If Smallpox Strikes Portland. . . ." *Scientific American* (March 2005): 54–61.

Barrett, Richard. "The Islamic State Goes Global." *Sentinel*, 8, no. 11 (November/December 2015): 1–4.

Barry, Dan, et al. "'Always Agitated. Always Mad': Omar Mateen, According to Those Who Knew Him." *New York Times* (June 18, 2016). https://www.nytimes.com/2016/06/19/us/omar-mateen-gunman-orlando-shooting.html (accessed November 5, 2018).

Batal al-Shishani, Murad. "Understanding Strategic Change in al-Qaeda's Central Leadership after Bin Laden." *Terrorism Monitor*, 9, no. 23 (June 9, 2011). https://jamestown.org/program/understanding-strategic-change-in-al-qaedas-central-leadership-after-bin-laden/ (accessed May 8, 2018).

Beinart, Peter. "America's Most Prominent Anti-Muslim Activist Is Welcome at the White House." *The Atlantic* online (March 21, 2017). https://www.theatlantic.com/politics/archive/2017/03/americas-most-anti-muslim-activist-is-welcome-at-the-white-house/520323/ (accessed September 21, 2018).

Bennhold, Katrin. "Jihad and Girl Power: How ISIS Lured 3 London Girls." *New York Times* (August 7, 2015). https://www.nytimes.com/2015/08/18/world/europe/jihad-and-girl-power-how-isis-lured-3-london-teenagers.html (accessed November 19, 2018).

Berman, Mark. "One Year after the San Bernardino Attack, Police Offer a Possible Motive as Questions Still Linger." *Washington Post* (December 2, 2016). https://www.washingtonpost.com/news/post-nation/wp/2016/12/02/one-year-after-san-bernardino-police-offer-a-possible-motive-as-questions-still-linger/ (accessed November 4, 2018).

Berry, Maya, and Kai Wiggins. "FBI Stats on Hate Crimes Are Scary. So Is What's Missing." *CNN* (November 14, 2018). https://www.cnn.com/2018/11/14/opinions/fbi-hate-crimes-data-whats-missing-berry-wiggins/index.html (accessed December 1, 2018).

Blinder, Alan, et al. "Omar Mateen: From Early Promise to F.B.I. Surveillance." *New York Times* (June 12, 2016). https://www.nytimes.com/2016/06/13/us/omar-mateen-early-signs-of-promise-then-abuse-and-suspected-terrorist-ties.html (accessed November 5, 2018).

Blinder, Alan, et al. "Omar Mateen Posted to Facebook Amid Orlando Attack, Lawmaker Says." *New York Times* (June 16, 2016). https://www.nytimes.com/2016/06/17/us/orlando-shooting.html (accessed November 5, 2018).

Bloom, Mial, and Chelsea Daymon. "Assessing the Future Threat: ISIS's Virtual Caliphate." *Orbis*, 62, no. 3 (Summer 2018): 372–388.

Brisard, Jean Charles, and Kevin Jackson. "The Islamic State's External Operations and the French-Belgian Nexus." *Sentinel*, 9, no. 11 (November/December 2016): 8–15.

Buchanan, Michael. "London Bombs Cost Just Hundreds." *BBC* (January 3, 2006). http://news.bbc.co.uk/2/hi/uk_news/4576346.stm (accessed July 21, 2018).

Bunker, Robert J. "Strategic Insights: The Assad Regime and Chemical Weapons." Strategic Studies Institute (May 18, 2018). http://strategicstudiesinstitute.army.mil/index.cfm/articles/Assad-Regime-Chemical-Weapons/2018/05/18 (accessed December 9, 2018).

Callimachi, Rukmini. "The ISIS Files." *New York Times* (April 4, 2018). https://www.nytimes.com/interactive/2018/04/04/world/middleeast/isis-documents-mosul-iraq.html (accessed November 17, 2018).

Callimachi, Rukmini. "How a Secretive Branch of ISIS Built a Global Network of Killers." *New York Times* (August 3, 2016). https://www.nytimes.com/2016/08/04/world/middleeast/isis-german-recruit-interview.html (accessed November 27, 2018).

Cambanis, Thanassis, and Rebecca Collard. "How ISIS Runs a City." *Time* (February 26, 2015). http://time.com/3720063/isis-government-raqqa-mosul/ (accessed November 17, 2018).

"Can Hackers Take over Traffic Lights?" *Washington Post* (August 8, 2015). https://www.washingtonpost.com/local/could-a-hacker-gain-control-of-dcs-traffic-system/2015/08/08/7cb7cf94-201a-11e5-bf41-c23f5d3face1_story.html (accessed December 12, 2018).

"Cargo Plane Bomb Found in Britain Was Primed to Blow Up over U.S." *Guardian*, (November 10, 2010). https://www.theguardian.com/world/2010/nov/10/cargo-plane-bomb-us-alqaida (accessed June 22, 2018).

Casiani, Dominic. "Analysis: The Prevent Strategy and Its Problems." *BBC* (August 26, 2014). https://www.bbc.com/news/uk-28939555 (accessed December 8, 2018).

"Charleston Church Shooting: Who Is Dylan Roof?" *CNN* (December 16, 2016). https://www.cnn.com/2015/06/19/us/charleston-church-shooting -suspect/index.html (accessed November 11, 2018).

"Charlottesville: Who Is Suspect James Alex Fields, Jr.?" *BBC* (August 14, 2017). https://www.bbc.com/news/world-us-canada-40923489 (accessed November 12, 2018).

Coaston, Jane. "New Evidence Shows the Pulse Nightclub Shooting Wasn't about Anti-LGBTQ Hate." *Vox.* https://www.vox.com/policy-and-politics /2018/4/5/17202026/pulse-shooting-lgbtq-trump-terror-hate (accessed November 5, 2018).

Cole, Jennifer. "Operation Crevice Trial Ends." *Royal United Services Institute* (May 2, 2007). https://rusi.org/commentary/operation-crevice-trial-ends (accessed July 5, 2018).

Cox, Christopher. "Cyber Capabilities and Intent of Terrorist Forces." *Information Security Journal: A Global Perspective*, 24 (2015): 35–36.

Cruickshank, Paul. "The Inside Story of the Paris and Brussels Attacks." *CNN* (October 30, 2017). https://www.cnn.com/2016/03/30/europe/inside -paris-brussels-terror-attacks/index.html (accessed November 27, 2018).

Duffy Toft, Monica. "Networks Fighting Networks: Understanding Extremism and Radicalisation on a Smaller Scale." *Juncture*, 23, no. 1 (Summer 2016): 37–40.

Dugan, Paul. "Four Alleged Members of Hate Group Charged in 2017 'Unite the Right' Rally in Charlottesville." *Washington Post* (October 2, 2018). https:// www.washingtonpost.com/local/public-safety/federal-officials-to -announce-additional-charges-in-2017-unite-the-right-rally-in-charlotte sville/2018/10/02/60881262-c651-11e8-9b1c-a90f1daae309_story.html (accessed October 15, 2018).

Durakovic, COL Asaf, MC USA(R). "Medical Effects of Tranuranic 'Dirty Bomb.'" *Military Medicine*, 82 (March/April 2017): e1591–e1595.

"Engineers Who Hacked into L.A. Traffic Signal Computer, Jamming Streets, Sentenced." *LA Times Blog* (December 1, 2009). https://latimesblogs .latimes.com/lanow/2009/12/engineers-who-hacked-in-la-traffic-signal -computers-jamming-traffic-sentenced.html (accessed December 12, 2018).

Felter, Joseph, and Brian Fishman. "Al-Qaeda's Foreign Fighters in Iraq: A First Look at the Sinjar Records." *Harmony Project*. West Point: Counterterrorism Center, 2007. https://www.files.ethz.ch/isn/45910/CTCForeignFighter .19.Dec07.pdf (accessed July 21, 2018).

Fernandez, Miriam, et al. "Understanding the Roots of Radicalisation on Twitter." *WebSci 18: 10th ACM Conference on Web Science*, May 27–30, 2018. Amsterdam, Netherlands, ACM. Association for Computing Machinery. http:// dx.doi.org/doi:10.1145/3201064.3201082 (accessed November 21, 2018).

Fishman, Brian. "Revising the History of al-Qa'ida's Original Meeting with Abu Musab al-Zarqawi." *Sentinel*, 9, no. 10 (October 2016). https://ctc.usma .edu/revising-the-history-of-al-qaidas-original-meeting-with-abu-musab -al-zarqawi/ (accessed June 19, 2018).

Fruhlinger, Josh. "What Is Stuxnet, Who Created It and How Does It Work?" CSO (August 22, 2017). https://www.csoonline.com/article/3218104/malware /what-is-stuxnet-who-created-it-and-how-does-it-work.html (accessed December 12, 2018).

Gakuo Mwangi, Oscar. "Stat Collapse, al-Shabab, Islamism, and Legitimacy in Somalia." *Politics, Religion and Ideology*, 13, no. 4 (December 2012): 513–527.

Garrity, Patrick. "Paris Attacks: What Does 'Daesh' Mean and Why Does ISIS Hate It?" *NBC News*. November 4, 2015. https://www.nbcnews.com/storyline/isis-terror/paris-attacks-what-does-daesh-mean-why-does-isis-hate-n463551 (accessed December 17, 2018).

Gaub, Florence, and Julia Lisiecka. "Women in Daesh: Jihadist 'Cheerleaders,' Active Operatives?" *European Union for Security Studies* (October 2016). https://www.iss.europa.eu/sites/default/files/EUISSFiles/Brief_27_Women_in_Daesh.pdf (accessed November 19, 2018).

Genoways, Ted. "The Only Good Muslim Is a Dead Muslim." *New Republic* (June 2017): 31–41.

Gomez, Melissa. "Charlottesville Car Attack Suspect Pleads Not Guilty to Federal Hate Crimes." *New York Times* (July 5, 2018). https://www.nytimes.com/2018/07/05/us/charlottesville-plea-hate-crimes.html (accessed November 12, 2018).

Goodstein, Laurie. "Drawing Crowds with Anti-Islam Message." *New York Times* (March 7, 2011). https://archive.nytimes.com/www.nytimes.com/2011/03/08/us/08gabriel.html (accessed September 21, 2018).

Graham, David A. "The White-Supremacist Group That Inspired a Racist Manifesto. How Did the Council of Conservative Citizens Become America's Biggest White-nationalist Organization, and Why Do Politicians Keep Dealing with It?" *Atlantic* (June 22, 2015). https://www.theatlantic.com/politics/archive/2015/06/council-of-conservative-citizens-dylann-roof/396467/ (accessed August 23, 2018).

Greenberg, Andy. "Next-Gen Air Traffic Control Vulnerable to Hackers Spoofing Planes out of Thin Air." *Forbes* (July 25 2012). https://www.forbes.com/sites/andygreenberg/2012/07/25/next-gen-air-traffic-control-vulnerable-to-hackers-spoofing-planes-out-of-thin-air/#34ef4af45927 (accessed December 12, 2018).

Greif, Adi. "Double Alienation and Muslim Youth in Europe." USIP Brief (August 21, 2007). https://www.usip.org/publications/2007/08/double-alienation-and-muslim-youth-europe (accessed December 20, 2018).

Hamilton, Matt. "San Bernardino Shooting Suspect Endured Turbulent Home Life, According to Court Documents." *Los Angeles Times* (online, December 3, 2015). http://www.latimes.com/local/lanow/la-me-san-bernardino-shooter-endured-turbulent-home-life-according-to-court-documents-20151203-story.html (accessed November 4, 2018).

Hawley, George. "The Demography of the Alt-Right." Institute for Family Studies (August 9, 2018). https://ifstudies.org/blog/the-demography-of-the-alt-right (accessed October 10, 2018).

Holmes, Frank. "Global Cost of Terrorism Is at an All-time High." *Business Insider* (March 28, 2016). http://www.businessinsider.com/global-cost-of-terrorism-at-all-time-high-2016-3 (accessed December 16, 2017).

Horgan, John. "Deradicalization or Disengagement? A Process in Need of Clarity and a Counterterrorism Initiative in Need of Evaluation." *Perspectives on Terrorism*, 2, no. 4 (2008). http://www.terrorismanalysts.com/pt/index.php/pot/article/view/32/html (accessed December 6, 2018).

"How Serious a Threat Do You Think White Nationalism Poses to the United States?" *Statista: The Statistical Portal* (August 2017). https://www.statista.com/statistics/738161/public-opinion-on-the-threat-of-white-nationalism-in-the-us/ (accessed February 13, 2018).

Hunter, Ryan, and Daniel Heinke. "Radicalization of Islamist Terrorists in the Western World" (September 1, 2011). https://leb.fbi.gov/articles/perspective/perspective-radicalization-of-islamist-terrorists-in-the-western-world.

Ibrahim, Azeem. "ISIS in Libya: A Threat or a Deadend?" Strategic Studies Institute (September 2018). https://ssi.armywarcollege.edu/index.cfm/articles/ISIS-In-Libya/2018/09/26#end10 (accessed November 22, 2018).

"Is Islamism a Threat? A Debate." *Middle East Quarterly*, 6, no. 4 (December 1999). https://www.meforum.org/articles/other/is-islamism-a-threat (accessed March 28, 2018).

"Jason Kessler on His 'Unite the Right Rally' Move to D.C." NPR, *Morning Edition* (April 10, 2018). https://www.npr.org/2018/08/10/637390626/a-year-after-charlottesville-unite-the-right-rally-will-be-held-in-d-c (accessed August 13, 2018).

"Jihadi Bride Led the Way at Party Massacre." *Daily Mail* (December 6, 2015). https://www.dailymail.co.uk/news/article-3348102/I-think-married-terrorist-Tashfeen-Malik-shot-Syed-Farook-hesitated-attack-killed-14-FBI-investigate-radicalized-husband.html (accessed November 4, 2018).

Johnston, Patrick B., et al. "The Islamic State of Iraq and the Iraq War." *Foundations of the Islamic State: Management, Money, and Terror in Iraq, 2005–2010*. Santa Monica, CA: Rand, 2016.

Jordan, Javier, et al. "Strengths and Weaknesses of Grassroot Jihadist Networks: The Madrid Bombings." *Studies in Conflict & Terrorism*, 31 (2008): 17–31.

Karasin, Ekin. "ISIS: 'We Killed Your Children'. Terror Group Claim Responsibility for Manchester Bombing 'in the Midst of a Gathering of the Crusaders.'" *Daily Mail* (May 23, 2017). https://www.dailymail.co.uk/news/article-4534612/ISIS-claim-responsibility-Manchester-bombing.html (accessed November 29, 2018).

Karnowski, Steve. "Minnesota Terror Sentences Expected to Set National Pattern." *TwinCities* (November 19, 2016). https://www.twincities.com/2016/11/19/minnesota-terror-sentences-expected-to-set-national-pattern/ (accessed December 6, 2018).

Kessler, Robert. "Outbreak: The Pandemic Strikes." *EcoHealth Alliance* (2018). https://www.ecohealthalliance.org/2018/05/outbreak-pandemic-strikes (accessed December 10, 2018).

Keyes, Scott. "A Strange but True Tale of Voter Fraud and Bioterrorism." *Atlantic* (June 10, 2014). https://www.theatlantic.com/politics/archive/2014/06/a-strange-but-true-tale-of-voter-fraud-and-bioterrorism/372445/ (December 10, 2018).

Klausen, Jytte, et al. "Toward a Behavioral Model of Homegrown Radicalization Trajectories." *Studies in Conflict and Terrorism*, 39 (2015): 39–67.

Lee, Robert M., and Sergio Caltagirone. "Hackers Got into America's Power Grid. But Don't Freak Out." *Fortune* (September 11, 2017). http://fortune.com/2017/09/11/dragonfly-2-0-symantec-hackers-power-grid/ (accessed December 12, 2018).

Leonard, Frank. "Are Suitcase Nukes a Genuine Concern." *New Atlas* (June 9, 2011) https://newatlas.com/suitcase-nukes-fact-or-fiction/18506/ (accessed November 15, 2017).

Levitz, Jennifer, and John Kamp. "Charleston Shooting Suspect Became a Loner in Recent Years." *Wall Street Journal* (June 18, 2015). https://www.wsj .com/articles/charleston-church-shooting-suspect-dylann-roof-became-a -loner-in-recent-years-1434644808 (accessed November 12, 2018).

Lister, Tim, et al. "ISIS Goes Global: 143 Attacks in 29 Countries Have Killed 2,043." *CNN* (February 12, 2018). https://www.cnn.com/2015/12/17/world /mapping-isis-attacks-around-the-world/index.html (accessed November 29, 2018).

"Lone Wolf Attacks Are Becoming More Common—And More Deadly." *Frontline* (July 14, 2016). https://www.pbs.org/wgbh/frontline/article/lone-wolf -attacks-are-becoming-more-common-and-more-deadly/ (accessed October 20, 2018).

Mahler, Jonathan, and Julie Turkewitz. "Suspect in Dallas Attack Had Interest in Black Power Groups." *New York Times* (July 8, 2016). https://www.nytimes .com/2016/07/09/us/suspect-in-dallas-attack-had-interest-in-black -power-groups.html

Malloy, Darren. "Conversing with the Dead: The Militia Movement and American History." *Journal of American Studies*, 38, no. 3 (December 2004): 439–456.

"Manchester Arena Attack: Bomb 'Injured More Than 800.'" https://www.bbc.com /news/uk-england-manchester-44129386 (accessed December 17, 2018).

Mark, Carson, et al. *Can Terrorists Build Nuclear Weapons?* Washington, DC: Nuclear Control Institute, n.d. https://www.nci.org/k-m/makeab.htm (accessed December 11, 2018).

McGuinness, Damien. "How a Cyber Attack Transformed Estonia." *BBC* (April 27, 2017). https://www.bbc.com/news/39655415 (accessed December 12, 2018).

Mockaitis, Thomas R. "The Abbottabad Files: An Enduring Resource." *Georgetown Journal of International Affairs* (February 7, 2018). https://www.geo rgetownjournalofinternationalaffairs.org/online-edition/2018/2/6/the -abbottabad-files-enduring-impact (accessed August 8, 2018).

Nashino, Masami. "Muhammad Qutb's Islamist Thought: A Missing Link between Sayyid Qutb and al-Qaeda?" *NIDS Journal of Defense and Security*, 16 (December 2015).

"Norway Killer: Anders Behring Breivik Was a 'Mummy's Boy.'" *Daily Telegraph* (July 25, 2011). https://www.telegraph.co.uk/news/worldnews /europe/norway/8659746/Norway-killer-Anders-Behring-Breivik-was-a -mummys-boy.html (accessed November 12, 2018).

"Norway's Mass Killer Breivik Declared Sane." *BBC* (April 10, 2012). https:// www.bbc.com/news/world-europe-17663958 (accessed November 12, 2018).

Nowrashteh, Alex. "Terrorism Deaths by Ideology: Is Charlottesville an Anomaly?" *CATO Institute* (August 14, 2017). https://www.cato.org/blog /terrorism-deaths-ideology-charlottesville-anomaly (accessed December 14, 2018).

Oppenheim, May. "22 Million Americans Support Neo-Nazis, New Poll Indicates." *Independent* (August 22, 2017). https://www.independent.co.uk/news

/world/americas/us-neo-nazi-support-american-public-charlottesville
-white-supremacists-kkk-far-right-poll-a7907091.html (accessed December
2, 2018).

Ostaeyen, Pieter van. "Belgian Radical Networks and the Road to the Brussels
Attacks." *Sentinel*, 9, Issue 6 (June 2016): 7–12.

Pilcher, James. "Charlottesville Suspects Beliefs Were 'Along the Party Lines of the
Neo-Nazi Movement,' Ex-Teacher Says." *Cincinnati Enquirer* (August 13,
2017). https://www.cincinnati.com/story/news/local/northern-ky/2017
/08/13/charlottesville-suspects-beliefs-were-along-party-lines-neo-nazi
-movement-ex-teacher-says/563139001/ (accessed November 12, 2018).

Poole, Patrick. "London Tube Bomber Was Part of 'Deradicalization' Program."
PJ Media (September 20, 2017). https://pjmedia.com/homeland-security
/2017/09/20/london-tube-bomber-part-deradicalization-program/amp/
(accessed December 7, 2018).

Poushter, Jacob. *Majorities in Europe and North America Worried about Islamic Extremism.* Washington, DC: Pew Research Organization, Spring 2017. http://
www.pewresearch.org/fact-tank/2017/05/24/majorities-in-europe
-north-america-worried-about-islamic-extremism/ (accessed February 13,
2018).

Rapoport, David. "Four Waves of Modern Terrorism." In Audrey Cronin and
James M. Ludes, eds., *Attacking Terrorism: Elements of Grand Strategy.* Washington, DC: Georgetown University Press, 2004.

Reinares, Fernando. "Jihadist Radicalization and the 2004 Madrid Bombing Network." *Sentinel*, 2, no. 11 (November 2009). https://ctc.usma.edu/jihadist
-radicalization-and-the-2004-madrid-bombing-network/ (accessed July
19, 2018).

Reinares, Fernando, and Carola García-Calvo. "'Spaniards, You Are Going to Suffer:' The Inside Story of the August 2017 Attacks in Barcelona and Cambrils." *Sentinel*, 11, no. 1 (January 2018): 1–11.

Robles, Frances, and Nikita Stewart. "Dylan Roof's Past Reveals Trouble at Home
and at School" (June 16, 2015). https://www.nytimes.com/2015/07/17/us
/charleston-shooting-dylann-roof-troubled-past.html (accessed November 12, 2018).

"Rudolph's Mother: Son Not a Monster." *CNN* (August 22, 2005). https://web
.archive.org/web/20140715230302/http://www.cnn.com/2005/LAW/08
/22/rudolph.mother/index.html?_s=PM%3ALAW (accessed November
8, 2018).

"The Sarin Gas Attack in Japan and the Related Forensic Investigation." *Organization for the Prohibition of Chemical Weapons* (June 1, 2001). https://www
.opcw.org/media-centre/news/2001/06/sarin-gas-attack-japan-and
-related-forensic-investigation (accessed December 10, 2018).

Sawicki, John. "Why Terrorists Use Female and Child Suicide Bombers." *Health
Progress* (July-August 2016). https://www.chausa.org/publications
/health-progress/article/july-august-2016/why-terrorists-use-female
-and-child-suicide-bombers (accessed November 13, 2017).

"Search of Tsarnaevs' Phones, Computers Finds No Indication of Accomplice, Source Says." *NBC News* (online, April 23, 2013). http://usnews

.nbcnews.com/_news/2013/04/23/17877288-search-of-tsarnaevs-phones
-computers-finds-no-indication-of-accomplice-source-says?lite (accessed
November 4, 2018).

Serven Smith, Ruth, and Allison Wrabel. "'Serial Rioters' Charged in Rally Violence." *The Daily Progress* (October 2, 2018). https://www.dailyprogress
.com/news/local/serial-rioters-charged-in-rally-violence/article
_14d0ec88-c659-11e8-a61d-57feee131da1.html (accessed October 15, 2018).

Shoichet, Catherine E., and Josh Levs. "Al-Qaeda Branch Reveals Charlie Hebdo
Attack Was Years in the Making" (January 21, 2015). https://www.cnn.com
/2015/01/14/europe/charlie-hebdo-france-attacks/index.html (accessed
June 22, 2018).

Shrader, Katherine, and Associated Press, "Suitcase Nukes Closer to Fiction
Than Reality" (November 10, 2007). https://usatoday30.usatoday.com
/tech/science/2007-11-10-suitcasenukes_N.htm (accessed December 11,
2018).

Smithson, Amy E. "Grounding the Threat in Reality." In Amy E. Smithson and
Leslies-Anne Levy, *Ataxia: The Chemical and Biological Terrorism Threat and
the US Response.* Washington, DC: Henry L. Stimson Center, 2000.

Spencer, Amanda N. "The Hidden Face of Terrorism: An Analysis of the Women
in Islamic State." *Journal of Strategic Security*, 9, no. 3. *Special Issue: Emerging
Threats* (Fall 2016): 74–98.

"'Suitcase Nukes': A Reassessment." Middlebury Institute of International Security
(September 23, 2002). https://www.nonproliferation.org/suitcase-nukes
-a-reassessment/ (December 11, 2018).

Taylor, Alan. "Bhopal: The World's Worst Industrial Disaster, 30 Years Later." *The
Atlantic* (December 2, 2014). https://www.theatlantic.com/photo/2014
/12/bhopal-the-worlds-worst-industrial-disaster-30-years-later/100864/
(December 10, 2018).

Temple-Raston, Dina. "Jihadi Rehab May Be an Alternative to Prison for Young
ISIS Recruits." NPR (November 28, 2017). https://www.npr.org/2017/11
/28/566877270/jihadi-rehab-may-be-an-alternative-to-prison-for-young
-isis-recruits (accessed December 6, 2018).

Thornton, Thomas P. "Terror as a Weapon of Political Agitation." In Harry Eckstein, ed., *Internal War: Problems and Approaches.* Westport, CT: Greenwood,
1964.

"Underwear Bomber Abdulmutallab Sentenced to Life." *BBC* (February 16, 2012).
https://www.bbc.com/news/world-us-canada-17065130 (accessed June
22, 2018).

"United States Crime Rates, 1960–2017." http://www.disastercenter.com/crime
/uscrime.htm (accessed November 30, 2018).

Valverde, Miriam. "A Look at the Data on Domestic Terrorism and Who's Behind
It." *Politifact* (August 16, 2017). https://www.politifact.com/truth-o-meter
/article/2017/aug/16/look-data-domestic-terrorism-and-whos-behind-it/
(accessed December 1, 2018).

Velicof, Mihai, and Simona Miclăuǔ. "An Analysis of Radiological Dispersal
Devices in Terms of Nuclear Hazard." Land Forces Academy of Romania.
Technical Sciences, 58, no. 2 (June 2010): 267–276.

Warrick, Joby. "FBI Investigation of 2001 Anthrax Attacks Concluded; U.S. Releases Details." *Washington Post* (February 20, 2010). http://www.washingtonpost .com/wp-dyn/content/article/2010/02/19/AR2010021902369.html (accessed December 10, 2018).

"*Washington Post-ABC News* Poll" (August 16–20, 2017). http://apps.washingtonpost .com/g/page/politics/washington-post-abc-news-poll-aug-16-20-2017 /2235/ (accessed December 2, 2018).

Weaver, Mary Anne. "The Short, Violent Life of Abu Musab al-Zarqawi." *Atlantic* (July/August 2006). https://www.theatlantic.com/magazine/archive /2006/07/the-short-violent-life-of-abu-musab-al-zarqawi/304983/ (accessed June 20, 2018).

Williams, Phil. "In Cold Blood: The Madrid Bombings." *Perspectives on Terrorism*, X, no. 9 (2008): 19–24.

Zimmer, Ben. "The Phrase 'Lone Wolf' Goes Back Centuries." *Wall Street Journal* (online, December 19, 2014). https://www.wsj.com/articles/the-phrase -lone-wolf-goes-back-centuries-1419013651 (accessed May 9, 2018).

Websites

Anti-Defamation League. https://www.adl.org

Counter Extremism Project. https://www.counterextremism.com

Global Terrorism Database. https://www.start.umd.edu

Life after Hate. https://www.lifeafterhate.org

Living Islam. http://www.livingislam.org

Mapping Militant Organizations. http://web.stanford.edu/group/mapping militants/

Quilliam Foundation. https://www.quilliaminternational.com

Southern Poverty Law Center. https://www.splcenter.org

West Point Counterterrorism Center. https://ctc.usma.edu

Index

About the Author

THOMAS R. MOCKAITIS is professor of history at DePaul University. He presents programs with other experts through the Center for Civil-Military Relations at the Naval Postgraduate School at venues around the world. Professor Mockaitis was the 2004 Eisenhower Chair at the Royal Military Academy of the Netherlands. He has also lectured at the NATO School, the U.S. Marine Corps Command and Staff College, and the Canadian Forces Staff College, and he has presented papers at the Pearson Peacekeeping Center (Canada), the Royal Military Academy Sandhurst (UK), and the Austrian National Defense Academy.

A frequent media commentator on terrorism and security matters, Dr. Mockaitis has appeared on public television, National Public Radio, BBC World News, all major Chicago TV stations, and various local radio programs. He appears regularly as a terrorism expert for WGN-TV News. He is the 2008 recipient of the DePaul Liberal Arts and Sciences Cortelyou-Lowery Award for Excellence in Teaching, Scholarship, and Service.

Dr. Mockaitis is the author of numerous books and articles, including *The COIN Conundrum?* (Carlisle Barracks, PA: Strategic Studies Institute, U.S. Army War College, 2016); *Soldiers of Misfortune?* (Carlisle Barracks, PA: Strategic Studies Institute, U.S. Army War College, 2014); *Avoiding the Slippery Slope: Conducting Effective Interventions* (Carlisle, PA: Strategic Studies Institute, U.S. Army War College, 2013); *The Iraq War: A Documentary and Reference Guide* (Santa Barbara, CA: Greenwood, 2012); *Osama bin Laden: A Biography* (Santa Barbara, CA: Greenwood, 2010); *Iraq and the Challenge of Counterinsurgency* (Westport, CT: Praeger, 2008); *The "New" Terrorism: Myths and Reality* (Westport, CT: Praeger, 2007); *The Iraq War: Learning from the Past, Adapting to the Present, and Preparing for the Future* (Carlisle, PA: Strategic Studies Institute, U.S. Army War College, 2007); *Peacekeeping and Intrastate Conflict: The Sword or the Olive Branch?* (Westport, CT: Praeger, 1999); *British Counterinsurgency in the Post-Imperial Era* (Manchester, UK: University of Manchester Press, 1995); and *British Counterinsurgency: 1919–1960* (London, UK: Macmillan, 1990). He coedited *Grand Strategy and the War on Terrorism* with Paul Rich (London, UK: Frank Cass, 2003) and *The Future of Peace Operations: Old Challenges for a New Century* with Erwin Schmidl (a special issue of *Small Wars and Insurgencies* [London, UK: Taylor and Francis 2004]). He has also published numerous articles on unconventional conflict.

His most recent book, *Conventional and Unconventional War: A History of Conflict in the Modern World* (Santa Barbara, CA: Praeger) was released in February 2017. Dr. Mockaitis earned his BA in European history from Allegheny College and his MA and PhD in modern British and Irish history from the University of Wisconsin–Madison.

www.ingramcontent.com/pod-product-compliance
Lightning Source LLC
Chambersburg PA
CBHW050512280326
41932CB00014B/2291

* 9 7 9 8 7 6 5 1 2 6 3 3 2 *